# Captain James Carlin

STUDIES IN MARITIME HISTORY
*William N. Still, Jr., Series Editor*

Recent Titles

# Captain James Carlin

## Anglo-American Blockade-Runner

### Colin Carlin

The University of South Carolina Press

© 2017 University of South Carolina

Published by the University of South Carolina Press
Columbia, South Carolina 29208

www.sc.edu/uscpress

Manufactured in the United States of America

26 25 24 23 22 21 20 19 18 17    10 9 8 7 6 5 4 3 2 1

Names: Carlin, Colin, author.
Title: Captain James Carlin :
Anglo-American blockade-runner / Colin Carlin.
Description: Columbia, South Carolina : University of South
Carolina Press, 2016. | Series: Studies in maritime history
Includes bibliographical references and index.
Identifiers: LCCN 2016047772 | ISBN 9781611177138 (hardcover : alk. paper)
Subjects: LCSH: Carlin, James 1833–1921. | United States—History—
Civil War, 1861–1865—Blockades. | Ship captains—South Carolina—
Charleston—Biography. | Charleston (S.C.)—History—
Civil War, 1861–1865. | Charleston (S.C.)—Biography.
Classification: LCC E600 .C28 2016 | DDC 973.7092 [B]—dc23
LC record available at https://lccn.loc.gov/2016047772

This book was printed on recycled paper with
30 percent postconsumer waste content.

*William Kirkpatrick of Málaga:*
*Consul, Négociant and Entrepreneur, and Grandfather of the Empress Eugénie.*
Glasgow: Grimsay Press, Scotland, 2011.

In Spanish translation:
*William Kirkpatrick de Málaga, Cónsul en Málaga. Afanoso Industrial, y Abuela*
*de la Emperatriz Eugenia, consorte de Napoleón III, Emperador de Francia.*
Glasgow: Grimsay Press, Scotland, 2012.

For Olivia, James, Rose Agnes, Polly Ella, and Thomas Peter.

For if ever a cool head, strong nerve, and determination of character were required, it was while running or endeavoring to run through the American blockade of the Southern States. It must be borne in mind that the excitement of fighting, which some men (inexplicable I confess to me) really love, did not exist. One was always either running away, or being deliberately pitched into the broadsides of the American cruisers, the slightest resistance to which would have constituted piracy; capture without resistance, merely entailed confiscation of cargo and vessel.

Captain A. Roberts,
*Never Caught*, 6

# Contents

. . .

. . .

* * *

# Illustrations and Maps

. . .

## Illustrations

• • •

## Maps

# Preface

. . .

On the veranda of a colonial-style house in Africa, my father and I puzzled over the broad-nibbed script on the flyleaf of a well-worn pocket Bible. A dedication in heavy black ink showed that the Bible had been presented to Captain James Carlin. On the front flyleaf was a roll call of the sea captains with him in Fort Lafayette in 1862. Also listed were the names of their ships and the date and place of their capture. On the rear flyleaf was a record of the names and birthdates of his numerous sons and daughters. What were we to make of this? All we knew was that our ancestor, Captain James Cornelius Carlin, had been a gunrunner in the American Civil War and that he had disappeared from family view under mysterious circumstances in the early 1880s.

My great aunts, James Carlin's daughters, believed that their father had been a Rhett Butler–like figure and that their Louisiana-born mother, Ella Rosa Imogene, had been, as it were, a "bit player" in *Gone With the Wind,* the 1939 film that created an image of the Old South for cinemagoers in the mid-twentieth Century. Her daughters knew that Ella Rosa and James had a romantic past, and there were tales of an elopement and a dramatic shipboard escape. Ella Rosa, too, had her own mysteries as she claimed to be a niece of the Empress Eugénie, consort to Napoleon III of France. We knew almost nothing of all this and could visualize little more than the images shown in the Hollywood film.[1]

While James Carlin's life and his romance with Ella Rosa may have had parallels with that of Rhett Butler, the fictional blockade-runner, the Charleston merchant and ship owner George Alfred Trenholm was probably the character Margaret Mitchell actually had in mind when creating Butler. However, Trenholm was not a blockade-running captain, and James Carlin appears a better fit for this swashbuckling character.

Carlin was listed as captured on the *Memphis,* and we assumed that this was the name of his swift gunrunning frigate that had become an icon of family lore. In those pre-Internet days, there was no instant search engine to query, and the *Memphis* remained a mystery. A few years later I was living in London and occasionally spent the odd day in the British National Archives looking for the SS *Memphis* in British shipping records. I searched for traces of James Carlin's career in the merchant marine: a master's certificate or the like. Over a couple of years, I found some references to a *Memphis* of the correct date but no trace of Carlin in the British Merchant Navy or the Royal Navy.

Then, one of the ever-helpful archive staff suggested that I look in an Admiralty series for "Special Cases." There I found a file named "The Case of the Memphis," which I called up. It was not very hopeful, and I had a number of other files on order at the same time to make good use of my time. In due course, the archives bleeper told me that I had records to collect, and I went to the counter. My file was in the usual stiff cardboard box, so I had to carry it to my desk before I could undo the pink ribbon—red tape—and lift off the lid. I was expecting to see a folder of loose notes on the *Memphis*. In fact I found a handsome volume, bound in leather with marbled covers.

On the front was a label, "The Case of James Carlin."[2] One does not really whoop for joy in the hush of the Public Record Office reading room, but I did the next best thing. All that follows resulted from that discovery. In a long series of official copies of letters was an extensive correspondence concerning the detention of James Carlin in Fort Lafayette, New York, and the vigorous efforts by his father and the diplomats of the British Foreign Office to have him released. Other documents were to show his involvement in even more dangerous events. The *Memphis* was no swift frigate and did not belong to James Carlin. It was just a large merchant steamer, but its story and that of my great-grandfather's involvement in its tribulations are the centerpiece of his story.

I have chosen to include extensive passages from the official records that document the more dramatic periods of Carlin's life. In the absence of more personal letters, these give a vivid flavor of the times in which he lived and a window to his past. His own reports and business correspondence give us our best glimpses of his character as revealed by his actions and reactions.

Further discoveries explain why his exploits had remained a family secret. Under the British Foreign Enlistment Act of 1819, British subjects who were proved to have aided recognized belligerents in a dispute in which Britain remained neutral were liable to very extensive fines and the confiscation of their vessels. The act specifically covered enlistment in foreign military or naval forces or the building, equipping, or dispatching of ships for employment in foreign military forces or their fitting out or armament for such enterprises. While a few of the scores of British skippers who had run the blockade published colorful accounts of their exploits, they tried to keep their identities and the names of their ships anonymous. No wonder the details of James Carlin's various activities remained unknown. He made a career of breaking the spirit, if not always the legal niceties, of this long-established act of Parliament.

Captain James Carlin is often mentioned in naval histories of the American Civil War. Stephen R. Wise, Eric J. Graham, and many others have scoured the records and have charted the movements of the ships that imposed the blockade and those who tried and usually succeeded in evading them. This study does not attempt to follow James Carlin on every voyage, or to list every ship he commanded. The literature now has so many conflicting numbers that it is probably impossible to resolve the many inconsistencies about ship names, their commanders, and their various arrivals and departures.[3] Instead, I have concentrated on those of his exploits documented in detail by Admiralty courts in America and Britain and in other official records. These also give us a unique description of an expedition to land guns and insurgents onto the Cuban coast in the face of the British Royal Navy and the Spanish authorities. Carlin's adventures have been set in their wider social and historical context to give today's readers a sense of the period and perhaps a glimpse of the man and his motives.

# Acknowledgments

. . .

I have made extensive use of documents found in the United States by Christopher Carlin.

Lynda Worley Skelton's thesis "The Importing and Exporting Company of South Carolina, 1862–1876" and her similar but shorter article in *South Carolina Historical Magazine* were invaluable sources for the section on the Bee Company, later incorporated as the South Carolina Importing and Exporting Company. These were supplemented by letters in the Bee Company collection in the South Carolina Historical Society in Charleston.

Madeline Russell Robinton's *An Introduction to the Papers of the New York Prize Court, 1861–1865* provided the foundations of the chapters on the *Memphis* case and the events behind the efforts to release James Carlin from Fort Lafayette.

Douglas H. Maynard's thesis "Thomas Dudley and Union, Efforts to Thwart Confederate Activities in Great Britain" gave useful background on Confederate affairs in Liverpool.

There is a wealth of material on the blockade and the runners in the British Foreign Office and Admiralty files in the National Archives in Kew, London. Similarly, the Colonial Office, Foreign Office, and Admiralty files are invaluable for the study of events in the Caribbean and Cuba in the period 1860–75 and beyond.

I looked at various sources to try to determine James Carlin's movements during his blockade-running days and determine the number of trips he made through the blockade. But without many laborious hours spent over microfilm of Record Group 365, which contains the Register of Export Duty on Cotton (Charleston), as well as similar registers in the U.S. National Archives, it would be impossible to come to even a reasonability secure figure. Marcus W. Price has already done much of this work in his "Ships That Tested the Blockade of the Carolina Ports, 1861–1854." But, as in the case of the *Ella and Annie*'s sailing from Charleston, there are uncertainties in this data, distorted as they were by deliberate subterfuge and propaganda.

The late Dr. Charlie Peery's enthusiasm for Confederate naval history and the blockade runners of Charleston stimulated my search for James Carlin and his exploits. Charlie welcomed me to Charleston and introduced me to Ethel Trenholm Seabrook Nepveux, doyenne of Charleston Confederate history.

Dr. Peery also had James Carlin and the crewmembers of the *Torch* added to the names on the memorial to the first submarine, the *Hunley,* in White Point Gardens, Charleston, South Carolina. I am grateful to both Stephen Wise, author of the invaluable *Lifeline of the Confederacy,* for unpublished material on the Waddells and to Eric J. Graham, author of *Clyde Built,* for information on the Leslie family and much else.

All along the way Chris and Liz Carlin worked assiduously at filling in the gaps in the story of James Carlin, coming up with inspired leads. They have searched numerous coastal museums, archives, and libraries up and down the United States and found many vital clues and valuable new sources. I remain extremely grateful for Liz's quiet council, now sadly missed. Chris's continuing help and encouragement have been essential to the completion of this project and both are very much appreciated.

The late Captain William Carlin White, U.S. Navy (Retired), James's great nephew, provided a vital letter revealing something of the old blockader's last year and the photograph on the title page. I am indebted to Sally Purinton, a descendent of James Carlin Jr., who provided a compelling photograph of Captain Carlin in later life. Bea Savory (née Carlin) kept me going with contributions on family history. Sydney Stevens of Oysterville, Washington, completed the story of James Carlin Jr. and his family.

Fred Carlin, attorney of New York, unraveled some of the mysteries of James's last years. Graham Hopner of Dumbarton Library provided information on the ships built in the Denny yard.

Niels H. Frandsen, archivist at the Greenland National Archives, Nuuk, was very helpful on Greenland trade prohibition. I have a host of librarians, archivists and their staff, and many others to thank for their patient and conscientious efforts to answer my too-numerous queries. I am greatly indebted to them all.

Very special thanks are due to my cousin Dr. Martin Foster and to Martin Prentice for reading through the text and coming up with many suggestions and corrections. Dr. Rebecca Prentice has provided valuable source material and guidance on current American thinking on contentious issues. Once again, I am extremely grateful to Catherine Kirkpatrick for the generous contribution of her time and skill to improving my literary efforts.

I am particularly grateful to Alexa Selph for her sharp-eyed work on the index and to Lynne Parker for her excellent work on the maps. I must give special thanks to the staff of the USCP for their invaluable help in preparing this manuscript.

All errors, misunderstandings, and omissions are entirely due to my own shortcomings.

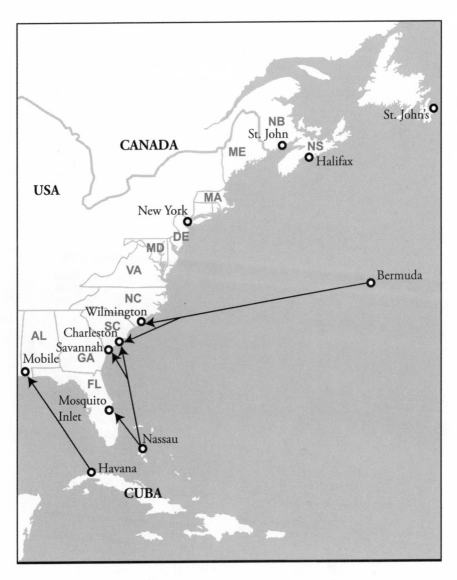

The Main Routes of the Blockade Runners into the Confederacy.

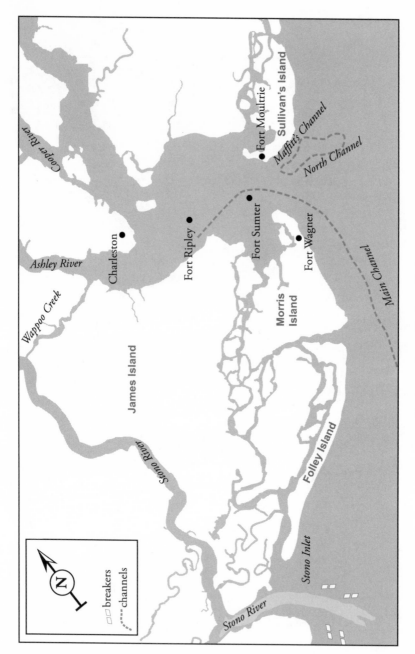

The Approaches to Charleston Harbor.

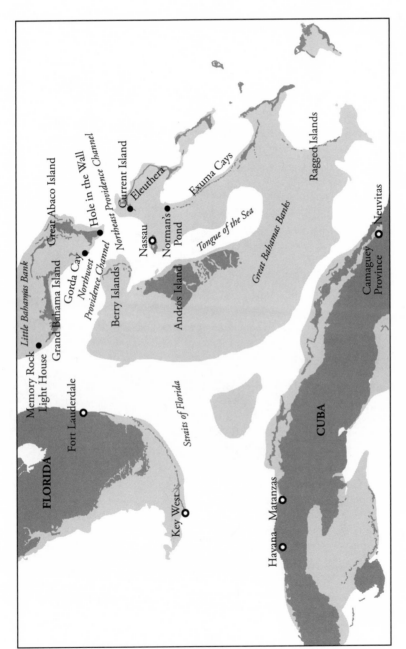

The Bahamian Islands and the North Coast of Cuba.

Captain James Carlin, *carte de visite.*
Courtesy of the Loxahatchee River Historical Society.

James Carlin in later life.
Courtesy of Mrs. Sally Purinton.

# Introduction

. . .

This is an intimate portrait of a leading blockade-runner during the American Civil War and gunrunner during the Cuban Ten Years' War of Independence. Others have written of the naval captains of the Confederacy, such as Raphael Semmes, John Newland Maffitt, and their colleagues. Some blockade-runners described their adventures, but they remain shadowy figures, most of whom soon merge into obscurity. Where did they come from, why did they take such enormous risks, and what did they do after the war? This biography attempts to answer some of these questions by examining the life of a prominent member of their fraternity, showing his origins, how he qualified as a runner, and what happened in the remaining fifty-five years of his life.

James Carlin's daring and perhaps reckless exploits took place against the backdrop of the American Civil War, or, as it was often called in the South, the War Between the States. On one side were the Confederate States of America, determined to secede from the United States; on the other were the Northern states, determined to preserve the Union.

While the issue of slavery caused bitter antagonism between the North and the South, the longstanding dispute about states' rights and restraints on Southern trade were also significant factors for the South. The Southern states, whose cotton-based economies depended on slave labor, believed they had the right to secede and thus preserve their independence. When Thomas Jefferson remarked that "the South was zealous of their Liberty," he had in mind the liberty of these states from Federal interference, rather than the freedom of their slaves. For the North the initial and principal aim was the preservation of the Union.

This, the cataclysmic event of mid-nineteenth-century America, is commonly thought of as the war the North fought to end slavery in the Southern states. What follows is not a neo-Confederate paean; nor is it a romantic take on the Old South. Rather, it shows the tragic nature of the Civil War and examines aspects its aftermath. These events and the motives of the participants can best be understood, if not excused, in the context of their times.

We recognize the Civil War period from television documentaries in which tripod-mounted cameras, in want of any moving images, pan across Mathew Brady's crisp, wet-plate photographs of ragdoll-like casualties strewn across the picket fence lines, showing us a foretaste of Flanders's muddy wastes. The Civil War was a grisly dress rehearsal for the Prussian invasion of France in 1870 and the greater catastrophe of the First World War in Europe. Six hundred thousand Americans died, and millions fought, brother against brother, new immigrant against "plantation aristocrat," in a conflict that left the South ruined and embittered. The ebb and flow of the great land battles regularly followed the blockade-runners' efforts to keep up the vital supply of munitions.

Slavery and racism are now central issues when writing of the American Southern states of this period. The starred saltire of the Confederate battle flag is familiar to us today as an icon of the American South. In the early 1860s this flag symbolized the courage with which young men from the Southern states went out to meet their deaths for a cause they believed was right. Many thought that they were fighting for a God-given way of life that held chivalry and honor as high ideals. They idealized a rural plantation culture, derived from a hundred-year-old concept of British county life that set them against the industrialized northern states of smokestacks and hard graft in the get-rich-quick culture of the New York immigrant. In reality, the South was fighting to preserve the institution of slavery.

The "moonlight-and-magnolia" planter idyll was far from the reality of life across the Old South. In 1860 there were only some twenty-three hundred great plantations with one hundred or more slaves, and about eight thousand owners of fifty slaves combined with substantial land holdings. Forty-six thousand out of 1.5 million heads of families met the rough guide for planter status: twenty or more slaves and some land. The many smaller plantations were quite primitive and bore little resemblance to Tara of *Gone With the Wind.* The enthusiasm for states' rights and secessionist pressure in the legislatures of the South demonstrate that planter interests prevailed in what has been characterized as "an un-American aristocratic tradition."[1]

The planters held power in Southern society and politics because non-planter whites aspired to planter status and generally accepted planter values and ideology. Southern whites were generally a homogeneous society of British origin that had avoided the mass immigration from continental Europe that characterized the Northern states. They "blended the traits of aristocracy and democracy within the same social structure." Ties of locale, kinship and shared experience bonded both rich and middling whites in a generalized "folk culture" that fed into the sense of patriotism that sent their sons off to a futile war.[2]

Slaves represented the industrial capital of the South, and it seemed impossible to devise an alternative that would not bankrupt the plantations and ruin the Southern states. During the course of the war, President Abraham Lincoln recognized that this gave him an opportunity to put further pressure on the South, and on 1 January 1863 he issued the Emancipation Proclamation, freeing all slaves in the rebel states.

Southern commercial and trade resentments also contributed to the clamor to break from the Union. Charleston and other ports of the South were aggrieved that they were not permitted their share of direct seaborne trade with the rest of the world. This was an especially contentious issue among merchants and exporters resentful that Northern ports monopolized transatlantic commerce, with much Southern produce being shipped abroad via New York.

President Lincoln and his secretary of state, William Henry Seward, were well aware of the disparity between the two sides. The Northern industrial sector was some thirteen times the size of that in the Southern states. The North could manufacture the munitions it needed for its war effort, while the South would have to import all its arms from Europe. Washington was mindful of the harm done to the United States by the British blockade during the War of 1812. Lincoln declared a general blockade of the Southern coastline on 19 April 1861 to ensure that this imbalance was maintained and that the South could not exchange its cotton for vital war supplies.

This was an extremely ambitious project. With some three thousand miles of coastline for Northern ships to patrol, the blockade was always going to be porous, and its very legitimacy would be questionable under international law. As the London *Economist* commented at the time, Lincoln was "endeavouring to establish the greatest blockade ever known or contemplated since navigation has been an art. We cannot believe that it will succeed; we have no faith that such a blockade can be effectual; and upon our government will lie the difficult, the delicate, but the pressing duty of enabling our ships to disregard it with impunity as long as it is ineffectual."[3]

The British government, under the leadership of the wily old Whig politician Lord Palmerston (Henry John Temple), appeared somewhat ambivalent in its views about the war. Palmerston and his foreign secretary, Lord John Russell, were conscious of the strong anti-British element in the North and wanted to avoid an all-out conflict and to protect British Canada from American expansionism. While Palmerston was sympathetic to the Cavalier Southern cause, he was strongly opposed to slavery. He was well aware of Lancashire's dependency on Southern cotton, but he was also conscious of Britain's need for North American wheat. Essentially the government favored a diminution of American power and saw the breakup of the Union as a benefit to Britain as a world power. France, too, under Napoleon III, saw advantages in the transformation of the balance of power across the Atlantic.[4]

This is the story of one man and the small part he played in the titanic struggle between the American peoples, a struggle between two ideals—that of a romanticized notion of chivalry and honor fatally flawed by slavery and the racial brutality it entailed, and a stricter nonconformist morality compromised by city slums, rural poverty, and industrial exploitation.

James Carlin's involvement was not one of heroic participation in the immense land battles that have come down to us as typifying the horror of the American Civil War. However, his part exemplifies elements that were new to warfare. As the senior captain of the South Carolina Importing and Exporting Company, overseeing eight other blockade-runners, he helped keep the munitions flowing to the troops on the front line. He also played a key role in a pivotal experiment in the application of new technology to naval warfare.

James Carlin's main contribution was to the blockade-running effort that sustained the Confederacy for bitter years beyond what would otherwise have been the fighting capacity of a purely agricultural economy. The blockade-runners brought in thousands of tons of arms and munitions, while exporting tens of thousands of bales of cotton, which underwrote the financial viability of the Southern states up until their collapse in 1865.

The family's romantic legend has James Carlin making some one hundred trips through the blockade. However, this is not borne out in the research of leading authorities such as Stephen Wise or Marcus W. Price, who credits him with some twenty-five runs in Charleston and Wilmington but does not take into account runs through to other Southern ports.[5] It is probably impossible to establish the actual number with any accuracy. We know most of the ships he commanded at various points but cannot verify that he was actually on board for all their voyages. From existing records and newspaper reports we can tally about fifty one-way trips in which he probably served as captain, pilot, or supercargo, or was just an ordinary passenger. This seems a more likely number from the available evidence and assumes that he was on vessels he was known to command at the time of their recorded arrival or departure at ports across the South. This makes him one of the leading blockade-runners as promoted in the Charleston newspapers that frequently lauded his successes. But propaganda and deception tactics also played a role in these reports.

Carlin also used his skills and his experience to design efficient vessels to continue the trade commanded by captains he had selected and trained. The rewards for successful captains were enormous by the standards of any period. The blockade-running commanders were paid more per trip than many a man could earn in years of labor.[6]

This was a conflict where science, technology, military logistics, and manufacturing innovations led to a new form of combat, which we recognize now as modern warfare. The revolutionary weapons devised by the Confederate States Navy exemplify this. While there were no great massed naval battles, there were ships, devices, and battles that were so revolutionary in concept that they showed the way for naval warfare into the twentieth century.

Charleston was central to the blockade-evading efforts of the Confederacy. The city was located on a spacious harbor some seven miles from the open sea. Ships with a draft of up to eighteen feet could enter the harbor by a variety of routes: through the wide estuary of the converging Cooper, Ashley, and Waldo Rivers and through other, narrower channels such as the Stono River and Wappoo Creek, a shallow cut-through that connected the Stono River with Charleston Harbor. "The bay is almost completely landlocked, making the harborage and roadstead as secure as they are available," noted a Charleston directory of the time.[7]

The port was connected to the Southern railways lines and was thus tied into the communications network for the entire region. The railroad system went as far as Mobile, Alabama, on the Gulf Coast and to the banks of the Mississippi River. Despite its deficiencies, the Confederate authorities made extensive use of the network for transporting men and munitions to points of need and bringing inland cotton to the coast.[8]

At Charleston, Wilmington, and other ports, blockade-runners chose dark nights to hit the coast just north or south of their target harbor, running close into the shore and then turning down the surf line until they could slip into the shallow estuary openings. In this way the spray from the breaking surf and morning mists helped to obscure their "sky-coloured" ships.[9] The deep-draft Union warships could not get close enough inshore in these shallow waters beset with sand bars and banks to challenge the runners effectively. Ship owners soon realized that specialist knowledge of the coast was needed for these navigationally exacting dashes though to Charleston or Wilmington.

James Carlin's watching spirits, his "kindly fates," had prepared him to become just such a specialist blockade-runner. He was a skilled seaman who had gained an intimate knowledge of the coast of the Carolinas as a pilot with Dr. Alexander Dallas Bache's U.S. Coast Survey Department. He used this knowledge to become the top-ranking captain in the South Carolina Importing and Exporting Company (I&E Company), holding the substantive rank of senior captain or "commodore" in the merchant navy. His later adventures off the Cuban coast caused turmoil among the colonial governors and the Royal Navy admirals who administered Britain's interests in the Caribbean. In his seafaring exploits, James Carlin left his adversaries shaken and stirred, but he met his ultimate fate many years later in New York.

# Chapter 1

# Early Days, 1833–1848

• • •

The North Norfolk coast fringes the bulge of eastern England that juts out into the North Sea. It is a land of dunes, salt marshes, and enormous skies, where the horizon dissolves into a haze of washed blues and greys. To the east, the coast turns south to form the northern entrance to the English Channel. Westward, at the faded Edwardian bathing resort of Hunstanton, the dunes give way to cliffs rising to some two hundred feet above the currents and tidal sandbanks of the Wash, a great square of open water that looks like a bite taken out of Norfolk. In reality it is a multiple estuary for rivers draining the Fenlands. High on the cliffs overlooking this wide expanse is an ancient lookout point on the pre-Roman Icknield Way.

St. Mary's Church, Old Hunstanton, North Norfolk.
Courtesy of Francis Frith Collection.

Straddling a cleft in these cliffs is the village of Old Hunstanton, where James Carlin was born in December 1833. Early in the New Year he was taken to the Parish Church of St. Mary the Virgin, where he was baptized on 5 January 1834 at the church's ancient Norman-style font. His baptismal record shows only one forename, James, but at some point he added Cornelius, the name he was known by in later generations of his family.[1]

Later there was a lighthouse and then a Coast Guard station. The station cottages nestle on the side of the gap in the cliffs leading down to the beach that was the site of an early landing point for the Wash and joined up with the Roman Road through Lincolnshire to York and beyond. Somewhere in the Wash, King John lost his treasure as he scrambled across the treacherous sand banks, escaping the flood tide.

Across the Atlantic the estuary of the Ashley and Cooper Rivers is a similar, though warmer, seascape of rolling sea mists, currents, and hidden, mobile sandbanks. Here Carlin made his reputation as, in the words of the *Charleston Mercury* of May 1, 1863, "one of the most successful of the runners."

Old naive gouache of the Norfolk Saltings off the North Sea coast.
Author's collection.

James's family were not from Norfolk, although he often referred to Hunstanton and his English birth and called himself an Englishman. His elder sister, Eleanor, was born in Aldeburgh, Suffolk, and his younger brother, Charles Robert, was born in Carrickfergus, just to the north of Belfast, and made a point of calling himself an Irishman. Their father, also James Carlin, was a commissioned boatman in the British Coast Guard Service. His seaman's records show that he came from near Rathmullen on the coast of County Donegal, but he started his Coast Guard service at Aldeburgh on the east coast of Norfolk.[2]

James Carlin Sr. never progressed beyond commissioned boatman, probably because of a lack of education, but he was said to be of good character and was well regarded in the Carrickfergus area in his later years. He came from a maritime family who served for generations in the Royal Navy as petty officers before taking up the comfortable billets of the shore-based Revenue Service.[3] Seafaring on the great warships of the time took a physical toll on the older men, and the navy recognized that long service warranted reward.

London Road, Brancaster, North Norfolk, in the 1880s.
The Coast Guard cottages are to the right, just behind the girls in their smocks. Author's collection.

In the Dublin Archives there are a series of letters from ex–Royal Navy seamen named Curlin/Curling, both also referred to as Carlin,[4] seeking appointments as boatmen for their sons and nephews in the Revenue Service. This would have been the way young James Carlin Sr. from Rathmullen was granted a highly prized post in the Coast Guard. The name probably became standardized as Carlin when the Royal Navy took over the Irish Coast Guard in the 1840s. This naval tradition is strengthened by family lore. The Carlins were part of the Anglo-Irish Protestant hegemony that governed Ireland in the days before the Republic, but they were not of the Anglo-Irish Ascendancy.

James Carlin Sr. married Susan Melles on 23 March 1831, while he was stationed in Aldeburgh. She was from an established Norfolk family that owned a glazing, plumbing, and engineering business. His Irish charm had attracted the older sister, Susan. She was twenty-eight, the third oldest of eight brothers and sisters, some of whom had married before her.

James Carlin Sr. and his new wife were quickly moved from Aldeburgh to Hunstanton "for the good" of the service. This was the usual practice for Coast Guards who married a "native" woman, as it was thought necessary to ensure that the men were not compromised by family ties that could ensnare them in local smuggling gangs.

From Hunstanton, James Sr. and his family were posted to Brancaster, a few miles to the east along the North Norfolk coast. Brancaster was then the best harbor between Kings Lynn and Yarmouth. The Coast Guard cottages, where the service families lived, still line London Road in Brancaster, and many are now much-prized homes. James Sr. may well have been present in November 1832 when officers at the Brancaster station seized a large "tub boat" and shared the prize money on 5,565 pounds of tobacco and 650 gallons of brandy.[5]

The Carlin family then moved to Cranfield on Carlingford Lough in Northern Ireland and later to Blackhead near Larne and Port Muck on Isle Magee, all Coast Guard stations in Ulster in the North East of Ireland.[6] The British Coast Guard Service had been heavily strengthened in the years following the Napoleonic wars. By the late 1830s the authorities believed that the worst of the smuggling on the English mainland had been overcome with a combination of reduced customs tariffs and a triple-guard strategy. This consisted of offshore cruisers tackling the provisioning craft that brought bulk supplies of contraband from the continent to within reach of the smugglers' small craft. Regular coastal patrols took care of the inshore routes, while onshore riding officers patrolled the shoreline and cliff tops.

The success of this strategy in England allowed large numbers of men to be redeployed to secluded spots on the Irish coast where there was still active smuggling. The service also took action against illicit distilling, causing much local hostility. The more remote stations suffered occasional attacks from Fenian nationalists. As a consequence, the men and their families were isolated from their Irish neighbors.

We can imagine that a lad in these surroundings would have delighted in the lore of the smugglers and all their romanticized ruses and tricks. From his father and his colleagues, he would also have learned the tactics the Coast Guards used to foil them. James came to the business of gunrunning with a useful background that must have helped him through some of his more hair-raising adventures on the coast of the Carolinas and in the Caribbean.

# Chapter 2

# Navigation School,
# the Apprentice, 1850–1856

. . .

James Carlin grew up in the British Coast Guard stations close to Carrickfergus, the market town of County Antrim. The service was noted for the care it took to provide education for the children of its officers who were often stationed in remote and isolated places. It also had the largest lending library then in existence. He would have been imbued with a seafaring tradition, "born to the sea," in the expression of the times. Male conversation would often have been of ships and tides, currents and storms. Steamships were now common in coastal waters, and there would have been technical discussions about the merits of the unreliable engines against the vagaries of the wind and the weather. James Carlin must have stood out from his peers as his father found a way to give him a good education for that time and place.

The Carlin family had a connection with Carrickfergus as James's father retired to a village near that ancient town after his long service. This is significant for his son's career because Carrickfergus was the location of the Larmour Navigation School. While no school register exists showing that James Carlin attended the school, his skill as a navigator and his service with the U.S. Coast Survey suggests that he may well have been a pupil.

William Larmour tutored in the houses of the local gentry, and many of his pupils went on to make careers as officers in the Merchant Navy. Larmour's school was at Joymount Bank. He also had another school at Union Hall at 4, High Street, Carrickfergus, the home of the local Scientific and Literary Society. There was the opportunity for James to have a sound education and instruction in navigation from Larmour himself. Larmour's obituary commented, "As a teacher of navigation, Mr Larmour earned a wide reputation, his pupils having navigated every sea in the known world; and some twenty years ago [in 1863], a number of his pupils, who were then captains in the merchant service, presented him with a valuable gold watch, as a token of their esteem for him as their instructor."[1]

James's nephews, the sons of his sister Eleanor, were all educated at the Royal Naval Hospital School in Greenwich in southeast London.[2] Their mother had died young, leaving her husband, James Edmunds, a station officer in the Coast Guard, with five semi-orphans. The boys regularly made the long journey to and from Ireland to benefit from the naval education that the Greenwich school provided. Some reached senior warranted ranks as engineers or engine room artificers in the Royal Navy. The 1848 syllabus for this school shows that the students were instructed in navigation and nautical astronomy, including geometry, algebra, and elementary trigonometry. They practiced marine surveying on the Thames.[3] Larmour's school would have followed a similar course to qualify boys for entry as officers in the merchant marine.

On 13 March 1849 James was apprenticed to Fitzsimmons of Belfast, ship owners, with the intention of qualifying as a merchant marine officer at the completion of his four-year term.[4] The apprenticeship records show that James was born in 1833 at Hunstanton, Norfolk, and that he was five feet five and a half inches tall, aged sixteen, and resided in Belfast. He had brown eyes, brown hair, and some damage to his left middle finger.[5] By April of that year, he had signed as a crew-member on Fitzsimmons's vessel the *Diamond*.

Nicholas Fitzsimmons was a long-established Belfast merchant and ship owner, and an agent for the Lloyds of London, the Glasgow and Liverpool Underwriters Association, and the Belfast Steam Packet Company. His offices were at 12 and 18 Corporation Street, Belfast. From the earliest years of the century, Fitzsimmons had run a series of copper-bottomed sailing vessels across the Atlantic to New York and as far as New Orleans. His advertisements emphasized the faster sailing advantages of their cleaner, copper-sheathed hulls.[6]

By 1 April 1854, only a year out of his apprenticeship, James Carlin was serving as a master's mate and pilot with the U.S. Coast Survey Department, having been recruited at the "friendly invitation" of a fellow officer.

Quite how he made his way from a lowly merchant marine apprentice to pilot in an elite U.S. service is unknown. However, there was a Fitzsimmons Wharf in Charleston, South Carolina, belonging to the wealthy family of Christopher Fitzsimmons, a merchant of an earlier generation. Charleston was then the third most important port in America. Carlin may well have spent the intervening years on a Nicholas Fitzsimmons ship running between Belfast and American ports, becoming familiar with the Carolinas and the northern Caribbean in the process.

James Carlin's invitation to join the U.S. Coast Survey by a fellow officer suggests that he had received a recognized education in navigation. His general literacy, competent report writing, and quick grasp of maritime legalities show a reasonable education for the period. His close association with the U.S. Naval officers and other outstanding figures in the Survey introduced him to American life and manners, raised his ambitions, and prompted his interest in his children's education. He was to send three sons to study at Göttingen and Heidelberg Universities in Germany and also ensured that his daughters were well educated by the standards of the period.

Chapter 3

# The United States Coast
# Survey Department, 1856–1860

. . .

J ames Carlin had been invited to join a select group of men. The United States
Coast and Geodetic Survey Department (the Survey) was an elite service. Most
officer appointments were directly seconded from the U.S. Navy and a number of
Coast Survey officers went on to distinguished careers in both the U.S. and Confederate Navies. The Survey also employed a corps of noncommissioned officers
in the role of ship's masters, master's mates, and pilots. Some of these were civilian
merchant seaman; others, such as Master's Mate William Budd, were from the
United States Navy. These were the men with practical skills in ship handling that
ensured the safety of the Survey vessels, while specialist naval officers and civilian
assistants directed the survey work and the scientific investigations and took command of the Survey vessels.

The Survey was formed in 1807 to study the coasts of the United States and
supply nautical charts and navigational aids for the use of seafarers. Over time, it
developed a reputation for innovative oceanographic research. Its work was highly
valued by sailors, ship owners, port authorities, and merchants, and was regularly
praised in the press for its contributions to maritime safety. The scope of the Survey
was continental, with parties working in nine sections from Maine on the Atlantic
Coast, around Florida and the Keys, to the Gulf Coast and the Texas border. Further work was undertaken on the Pacific Coast.

Dr. Alexander Dallas Bache extended the geodetic work of the Survey far beyond its original remit, and innovative scientific work was done on astronomy,
terrestrial magnetism, and telegraphy as a means of determined longitude.[1] Research was done also on the Gulf Stream, examining the deep water beyond the
coastal shelf and recording the bands of alternately warm and cold water within
the current and the offshore "cold wall" between the main current and the inshore
coastal waters. This would prove to be vital information for James Carlin in his
later exploits.

Dr. Bache, a noted scientist and a leading member of the American scientific establishment, was appointed superintendent in 1843. He was a prominent figure among the Greek-style Olympians of the Bache-Franklin family's American Philosophical Society. Bache, a great-grandson of the enlightened scientist and diplomat Benjamin Franklin, graduated at age nineteen from the U.S. Military Academy at West Point with the highest honors and went on to be recognized as one of America's leading scientists.[2]

Dr. Alexander Dallas Bache (1806–1867), LL.D. (hon.), 1837, with surveying instrument, stereoptic view. From the collection of the University of Pennsylvania Archives.

Dr. Bache served in the U.S. Army Corp of Engineers and taught at West Point before becoming a professor of natural philosophy and chemistry at the University of Pennsylvania. He conducted experiments into the earth's magnetism using the scientific methods being developed at Göttingen University in Germany.

Bache sought to establish strong links between American scientists and prominent German academics of the standing of the mathematician Carl Friedrich Gauss and the geographer and explorer Alexander von Humboldt. When visiting England and Scotland, he noted that German universities were then rated superior to their British counterparts.[3]

Bache's pro-German stance worked well with nationalistic, anti-British elements in both the Whig and Democratic Parties of Washington of that time. He took the German professors at Göttingen as his scientific mentors and sought to emulate their science and learning.

Bache was determined to use the Survey as the seedbed for U.S. scientific talent and recruited many promising young men who were to reach eminence in later life. James Abbott McNeill Whistler (1834–1903), the great American painter, learned the art of etching while working for the Survey Department in Washington before moving to Paris to study art and then on to London. In 1866 ex-Confederate officers in London brought Whistler into an abortive plan to sell steam-powered torpedo boats to Chile for use in their struggle for independence from Spain.[4]

By 1845 Bache's extensive Washington contacts included his uncle George M. Dallas, the U.S. vice president, and his brother-in-law Robert Walker, the secretary of the treasury. The American scientific establishment was then divided between an anti-British group led by Bache and a pro-British clique that included Matthew Fontaine Maury, a leading hydrographer, U.S. naval officer, and chief advisor to George Bancroft, the secretary of the navy. For some twenty years Maury had carried out innovative research into ocean currents and seasonal weather patterns, enabling seafarers to plan more efficient sea routes.[5] Maury became chief scientist to the Confederacy, while Bache, an intensely political operator, stuck to his Union post during the Civil War and led President Lincoln's military intelligence team.

Maury probably made the greater contribution to oceanography but was much disliked by Bache and his faction, and he was further scorned by them when he resigned from the U.S. Navy to join the Confederate forces. From as early as 1850, Maury had been alarmed at the growing forces threatening to dismember the Union.

Later, when James Carlin was a prisoner in Fort Lafayette, he sought Dr. Bache's help, saying that he, too, was "one of his followers in Science."[6] But Bache was having none of it. Carlin was tarred with the same brush as Maury, Maffitt, and other U.S. Navy officers who had gone to the South, and Bache had neither time nor sympathy for any of them.

Carlin's remark shows that he was familiar with these luminaries and saw himself as a member of their company. He would have spent many weeks with the scientific officers on the Survey schooners and small steamers as they charted the shoreline and inlets of the Atlantic and Gulf Coasts and during the off-season months, when they wrote up their results at the Survey headquarters in

Washington, D.C. Their company would have expanded his view of the world and the boundless possibilities of America.

Much of the Survey's work was conducted on entrances to the main harbors to keep mariners updated as the currents changed channels and sandbanks shifted. They also charted the creeks and channels of the offshore sea islands and farther inland on the tideways and estuaries of the larger rivers. This involved extensive use of small boats, as parties were sent ashore to establish base points for triangulations to fix the positions and chart the turns and bends of the channels and rivers. Other parties were sent downstream to sound the depth of water and record the material on the bed of the inlet or estuary or the outwash of the rivers into the open sea. The mud or silt and gravel with mollusk shells nearer the open sea were brought to the surface on the tallow at the end of the sounding leads. This information, when transferred to charts, was helpful to seafarers attempting to fix their position as they left the deep blue waters of the Gulf Stream and maneuvered in towards the coast.

There were scattered plantations along the banks of these waterways, some with porticoed mansions and slave quarters. And while there were some substantial properties, most were on a fairly modest scale. The day-to-day management of the plantations was often left in the hands of overseers, who risked mosquitoes, malaria, and sometimes yellow fever by staying on the plantations throughout the year, including the hot and dangerous months of high summer. The owners of the larger plantations had townhouses in coastal cities such as Charleston, Savannah, or Beaufort, where they and their families could avoid the worst of the dangers, escaping some of the heat and the fevers.

While James Carlin's day-to-day service is not recorded in the annual reports of the Survey, the movements of the ships he served on and their commanders are described in some detail in a letter from Bache to Secretary of State Seward. From 1 April 1856 through to the end of 1857, he was employed as a pilot on the schooner *Gallatin,* with Lieutenant John Newland Maffitt in command.[7] Both Carlin and Maffitt had an Irish background, and they clearly formed a bond during this period. They were to serve together on the blockade-runner *Cecile* and were involved together in other ventures. Newspaper accounts of their exploits in the earlier period of the war often linked Carlin and Maffitt with the prewar work of the Survey along the Southern coast.[8] While no evidence has been found to explain how James came to join the Survey, Maffitt may well have been the "fellow officer" who invited him to join up.

The *Report of the Superintendent* for 1856 shows that they surveyed the sea approaches to Charleston and reexamined Maffitt's Channel, the deep-water access to the inner harbor. Earlier in 1852, Maffitt had determined that this channel was worth deepening and enlarging. This dredging work was carried out by a consortium of local interests and had transformed Charleston's maritime trade, allowing deep-draft vessels access to the cities' wharves.

Dr. Alexander Bache, seated. Courtesy of Library of Congress.

Section V of the Survey, commanded by Maffitt, conducted the inshore hydrography of the coast of South Carolina between Charleston and Savannah, using three surveying vessels. With the schooners *Bancroft* and *Crawford,* Maffitt recharted Maffitt's Channel and completed further survey work at the entrances of Port Royal Bay, Broad River, and Beaufort River and the shoreline of St. Helena bar and sound, as well as inshore soundings between the coast and Martin's Industry. Lieutenant Hunter Davidson on the *Gallatin* also made inshore soundings starting two miles northeast of the mouth of North Edisto River, while continuing to connect with the work at St. Helena bar by Maffitt and his team. Davidson then completed the hydrography of the bar and the harbor at South Edisto River and made a reconnaissance of the entrance of North Edisto to chart changes since the original 1851 Survey.

These operations demonstrate that Carlin obtained specific knowledge of the entrance to Edisto River just south of Charleston, which was to be highly useful to him a few years later. His familiarity with the Edisto River suggests that he was, as reported, pilot or master on the *Gallatin* during this operation and was not farther down the coast with Maffitt.

His work in this area may also have played a role in his courtship of Ella Rosa Jenkins, who was to become his wife. The Carlin family has always understood that he had first met her during such an expedition, when he and the crew of the Survey vessel had been invited to a plantation house for an evening of refreshments, no doubt dancing under the magnolias.

Maffitt's report for Section V records that the Survey team made 107,855 soundings, took 9,527 angles (for triangulation), and covered 4,801 miles during the sounding exercise. They also took sixty-five bottom samples for classification and chart work, and established a dozen or so current- and tidal-measuring stations. As Dr. Bache said in his annual report, it was a highly credible performance in difficult conditions, and he commended "the zeal evinced by the hydrographic chief and to the energy of the officers associated with him." The crews also helped extinguish a serious fire in Beaufort and carried out work up the coast at Georgetown.[9]

It may not be just a coincidence that the party surveying the south Edisto and Charleston area returned to Charleston on 5 May 1857, the day James and Ella were married at 12 Tradd Street. It would seem that his shipmates were invited to the wedding.

On 30 December 1857 James Carlin left the schooner *Gallatin* and transferred the next day to the schooner *Crawford,* commanded by Lieutenant J. B. Huger, where he continued until 15 October 1858. Huger was assigned to resurvey the entrances and bars of the Cape Fear River that led to the city of Wilmington, North Carolina, a major port of call for the blockade-runners a few years later. Huger reexamined Maffitt's channel to observe the scouring effect that slowly deepened the dredged channel and undertook offshore hydrography between Cape Romain, South Carolina, and Fernandina, Florida. If Carlin spent this season with Huger's party, he would have become an expert on precisely those sections of the coast where he was to run through the blockading squadrons a few years later.

On 16 October 1858 Carlin transferred to the schooner *Varina,* under Lieutenant Charles M. Fauntleroy, who was assigned to survey the entrance and approaches of the Sapelo River and Sound, a five-mile waterway passing inland from Savannah, Georgia. Both the schooner *Varina* and the steam tender *Fire Fly* were used, giving Carlin the opportunity to handle both types of vessels in tricky conditions and bad weather. Soundings were taken up to ten miles offshore and north and south of the entrance and the bar at the mouth of the sound. The lead was cast 29,404 times. The leadsmen would have heaved the lead weight and line over the brow of the little ships and called "mark" as the lead hit bottom, reading the depth from the spacers on the line. It was a wet and tiresome task for the crew.

In December 1858 Lieutenant Fauntleroy's party returned to the North. Carlin arrived with the *Varina* in Baltimore, having commanded the schooner on its voyage back from Port Royal to Baltimore. He announced his arrival as follows:

Baltimore Dec. 15 1858
Sir
I have the honor to report my Safe arrival at this
    place with the US Sch. Varina at 11 pm of the 14th.
The Varina is now anchored off Fells Point . . .
I am sir, Respectfully your Obd. Svt.
James Carlin, Masters Mate, U.S. Sch. Varina[10]

Dr. Bache then ordered James to report to Lieutenant Fauntleroy, then staying at the Baltimore Hotel.

Lieutenant Fauntleroy was instructed to take the schooner *Varina* to Port Royal Sound and the Broad River and the area between Hilton Head Island and the mainland, including Daws Island, and complete the hydrography of the more important parts of its main tributaries, the Chechessee and Colleton. The parties worked some two or three miles up both these rivers. The bed of the Colleton River was examined and recorded; Foot Point at the rivers' confluence with Port Royal Sound was also "thoroughly sounded."[11] An extract from a report to Dr. Bache by Lieutenant Fauntleroy on the commercial advantages of the upper waters of Port Royal Sound, South Carolina, gives a flavor of the work involved:

UNITED STATES SURVEYING SCHOONER VARINA
*Colleton river, S.C.* May 21, 1859
SIR * * * The Hydrographic work was commenced at Pinkney's island, connecting with Lieut. Comg. Maffitt, in 1855. That survey shows that the bar of the Chechessee river affords twenty feet at mean low water, with a mean rise and fall of 6.6 feet. The depth increases in passing upward, and vessels that enter Port Royal sound will find in Colleton river at the Neck, and at its confluences with the Chechessee, a capacious, completely protected, and easily accessible anchorage, in from four to seven fathoms water.
\*    \*    \*    \*    \*    \*    \*    \*    \*    \*    \*    \*    \*    \*    \*
Colleton Neck, Foot Point, or Victoria Bluff, as it has more recently been called, is only eleven miles from the Charleston and Savannah Railroad, and, by reason of the fact before stated, offers a very eligible site for the purposes of trade and commerce. In the event of blockade of the southern coast by a naval power this point could be easily made a sure protection to the inland commerce passing between Charleston and Savannah. . . .
CHAS. M. FAUNTLEROY
*Lt. Comg. U.S.N. Assistant, Coast Survey.*[12]

Fauntleroy's perceptive remark about a blockading naval power demonstrates that by 1859 the U.S. Navy was seriously considering its tactics in the event of hostilities and had a clear understanding of the consequences of a blockade. James Carlin developed an insider's view of the U.S. Navy's thinking as he worked with his commander piloting the *Varina* though the coastal channels and sounds of the Carolinas and Georgia.

The *Fire Fly,* which had previously been a private yacht, had then returned to Charleston for repairs.[13] Writing on 16 May 1860 at the end of the survey season, Lieutenant Fauntleroy complained bitterly about the inability of the marine engineering shops in Charleston, including Cameron and Cox, to undertake the repair of the boiler of the *Fire Fly* in under four months. It is a curiosity of the seafaring history of these times that both straightforward mechanical repairs, and also the handling of cargoes, took an extraordinarily long time. Fauntleroy also wrote that he could not persuade the little steamer's engineer, Mr. Griffin, to stay in the South and do the work. The engineer wanted to return to his family and refused to bring them to the South because of his concern for their safety in those summer months. "Within a few days of the secession of South Carolina on 20 December 1860, the officials of that State seized two Coast Survey vessels, the Schooner *Petrel* and the small steam yacht *Fire Fly,*" Faunterloy noted.

He also added a postscript: "Mr J. Carlin has left the Survey and removed to Texas with his family. I do not know how I am to replace this valuable officer whose practical skill in Surveying & Seamanship was at all times equal to every demand made upon him."[14] This was a handsome compliment but does not offer an explanation for Carlin's actions.

On 30 April 1860 James Carlin left the schooner *Varina* and the Survey Department. There could have been very few men on the Atlantic Coast of America with as much knowledge of the routes one could use to evade the blockade that the U.S. Navy was to soon impose on the Southern states. He had charted the channels, plumbed the depths of the sounds and estuaries, and triangulated most of the coast from Fernandina to Cape Fear and beyond. He had also been part of scientific research into the Gulf Stream and the ocean's deeps offshore. Either by accident or design, he was exceptionally well prepared for the events ahead.

# Chapter 4

# A Romantic Interlude, 1857

. . .

Ella Rosa Imogene de Montijo Carlin. From Carlin family records.

James Carlin married Miss Ella Rosa de Montijo Jenkins while he was still with the Coast Survey. To this day she is an enigma. The Carlin family has many legends about her. Some of these may be elderly ladies' fantasies, others the "official version" for daughters-in-law and valued friends and relatives.

The Survey parties were well received at the plantation houses, where they provided welcome company for the isolated communities. The sailors, especially the young officers, caused great excitement among the daughters of these families. The crews were invited for meals and dances, and the Carlin great-aunts used to say that James first met Ella Rosa at one such occasion. They also said that he saw her later on the seawall at Charleston, or perhaps it was the river levee in front of the Ursuline Convent in New Orleans. He was sailing by, close inshore on his ship, and she was promenading with her school friends, twirling their parasols at the passing sailors. Pointing to Ella Rosa, he turned to his fellow seamen and said, "That's the girl I am going to marry!" They responded with cries of derision, but marry her he did. In recounting such stories, the imaginations of those sharp-witted women in their faded Kensington drawing rooms in London were fired by their mother's tales of her plantation girlhood and her romance with James. It was around 1940. *Gone With the Wind* had just hit the British cinema screens in all the wonders of Technicolor, and they frequently went back to see the film "just one more time."

James and Ella Rosa were married on 5 May 1857 by the Reverend William Black Yates at what was to become their home at 12 Tradd Street, Charleston, a house that belonged to the Ravenal family.[1] The Reverend Yates and A. F. Ravenal were both board members of the Marine Hospital. This raises a question: why were they married at home and not at a local church? "Parson" Yates was the Scottish Presbyterian pastor of the Seamen's Bethel, or Mariner's Church. As the bethel was intended to cater to the common sailors who visited the port, it may not have been a romantic venue for marriages, but there were other Episcopalian and Presbyterian churches in Charleston.

There may well have been additional reasons for a private wedding, not least the suspicion that Ella Rosa was in some way a runaway bride. No trace has been found of her antecedents despite very extensive searches over many years. Family sources suggest that this was a mixed marriage in the sense that James was raised as an Anglican, while Ella Rosa's story that she was Spanish makes it likely that she came from a Roman Catholic background.

Whatever the truth, their numerous children grew up as Anglicans, and two of them married the children of Anglican clergymen. The Reverend William Yates was to play a prominent part in their lives throughout their connection with Charleston. He might also have played a bigger role helping a runaway bride, or a young girl who was marrying against her parents or guardian's wishes across a religious divide. Carlin family traditions say that Ella Rosa's mother died in childbirth and that Ella Rosa was brought up in a convent. The nuns were accused of trying to "steal" her money. This suggests that she was an orphan under the care of the nuns or a remote guardian. We can speculate that these funds would have been her dowry and left with the nuns for safekeeping, who then refused to pay up when she ran off with a sailor. This money played an important part in James's future actions.

The Reverend Yates was a remarkable man. At an early age he survived a four-and-a-half-hour operation to remove a tumor from his left clavicle, showing astonishing fortitude in those days before anesthesia.[2] Renowned chaplain of the Seaman's Mission in Charleston, he was a mentor for James and his family and a trustee of their Charleston assets when they left for England. While their marriage was recorded in both Yates's marriage book and by the diarist J. F. Schaumer in his journal of day-to-day events in Charleston, there is no official record of the marriage, or of any license.

Ella Rosa's telling of her story suggests a plantation background. On the 1860 census she was listed as born in Louisiana, but she does not appear in any records in that state.[3] Was she a member of the Cuban Montejo family from Cuba and Louisiana, or from the extensive South Carolina Jenkins family of Edisto Island, an orphan whose name escaped the records? Dr. Jenkins's plantation and that of Mary Jenkins on St. Helena Island both fronted broad tidal creeks in the area James was surveying. Perhaps Ella Rosa was from the Jenkins family of Goose Creek a few miles inland from Charleston, where her Joyner sister-in-law's family had a small plantation.

The family legend relates that on her supposed deathbed (she recovered), Ella Rosa confided that she had a secret source of funds because she was the niece of the Spanish-born Empress Eugénie, consort to Napoleon III of France. This is an astonishing claim that raises many questions, not least the possibility that Ella Rosa's mother was an unrecognized half-sister of Eugénie. Ella Rosa's story implies that Eugénie's mother, the magnificent Maria Manuela Kirkpatrick y Grivegnée, Countess of Montijo, had a child at an inconvenient time in the early days of her marriage when her husband, a well known Liberal, was a prisoner of the Inquisition in Santiago de Compostella.[4] Maria Manuela was a woman with a reputation. She certainly had a very long-lasting and close friendship with George Villiers, who was to become Lord Clarendon, the British foreign secretary.[5]

Eugénie was, after her friend Queen Victoria, the most celebrated woman of her age. An astute politician, trendsetter, and sometime regent of France, Eugénie conducted French cabinet meetings in the absence of the emperor, and was consulted by European heads of state and diplomats during her long exile in England. She died in 1920.

Was Ella Rosa a fantasist? Was she hiding modest origins as an abandoned waif in the Charleston Orphan House? Of the $7,196 raised for this charity in early 1863, James Carlin had donated $2,000, or some $37,000 in today's terms.[6] This was only the largest in a series of donations from the Carlin family, which were regularly recorded in the Charleston newspapers. Was her story concocted later to hide funds that her husband was anxious to keep from lawyers or government agents?

The fact remains that Ella Rosa included de Montijo in the names of some of her children and that Carlin gave his wife's "previous" name as de Montijo a number of times when registering the birth of their later children after 1870. This was just after Empress Eugénie fled from Paris in dramatic circumstances following the debacle of the Battle of Sedan at the end of the Franco-Prussian War. She was brought across the channel in an English gentleman's yacht and went into exile in England. Her past prominence and friendship with Queen Victoria meant that she was mentioned frequently in the world press.[7]

Extensive research in the United States has failed to reveal a direct link to a Montijo family in the Carolinas or Louisiana, which would fit Ella Rosa's legend and timing. However, there were Montijos/Montejos in Camaguey Province, Cuba, who also owned plantations in St. Mary's Parish, Louisiana, where James Carlin leased an estate in 1870. They appear in New Orleans social diaries and were tobacco and cigar merchants in New York. The Montejo family was prominent in the Cuban liberation struggle. Mercedes Montejo Sherman was secretary of the Cuban Liberation Junta in New York when James Carlin was commissioned by the junta to run guns into the Cuban coast.

The Empress Eugénie had de Lesseps cousins in New Orleans and a great uncle in Richmond, Virginia, who founded the Gallegos Flour Mills that were reduced to iconic ruins after the Union army occupation. His will shows no legacy that would connect him to Ella Rosa.[8] Her numerous daughters and sons all believed that there was a family connection to Spain and the fabulous empress whose father was the Spanish grandee Colonel Cipriano Palafox y Portocarrero, later Conde de Montijo. Ella even named a daughter Maria Eugenia after the empress.

Whatever the truth or fantasy of her assertion, Ella Rosa, who affected a very Spanish style, seems to have come into substantial funds a few years after her marriage. In later life, in James's absence, she had the resources, both in terms of finances and character, to maintain a modest household in Victorian London and to educate her thirteen surviving children and ensure their "suitable" marriages

Jenkins may have been just an adoptive name. Ella Rosa may have been the Mademoiselle E. Richardson listed in the roll of the large Ursuline convent that fronts onto the Mississippi River in New Orleans. Richardson was a name that Ella Rosa also used as a form of maiden name in later life, and a prominent Richardson family in New Orleans married into the de Lesseps family, who were real cousins of the Empress Eugénie through her great-aunt, Catherine de Lesseps, the wife of Ferdinand of Suez Canal fame. The de Lesseps were also associated with the Beauregards of New Orleans, a connection that may have played a part in a later drama in James Carlin's life. Or it may all have been a dream. Whatever the reality, her story seems to have worked for both her and her husband, while giving her daughters a romance that equaled that of Scarlett O'Hara and her lover, Rhett Butler.

The plantation owners were also the very people who most resented what they perceived as the interference of the U.S. government in their affairs, particularly the ownership of their slaves, whom they regarded as vital to their economy and the maintenance of their capital and way of life. The Coast Survey parties were welcomed socially, but they had come to represent the North and Washington. The crews and ships retreated to Northern ports in summer months, and the more sophisticated and worldly planters knew that Dr. Bache was an abolitionist and strong opponent of the secessionist movement gaining strength in the South.

Given the growing anti-Washington sentiment, it is not surprising that the Survey was beginning to meet local hostility and opposition. The small parties went about unarmed and were highly vulnerable to intimidation, nuisance, and the theft or destruction of their equipment and valuable instruments. The history of the Coast Survey records that, in contrast with their former popularity, the surveying parties working along the Southern coastline in the winter of 1860–61 suffered harassment and threats, leading to the early termination of fieldwork and the return to Northern waters.[9] Trouble was brewing.

Ella's parents or guardians would have felt the anti-Union sentiments sweeping the South and may have had difficulty accepting a potential son-in-law employed by a Washington institution. James Carlin's noncommissioned rank may have excluded him from their usual social circle. Someone, somewhere, may have put pressure on him to become a landsman so that he could care for his family and ensure that they were not left alone in a troubled state or with freedom-seeking slaves while he was away for months at sea.

Carlin could have gathered up Ella Rosa and his small family and moved to the Coast Survey headquarters in Washington. Instead he chose to leave the Survey and head for Texas.

Suddenly, from somewhere, he had the financial means to make choices. The state elections and the vote for secession were still some seven months away. Was he unduly prescient or blithely unaware of the significance of the mounting tension between the Southern states and Washington?

Other factors may have influenced James Carlin's decision to quit the Survey. He now had a family, his first son, James Cornelius, having been born on 2 September 1859. (He and Ella Rosa may have lost an earlier first-born.) His young wife must have complained about the seasonal nature of her husband's work, which took him away from home for long periods. He had not entered through service with the United States Navy like the other officers, nor was he was an American citizen, and he would have known that he was unlikely to make commissioned rank in the Survey. However, the determining factor must have been the couple's sudden relative wealth. Carlin was leaving behind safe government employment and starting the rest of his life, a period that was to lead to a measure of fame and riches, but also to great excitements, turbulence, notoriety of a kind, disasters, and a sad conclusion. This was a time when Carlin seemed to be hunting for a role. He had a wife and son, and somehow he had money to hand and the freedom to explore the possibility of independent life onshore.

# Chapter 5

# Transition, 1860

· · ·

James Carlin left the Coast Survey Department on 30 April 1860. Two days previously the Carlins had purchased a female slave named Nora, aged about eighteen years, and her son, Peter, aged about six months, and "together with her future issue and increase."[1] The sale price was $900, equivalent to about $25,600 at today's rates.[2] Nora's previous owner had been Seaborn Richardson, who may have had some connection to Ella's family. This was no simple cash purchase. A bill of sale was drawn up and sworn before a notary public of the State of South Carolina.

At a time when the institution of slavery was being called to account in the most dramatic way, Carlin's decision to make such a large "investment" must have been driven by Ella Rosa and her domestic needs. Whatever his own views might have been, and there is no suggestion that he was an abolitionist, they were not strong enough to hold out against the wishes of his wife. Ella Rosa's domestic influence seems to have grown with their newly acquired affluence. They had the means to move on, and Texas was a slave state, so Nora could go with them.

The money surely came from Ella Rosa's dowry or from her family resources, as Carlin could not have found $900 from his pilot's pay of $38 per month. This sudden display of independent means reinforces Ella Rosa's romantic story. Perhaps she did come from a well-to-do family, although it is a very long step to claim that it was all somehow linked to a faraway empress in France.

This was a confused period in their lives, and the family appears to have been highly mobile, moving between Charleston, Savannah, and Texas. Their precise movements remain obscure. James and Ella Carlin left for Texas in early 1860. He resigned from the Survey in good order and kept the respect of his fellow officers, some of whom he was to encounter in various guises during the course of the Civil War and later in Liverpool.

By 19 July 1860 Ella, James, and their baby son were all living in New Braunfels, Texas, then an expanding commercial center supplying a developing agricultural economy. It was a largely German community organized fifteen years earlier by Prince Carl of Solms-Braunfels to relieve population pressures in Germany. The Comal County census of 19 July 1860 lists James Carlin's occupation as farmer.

In the house with the Carlins were Edward Jenkins, aged sixteen, who was born in Louisiana, and Emily Anderson, aged nine, who was born in South Carolina. There is no indication of the relationship among them all.

There were good reasons for Carlin to take his family out of Charleston for the summer months, particularly as young James was only a few months old. Dry, hot Texas was safer for children than the fever-ridden lowlands of the Carolinas during the dangerous summer months. Carlin must also have appreciated that war was coming. Political sentiment was becoming strongly secessionist, and it was time to move on. He was an Englishman. American squabbles could be left to the locals. Doubtless there were better prospects in the West, and he had a wife and family to support.

Social pressures from Ella Rosa may have also contributed to their decision. Somehow, they had the money to join the "planter" class, head west, and leave their old life behind. This was the destiny of many of the younger sons from the East Coast. The Mississippi Valley was already settled and young men headed to Texas for cheaper land, fresh soil for growing cotton, and new prospects. If Ella Rosa has gained access to her own capital, or her father had accepted James and funded their new life, then the move would suit an ambitious young couple.

Given the seasonal nature of the Survey's work Carlin may have become accustomed to take on inland survey contracts in the hurricane months of summer. His expedition to New Braunfels could have been a survey project undertaken for Charleston interests in Texas. As an ambitious, trained ship's master and surveyor, he had some good reasons for leaving the Coast Survey. Becoming a farmer in rural Texas was an entirely different matter.

The most comfortable way to make the journey was by steamer around the Florida Keys to the ports of the Gulf of Mexico and on to New Braunfels in Comal County, Texas. Overland travel involved long journeys by train and coach, a hot and even dangerous trip. Later events suggest that they called in at Nassau on New Providence Island in the Bahamas and established useful contacts in that small British colony. They would have called in at Havana, Cuba, where their ship could take on coal, water, and even ice to comfort the passengers. In 1859 luxurious Cunard mail ships included Nassau en route to and from Havana and New York. We can imagine James and Ella enjoying the exotic Spanish atmosphere. A "paseo" in an open carriage though the surrounding countryside would be a welcome break from the notorious stench of the city. From Havana they would have made their way to Comal County, Texas.

By 27 October 1860 Carlin or his agent had paid $550 cash to Henry Dietz for 218.5 acres of land, twenty-four miles southwest of New Braunfels on the waters of the Cibolo River. He also signed a $300 promissory note, payable on 31 January 1866, for the balance secured by a mortgage to Dietz. This was a wise precaution on the part of Dietz as Carlin failed to pay up. In a petition of 1866 Dietz stated that on 11 March 1861 James made a further agreement with him to pay the note by 10 May of that year. By 1866 James had abandoned the property and surrendered the mortgage.[3] In today's dollars $550 is the equivalent of some $8,000.[4]

Rumors of a slave revolt swept the South in the fall of 1860. These wild stories induced a sense of alarm into the already inflamed atmosphere caused by John Brown's raid on Harpers Ferry. The panic started in Texas, as the press reported slave plots, and unease spread through the Southern states.[5] At this point the little family moved from New Braunfels to Anderson in Grimes County, Texas. The township lies between Austin and Huntsville, northwest of Houston. This may have been a stop on the way home to Charleston or maybe Ella Rosa had friends or family in Anderson, then a fast-growing center on numerous stagecoach routes. It boasted five hotels and two steam sawmills. It had been the fourth largest town in Texas but declined in importance when it was bypassed by the developing railway network.

Carlin was soon back at sea as captain of a coastal packet boat plying between eastern Florida, Savannah, and Charleston, and later of a small schooner in which he had a share. Farming in Texas was not for the restless master mariner. A year or more later, toward the end of 1861, he claimed that he had been living in Nassau since the spring of 1860, a date that coincides with the Carlins' departure from Charleston. Ella and her small son, James, were passengers on the *Cecile* on a trip from Savannah, Georgia, to Charleston in early February 1860. For a time her husband was the captain of this steamer on a regular run into Charleston.[6] James Carlin was well set for the role he was to play in the events that followed.

Chapter 6

# The Blockade Is Declared, 1860–1861

. . .

D eteriorating relations between the states of the Union led to South Carolina's declaration of secession on 20 December 1860, followed by a night of wild excitement and jubilation in Charleston, then acting as the state capital. Six states followed South Carolina's lead, with four more states opting for the South during April 1861.

View of Charleston, South Carolina, just as the Civil War was about to begin.
*Harper's Weekly,* 26 January 1861. Reprinted with full permission from
Applewood Books, Publishers of America's Living Past, Carlisle, MA 01741.

The pace then quickened, with open hostilities breaking out over the Southern forts still in Federal government control. At 4:30 A.M. on 12 April 1861, South Carolina state forces shelled Fort Sumter in Charleston Harbor, turning the citadel into "an erupting volcano."[1] Some thirty-four hours later, the Federal garrison was forced to surrender. On 19 April, President Lincoln imposed a blockade of Southern ports stretching from South Carolina to the Texas border with Mexico. The blockade was extended to cover North Carolina and Virginia on 28 April. This had the effect of recognizing that a state of war existed between the North and the South, and the breakaway states were now seen as belligerents under international law.[2] The coastal blockade was planned as the first phase of General Winfield Scott's Anaconda Plan to overcome the insurgency by encircling the Confederacy and cutting off all succor. The second phase was to be a rapid thrust down the Mississippi River to divide the Confederacy.

To implement this strategy, a blockade board was constituted in June 1861 with Dr. Bache of the Coast Survey and Captain Samuel F. Du Pont and Commander Charles H. Davis for the U.S. Navy. Major John G. Bernard represented the U.S. Army.[3] Coordinated plans were made to seal off both the Atlantic and the Gulf ports of the Confederacy. The U.S. Army and Navy set about the task of closing down the South's supply routes from land and sea.

The president's announcement was based on the principles of the Declaration of Paris of 16 April 1856, which followed the negotiations that concluded the Crimean War. This was intended to convert what had been international common law to a form of statute law.[4] The United States was not among the powers that signed the declaration, as the State Department had reservations regarding the first principle, which banned privateering. The United States saw this prohibition as benefiting those nations with large navies. However, Secretary of State William L. Marcy, in response to the declaration, noted that the United States was in general agreement with the principles governing the imposition of blockades and the seizure of contraband of war.[5]

President Lincoln's two blockade proclamations caused confusion in the chancelleries of Europe. Under established international law, a nation could legally "close" the ports of its own rebellious states but could only "blockade" those of independent nations. Lincoln's statements were seen to imply recognition of the independence of the Confederacy. His action had serious consequences.[6]

The Europeans nations recognized "the belligerency of the South, but not its actual sovereignty."[7] This had the effect of granting the South the right in law to import and export goods other than munitions. It was later argued that Lincoln's words were taken as tacit permission for the cross-Atlantic trade that was to underpin the Confederate war effort. To be legal, a blockade had to be effective, although subsequently, as legal scholars Jack Goldsmith and Eric Goldsmith note, Lincoln unilaterally "changed the U.S. stance arguing that it did not have to be totally effective to be legally effective."[8] These differing interpretations led to much legal wrangling.

On May 1 1861 Secretary of the Navy Gideon Welles set out to clarify the government's position by issuing a set of "Instructions to Commander of Coast

Blockading Squadron." He was ordered to "duly notify all neutrals of the blockade and give it all the publicity in his power." Additionally, "No neutral or foreign vessel proceeding toward the entrance of a blockaded port was to be captured or detained if it had not received, from one of the Blockading Squadron, a special notification of the existence of the blockade which must be inserted in writing in the muster roll of the neutral vessel."[9]

"Cæsar Imperator" or the American Gladiators. *Punch*, 16 May 1861.
Courtesy of Bristol Record Office.

The blockade-running captains soon became aware of these instructions, and captured ships crews frequently tried to invalidate their capture by stating that they had not been stopped en route into a blocked port or, if they were stopped, that they had not been given a warning or proper notification of the blockade.

The declaration also stated that neutral ships could carry any goods from one neutral port to another, including "contraband of war," if those goods were intended for actual delivery at the port of destination and were to become part of the common stock of that country or port. However, if the intention was to transfer the contraband to a belligerent state, whether by the same ship or another vessel or overland (as was the case on the Mexican border), then the contraband became liable to seizure.

These principles were tested by the cases of the *Bermuda,* the *Springbok,* and the *Peterhof,* which were heard in the U.S. Supreme Court at the termination of hostilities.

Robert Bunch, the British consul in Charleston, reacted quickly to Welles's instruction and the arrival of the blockading squadron off the entrance to Charleston Harbor. On 13 May he reported on events to the British Embassy in Washington:

> My Lord [Lord Lyons K.C.B.]
>
> I have the honour to acquaint Your Lordship that on the morning of the 11th Instant a Blockade of this Port was instituted by the United States Steam Frigate "Niagara", Captain McKean, and it was currently reported that several Vessels, both English and others, have been warned off by the commander during that day. This morning the British Ship "A and A", of London, Hutchinson, Master, came into the Harbour and anchored off the city. Upon the Master presenting himself at this office, I required of him an explanation of his reasons for breaking the blockade, when he informed me that he had received no warning or instruction from the Blockading ship of the condition of affairs and knew nothing whatever concerning it. I took his affidavit of the facts and have the honour to transmit herewith to your Lordship a certified copy of it. The reasons given appear to me to be entirely satisfactory.
>
> But as I was not aware of the view of this which might be entertained of his conduct by the commander of the "Niagara", I deemed it advisable, in order to prevent subsequent complications and the possible seizure of the "A and A" on her departure from the Port, to visit the Frigate and hear Captain McKean's version of the occurrence.

We are then presented with the splendid vision of the British consul steaming out of Charleston harbor with the British flag flying at the masthead of his steam launch:

> I therefore hoisted the Union Jack on a steam boat and proceeded in search of the "Niagara" which I found at about fifteen miles from the city and seven from the mouth of the harbour—I was received with the customary honours and had a satisfactory interview with Captain McKean who concurred in the

correctness of the Statement made by the Master of the "A and A." He re-marked that when the Merchant Vessel anchored, the "Niagara" was engaged in supplying water to another British Ship, and also that he thought the "A and A" seemed to be aground for which reason he left her alone. I inquired whether the vessel would be allowed to come out with her cargo to which he replied that she would—

I next asked Captain McKean if he would allow the Masters of British Vessels arriving at the Port to come up to the City in their boats to secure orders from their consignee, which he declined to do but stated that if unsealed letters were sent to him for them, they should be delivered if they contained nothing improper. I also secured his promise to supply British vessels with water and provisions should they stand in need of them.

Captain McKean informed me that he expected eight or ten vessels to arrive in a very few days as a Blockading Squadron, and added that the Flag Officer was also expected. This was said in reply to the suggestion on my part that a single ship like the "Niagara" could hardly be considered as adequate to the Blockade of so extended a Coast as that between Charleston and Savannah. . . .

I should add that Captain McKean allowed twenty days for the departure of Neutral vessels counting from the evening of Friday 10th Instant.

I have etc—signed Robert Bunch.[10]

This letter was Consul Bunch's first report on the effectiveness of the U.S. Navy's blockade and thus the extent to which its failure invalidated it. He made the point again on 12 June 1862 in a letter to Lord John Russell, M.P., the British foreign minister, listing in detail all ships that had successfully entered the Port of Charleston without being stopped by the blockading squadron. It was a point that would be taken up by the Confederate government and used by the defense in subsequent Admiralty Court actions.

Their argument was based on Article No. 4 of the Treaty of Paris of 16 April 1856, which governed the rights of neutrals and the establishment of blockades. The article stated: "Blockades in order to be binding must be effective; that is to say, maintained by a force sufficient really to prevent access to the coast of the enemy." The use of the word "really" came in for much further discussion, but it was understood to mean that it should be interpreted in the "strictest manner."

Blockade-runners had to find a safe passage between these ambiguous lawyer's arguments. One wrong move and they risked execution as pirates or the firing squad as traitors. As we shall see, James and his lawyers would become adept at negotiating the legalities of both British and American admiralty law.

Both Confederate and Union supporters argued for the interpretation that suited them best, and British officials were reluctant to prosecute for fear of incurring large penalties for wrongful arrest or detention of vessels. While merchant shipping was a legitimate part of commercial trade within the terms of international law, equipping and arming merchant ships was prohibited.[11]

President Lincoln was well aware of the manufacturing deficiencies of the South and believed that a blockade that cut off industrial products and munitions, and also prevented the export of cotton, would soon bring the Confederacy to its senses. In the South, leading opinion was much different. Jefferson Davis, the new Confederate president, even declared in his inaugural speech of February 1862 that the blockade would be ineffective.

In the South everyone, including the Confederate naval authorities, believed that it would be impossible to close both the Atlantic and the Gulf coastlines, and that it would be no more than a "paper blockade."

By 1862 the English public, too, had become convinced that the blockade was ineffective and joined in the trade across the Atlantic. The U.S. consul in Liverpool, writing to Secretary of State Seward at the end of 1864, reported that "Members of Parliament, mayors, magistrates, aldermen, merchants and gentlemen are now daily violating the law of nations. Nine-tenths of all vessels now engaged in the business were built and fitted out in England by Englishmen and with English capital, and are now owned by Englishmen."[12]

The U.S. Navy found it was facing formidable problems. The distances were immense, and resupplying and coaling their vessels was a continuing headache. The navy's commanders had little local knowledge of the harbors and estuaries they had to close and had difficulties with unfamiliar tides and currents.[13] The journalist Thomas Cooper Deleon wrote that in the early days it was "so inadequate that traders ran in and out Southern ports with greater frequency than before."[14] He was to change his tune by 1863, when he wrote that "the blockade has become so thoroughly effective that blankets and shoes had almost run out and a large portion of the Army was barefoot."[15]

To modern eyes, one of the curiosities of the whole episode is that Southern substitution industries did not take off as some commentators had expected and hoped. The Confederacy expended its energy and its white manpower in the military effort, and little was left over for any attempts at larger-scale manufacturing. Many enterprises were forced to close because of the scarcity of labor.[16] However, near the end of the conflict, William Bee and others, including James Carlin, embarked on a large-scale mill project in Aiken County, South Carolina.[17]

While the plantation owners willingly sent their sons off to the war, their slaves were not diverted to the war effort but kept on the land to produce yet more cotton.[18] Planter interests prevailed. Imports were vital to sustain the army in the field, and the government in Richmond turned its attention to ways to circumvent the blockade and earn diplomatic and financial advantage from the European and North American demand for raw cotton.

# Chapter 7

# The Wildcatter
## Blockade Running Under Sail, 1861–1862

. . .

Most accounts of the men and ships that ran the blockade into the Southern states concentrate on the fast, low-profile steamers and their famous captains, the mixed collection of American pilots, local skippers, British Merchant Navy personnel, and even some half-pay Royal Navy officers passing time before their next command. British colonial shipping records from the West Indies show a large increase in registered tonnage over the early period of the blockade as local sailing vessels took up the new business. Between 1861 and 1862, the value of Bahamian exports increased by five times. Some early runs were made in rowboats. Small open craft, owned by the islanders, made the trip to Florida and returned piled as high as they dared with a few bales of cotton. With the introduction of specialist steamers, exports had reached £4,600,000 in 1864 from a base of £157,350 in 1860.[1]

On 1 July 1861 James Carlin visited Savannah, Georgia, and signed up in the service of the Confederate States Navy on the Savannah Station with the rank of pilot for an annual salary of $750.[2] In comparison, a captain received $1,250, a master's mate $300, and a midshipman $500. These salaries provide a useful gauge of the standing of these ranks at a time when sail was giving way to steam. There is no record of Carlin ever receiving this salary, nor were any deductions made for the Hospital Fund. For the period 1–31 July he received a total credit of $55.31, which included a $6.00 credit for undrawn rations. While this amount is ticked off along with all the credits for the other officers on this pay sheet, his is the only name without a countersignature, suggesting that he did not draw this pay, although he remained on the muster roll through at least 1864.

It is probable that, along with his other ex-Survey colleagues, he was directed to more useful employment running the blockade. The Confederate navy was desperately short of vessels and would not have been able to deploy him any more effectively at that stage of the war. As a "neutral" Englishman, he was decidedly more useful as a blockade-runner than as a naval officer for the Confederacy, a posting that would have required a change of nationality.

The trade carried by coastal or interisland vessels was considerable, especially in the earlier period of the blockade before the U.S. Navy deployed more ships and created a more effective cordon. These Bahamian "wildcatters" were not associated with large overseas merchants. The boats carried local produce selected to take advantage of shortages in the South. They often ran from small cays or the beaches of the Bahamas, avoiding the scrutiny of both British and American officials in Nassau.

While they sometimes carried military supplies for the Confederate forces, the quantities were small, although the salt they carried was a vital strategic commodity for the Confederacy. W. C. Thompson, the U.S. vice consul in Nassau, reported that the wildcatters formed "a very large amount of blockade running done by sailing vessels of which there is no record."[3] They also developed techniques for avoiding the blockading squadrons. The U.S. Navy found it difficult to find these little vessels when they lowered their sails and turned end on to the warships, thus presenting a low profile that was almost invisible among the Atlantic swells.

Between June and the end of 1861, well over two hundred small sailing vessels arrived at Southern ports.[4] Shortages were sending prices up. A growing cash economy reduced credit provision and restricted trade. Fernandina, Jacksonville, the Indian Rivers, and Jupiter—all in northeast Florida—were favored destinations for the smaller wildcatters in these early days. James started his blockade-running career in just such a sailing vessel, utilizing his intimate knowledge of the coast to run small cargoes into Charleston.

From the second half of 1860, James Carlin was skipper of the *Mary Adelaide,* a small two-masted schooner trading local produce between the Southern states, the Bahamas, and the northern coast of Spanish-held Cuba. A subsequent court action suggests that he captained this vessel in the months just before and after President Lincoln's proclamation of the blockade on 19 April 1861. The court transcripts give us a very detailed picture of an early attempt to run through the blockade in a small sailing schooner.[5]

The ownership of the *Mary Adelaide* at this stage is not clear. Carlin may have owned half the vessel, but he was its master in mid-August when it ran the blockade out of Charleston with a cargo of rice, cleared for Matanzas on the northern coast of Cuba. The vessel was built in 1847 in Worcester, Maryland. The schooner was of some 60 tons, British measure, caravel built, with a single deck and square stern, measuring 68 feet long with a beam of 21 feet. Carlin would have found a vessel of this size and type very familiar from his days with Coast Survey Department schooners such as the *Gallatin.*

In August 1861 the *Mary Adelaide* left Nassau, heading for Matanzas. The captain and crew would have directed the ship for the northern tip of Andros Island, intending to cut through Providence Channel to the Straits of Florida for a clear run to northwest Cuba. The eastern side of the straits is skirted for a hundred miles or so by the Grand Bahamas Banks. This string of reefs and keys starts some fifty miles off the coast of Florida at about the latitude of Fort Lauderdale and extends to the southern group of Bahamian islands paralleling the northern coast of Cuba. While Carlin had probably made a number of similar trips, this was a very dangerous stretch of water. Sailing through it successfully required local knowledge and skilled navigation.

The little ship must have been carried off-course by the Gulf Stream. As the strong current of warm water rounds the tip of Florida, a westerly branch escapes into Northwest Providence Channel and influences flow along the banks. The *Mary Adelaide* was "wrecked" on these banks in unknown circumstances.[6] August is the beginning of the hurricane season, and the crew might have met the remains of bad weather farther to the south or west.

This "wreck" may not have been what it seemed, as the banks are shallow coral beds. A section of hull was likely stove in on a coral head in some eight feet of water. Temporary repairs can often be carried out *in situ* with tarred canvas coated in oakum, and the vessel can then be pumped out and returned to port. The schooner was reported to have sustained sufficient damage to be pronounced unseaworthy, but it was rapidly patched up and sent for sale in Nassau. The *Mary Adelaide* had taken James's fancy. He had sufficient confidence in the "damaged" vessel to arrange for a partner to buy it for $600 when the previous owner sold the little trader at auction in Nassau.

Doubt remains about this accident. Was it a ruse to ease out a previous shareholder, or was it an excuse to transfer the ownership to neutrals and bring it under British register? James Carlin would have been aware of the pace of events in Charleston. As historian Stephen Wise notes, "numerous Charlestonians saw tremendous opportunities to exploit the national split to their own advantage."[7] Carlin would have appreciated that there were fortunes to be made once the naive optimism of the likes of the blowhard Colonel Louis T. Wigfall gave way to commercial reality and the scale of the South's import requirements became clear. (Wigfall was well known for having rowed out to Fort Sumter alone and making an unauthorized demand for its surrender to its bemused commander. He was later a Confederate senator.) Carlin had the schooner seaworthy again very quickly. The damage must have been slight; big profits were in the offing.

Carlin had a busy month that September as the *Mary Adelaide* is listed as arriving in Nassau on 4 September with a cargo of rice consigned from Charleston.[8] By now it would have become obvious that the little schooner could no longer be on the Charleston shipping registry. On 21 September 1861 the previously "foreign owned" schooner *Mary Adelaide* was entered into the British shipping registry by Nassau authorities as the *Alert*. The owner was given as Joseph Roberts of Nassau, New Providence.

Further details are given in the Certificate of British Registry, a magnificent document exhibiting all of Queen Victoria's authority by sporting a huge royal coat of arms.[9] Here, a Joseph Roberts of Nassau, whose occupation is given as "clerk," is shown as full owner of all sixty-four shares, while Carlin is shown as the master with no certificate of competence or service number given. This implies that he never took the usual British or U.S. examinations for ships' officers and masters, and his time in the Coast Survey was seen as sufficient qualification to command vessels. Joseph Roberts was a resident merchant in the Bahamas who became highly active in blockade running, using his British nationality to provide legal cover for his activities.[10]

James Carlin was in Nassau during August and early September 1861 while the *Mary Adelaide* was being repaired. Whether his wife, Ella Rosa, was with him is unknown, but it seems unlikely, as she was heavily pregnant with their second child. William Yates Carlin was born in Charleston on 13 September 1861. William had been named in appreciation of the Charleston pastor and his parents' joint guardian angel, the Reverend Yates, whose wife would have supported Ella Rosa during her husband's frequent absences.

At the end of October 1861, Carlin stated in court that he was living "at Nassau New Providence one of the Bahamas islands, and had been sailing out of there off and on for the last year and a half."[11] He added that he had lived in the United States for the four years prior to that, and had passed the last seven years in England, the Bahamas, New York, Charleston, and Texas. He said that his family was living in Charleston and before that had resided in Anderson, Texas.

Robert Roberts, a Welshman, joined the vessel as first mate at about this time. There is no record that he was related to the part owner Joseph Roberts, also of Nassau, but he was allowed some personal cargo. Joseph Roberts's son Richard, a merchant captain, also became an active blockade-runner.[12] James's younger brother Charles Robert Carlin joined the crew, having shipped with them from Charleston.

The *Alert* sailed out of Nassau's notoriously shallow harbor on Sunday, 22 September, with thirty-four hundredweight of molasses and some barrels of sugar on board. The merchants and seamen of Nassau were very aware of the movements of the Union naval ships watching for vessels emerging from the harbor entrance. These were deep-draft warships, so patrolling was restricted to the north of New Providence in Northwest Providence Channel and in the depths known as Tongue of the Ocean to the west.

Carlin's route was governed by the tides that limited access to the harbor and the probable position of the Union blockading squadron. While the risk of capture in offshore British waters was remote, he would not have wanted to be boarded and searched or reported to the inshore blockading squadrons.

The shallow draft of the *Alert* allowed the little schooner to slip out of the back of Nassau harbor between Hog Island and Fort Montague Point and to head out over the banks. Carlin took on a southeasterly course over very shallow, difficult waters to Norman's Pond on the cay of the same name, in the long string of small islands known as Southern Exuma Cays. Norman's Pond Cay encloses a shallow lagoon that was worked as a saltpan. The *Alert* loaded eight hundred bushels of sea salt, then in great demand for preserving meat for the Confederate army. The Bahamas had exported salt to North America for generations, and this local industry provided seasonal work for many Bahamians and, along with salvage, was a mainstay of the islands' economy. The *Alert* then headed north for Current Island at the western tip of Eleuthera Island.

Current Island is no more than a long straggling spit of land separated from the main part Eleuthera by a narrow cut. Here the *Alert* took on board 20,000 oranges and limes, 3,000 pineapples including *pina blancas* (the choicest variety), 220 hands of bananas and plantains, and 400 coconuts. Also, 2,000 cigars in 67 boxes and a barrel had been loaded in Nassau. Some of the cigars belonged to Robert Roberts, the mate, who also owned the navigation quadrant. The cigars were a personal speculation, a common perk for sea officers, especially if the goods took up little cargo space. This cargo typifies the local produce that was being carried by the Bahamian wildcatters.

There was also a barrel of bread, or ship's biscuit, and a bundle of bark, probably quinine, which was valuable as a remedy for malarial fevers. One witness stated that James Carlin bought the fruit and salt, but whether he did this on his own account or for Joseph Roberts is not known, although he stated that the cargo was jointly owned, about half each.

While Carlin and his crew were sailing over the shallow and dangerous waters to the west of Eleuthera and Exuma Cays, he would have felt relaxed about the risk of meeting any Union warships; these were dangerous waters for any vessel. The Union navy would not have ventured from the known deep-water channels into these shallow seas littered with a graveyard of coral heads. The risk of sighting one of their warships was more serious in the open water from Current Island across the Northeast Providence Channel on course to Charleston 560 miles away, as Union warships lurked off the Berry Islands at the choke point between the Northwest and Northeast Channels.[13] This route was marked with British-built lighthouses, allowing for accurate, if anxious, night navigation.[14] When in the shoal water, Carlin and his crew would have been dependent on using buildings, casuarina trees, and tree trunks stuck in the sand to establish position and find safe channels. In these conditions navigation came down to local knowledge, and night passages would be terrifying and a genuine test of seamanship.

From Current Island the *Alert* set sail across the deep, ultramarine waters of the Northeast Providence Channel, leaving Great Abaco Island well to starboard to avoid the notorious reefs between Hole in the Wall and Gorda Cay. They sailed on past Grand Bahama Island, entering the Northwest Providence Channel in daylight on course for Memory Rock Lighthouse. This marked the western limits of the Little Bahamas Bank and entry to the Florida Straits, where they followed the Gulf Stream heading north.

The crew agreement shows James Carlin as master with no salary stated. Robert Roberts is listed as mate. He signed on for a monthly wage of thirty dollars and described himself as a seafaring man from Wales, who had hardly spent more than two weeks on land for the last seven years. The steward, or cook, Joseph Francis from Lima, Peru, signed with an "X" for twenty-five dollars in pay. The three seamen, including Charles Carlin, were signed on for eighteen dollars each.

Officially, the *Alert* was bound for St. John in New Brunswick, Canada, which would be a logical destination in September for a cargo of West Indies fruit that included bananas and limes. But St. John was also a cover destination used by many blockade-runners in their attempts to legitimize their ship's papers. It was a well-understood ruse; the customs officials in Nassau gave "the vessels clearances as British Vessels sailing for British ports."[15] This was later cited as a contributory British fault in the postwar case that the United States brought against United Kingdom authorities for reparations in what became known as the Alabama Settlements.

We know the details of this voyage because the *Alert* met its nemesis off the shores of South Carolina, and the case ended up in court in Baltimore. Testimony of the witnesses to the Baltimore Prize Commissioner give varying accounts of the last voyage Carlin took in the *Alert* and give us unique insight into a blockade run in a sailing vessel in the period before the general introduction of specialized fast steamers.[16] These events took place in the period prior to the Union invasion of Port Royal some sixty miles south of Charleston, when few had any notion that the war was going to drag for another four years.

Although the blockade was being evaded easily and many ships were bringing war supplies into the Southern ports, these were early days, and both the methods and the rules of engagement had not been developed. From the tactics James Carlin employed, it is apparent that he had been involved in earlier runs though the blockade into Charleston but had not perfected the timing of his approach. He also seems to have had bad luck or poor judgment with his appreciation of the wind and weather conditions on a mid-September dawn off Stono Bar, just south of the point where the coast folds back into the bay that forms the entrance to Charleston Harbor.

We take up Carlin's story as he told it to the Prize Court. Twelve hours clear of Current Island, on the morning of Wednesday, 25 September, it started blowing hard from the east and continued fresh until the ship had cleared Memory Rock at the west end of Great Bahama at about 5:30 that afternoon. The gale then increased. With the wind on the beam, the *Alert* was able to maintain its course for, in Carlin's words, "St John, New Brunswick." He stated that he "followed the course of the Gulf Stream, the usual route for such a voyage, bearing as close into the wind as the weather would admit." The little schooner was hard pressed, and it must have been a wet and anxious night for all aboard as they wondered if worse weather was on its way, unseen in the darkness to windward.

That anxiety increased when the vessel "started," or pulled, the main bolt of the starboard chains, securing the starboard rigging of the main mast to the hull. This split the planks on the ship's windward side through which the bolts passed. As these were below the waterline, the damage caused the vessel to take on water. The danger grew as the ship heeled and lurched into the waves and the pumps had to be kept going continuously. If the alarm was as real as Carlin maintained in his statement, the crew must have feared for the mainmast and for their lives.

The usual route Carlin spoke of, between Nassau and St. John, would have put the *Alert* sixty to seventy miles off the coast of the Southern states. The schooner kept its northerly heading as close to the usual Gulf Stream course as the fresh easterly winds and damaged tackle would allow. On the evening of Friday, 4 October, when the vessel was off Charleston, the wind "hauled," or shifted, more to the bow of the vessel. It was now blowing directly against the flow of the Gulf Stream, raising shorter, steeper waves, making for a desperately uncomfortable sea state.

With strong winds blowing from the northeast, ensuring that the *Alert* could no longer maintain its course, Carlin consulted the mate, Robert Roberts, who told the court in Baltimore that "she was not worthy to venture on to St. John." Carlin and Roberts decided that it would be prudent to seek help from the blockading fleet. The leak needed to be stopped and the mast secured. If the Union squadron was not found in the Charleston approaches, their plan was to declare Charleston a "Port of Necessity," thus giving the *Alert* the right, under international law, to seek repairs in the nearest refuge. Or that was the story they told in court.

At midday on Saturday, 5 October, the *Alert* was some thirty miles off Charleston in large waves but with little wind. Carlin may have used his knowledge of the deep-ocean temperature syncline, the "Cold Wall," to gauge how far he was from the coast, although he could probably tell this, even in the dark, from changes in the state of the sea. The variable speed of the strong current also introduced uncertainties, and the crew could not be sure of their position by calculating their time and speed alone. They would have had to start taking soundings as soon as they were close enough to shore. That evening a light wind sprang up from the northeast, and Carlin headed the ship toward the coast with the breeze now on the starboard quarter.

The crew must have been feeling their way inshore most of the night with the sails slatting in the light airs and heavy groundswell. They were casting the lead line as they went in. At 2:30 the next morning they found themselves near the shore and dropped anchor. Soundings, or seabed material, that were stuck to the tallow on the base of the sounding lead, combined with depth readings from the fathom markings on the line, had guided them in. But in the dark Carlin and crew would have been uncertain of their precise position in relation to the bar at the mouth of the Stono and thus had to wait for first light to attempt a crossing, with the anticipation of a dawn breeze or a rising tide.

Carlin stated in his interrogation that he had turned the badly leaking schooner toward land to seek help from the U.S. Navy. In any event, he found himself in the darkness, close inshore, having passed through the lines of the outer blockading squadron but uncertain as to the position of any warships maintaining the inner cordon. He was within sight of the loom of the breaking surf and would have been only too conscious of the set of the tide toward the coast. James Carlin's first experience of gunfire would come at the break of day on 6 October 1861.

Sunup found the ship about four miles from the mainland and some eight miles south of the Charleston Light House about half a mile seaward of Stono Inlet. With no wind and an adverse tide, the ship was in no condition to bear away under sail from the line of surf skirting the entrance to the inlet. Carlin ordered his boat out, and the crew started towing the *Alert* away from the breakers. They planned to make some sea room on an east-northeasterly course against the wind and the waves that were pushing the *Alert* toward the surf line. This was heavy work for the four members of the crew who had supposedly been pumping ship all night.

# Chapter 8

# The First Gunfire
## The *Alert*, October 1861

• • •

James Carlin claimed in his interrogation that he was seeking the blockading fleet.[1] Whatever the truth of this assertion, the United States Navy certainly found him. About half an hour after first light, just as the sun rose, the little schooner was spotted by the steam frigate USS *Roanoke,* with Captain John Marsden commanding, farther offshore to the south and west. It seems that neither Carlin nor his crew spotted the *Roanoke* as they continued rowing in a northeasterly direction toward the fleet on the outer blockade. At this time, he still had the palmetto flag of South Carolina flying at the hoist for the benefit of the Confederate batteries on the shore.

Captain Marsden signaled to Lieutenant Commander Louis C. Sartori on the USS *Flag,* to give chase and join the other vessels. The crew of the *Alert* was preoccupied with rowing. The first they knew of their imminent capture was the sight of the *Flag* steaming down on them at a distance of about ten miles, bearing east-northeast. This supports Carlin's assertion later that he was heading out toward the Union blockaders, pulling in an east-northeasterly direction with the rowers' backs to the approaching warship. When the *Flag* was about six miles off, Carlin must have seen that capture was inevitable, as he cast anchor and called in his rowers.

The Confederate battery on the Stono Bar (at the end of Folly Island where the U.S. forces later established Battery Delafield) then opened up with a ranging shot at the USS *Flag,* which fell short. Carlin later stated rather disingenuously that he could not tell if the shots from the shore were fired at the *Alert* or at the *Flag.* A correspondent of the *Philadelphia Bulletin* was on board the *Flag* at the time and gave a lively account of the affair that included Carlin's comments on his capture.

The Confederates were clearly warning the Union navy to keep its distance. It was at this point that Carlin claimed that he hoisted his English ensign with the Union Jack down, indicating that the vessel was in distress. Two or three more guns fired from the onshore battery, and a shot from the *Flag's* Parrot gun was promptly fired across the bows of the anchored *Alert*. The *Flag* then lowered its four sea boats and forty-two men, commanded by Lieutenant E. Y. McCauley, "dashed gallantly" to be the first boat to reach the *Alert*. They were all armed with Sharps carbines and Minié rifles, and each had a cutlass and revolver.[2]

The boats from the *Flag* pulled over to the *Alert* under gunfire from the Confederate shore batteries on Stono Island, which fired on the Union sailors up to eleven times. Two boats loaded with Confederate troops from the shore rowed out to intercept the navy boats from the *Flag,* but after approaching a short distance, they rested on their oars some way off, powerless to help the *Alert*. The Confederate boats remained out of sight of the *Flag*'s boats behind a line of breakers, and thus McCauley's party did not attack them. It is clear from the action of the military authorities on shore that the *Alert* was recognized as a blockade-runner. The batteries, about a mile and half off, had been quick to give assistance, although they were not able to drive off the Union naval forces.

Being of inferior force to the *Flag* and unarmed, Carlin and his tiny crew aboard the *Alert* were unable to make any resistance and were captured. Indeed, had they offered resistance, their legal position would have changed drastically. They would have faced accusations of piracy and the severest of penalties.

The *Alert* was only some fifty yards from the foam-crested breakers when it was taken in tow by the U.S. Navy sea boats and brought alongside the *Flag*. The crew were made prisoners. The ship was seized on latitude 32°35″, four miles from Stono Inlet at eight o'clock, and was brought beside the *Roanoke* by midday on that Sunday, 6 October 1861. The phrase "inferior force" and the statement that the *Alert* was "unarmed" appear significant in the context of the distribution and awarding of the prize money to the vessels involved in the capture. The *Alert* witnesses talked of two or three shots from the battery on the shore and seemed uncertain about where the shots were aimed. The Union naval officers, however, stated that eleven shots were fired at the four boats belonging to the *Flag* as they raced to the *Alert:* "At intervals the roar of the belching cannon rolled sullenly to us over the waves." With the prize money at stake, a little exaggeration would not go amiss. The officers claimed also that the pine-covered slopes back from the inlet were alive with at least two thousand rebels, who were running "hither and thither" and even climbing trees to get a vantage point. The Union officers congratulated themselves on a "beautiful achievement" in the very face of the enemy and its guns: "Every eye had been intent upon the waste of billows to catch the fall of the shell."[3]

In court Carlin asserted strenuously that he was not trying to run the blockade, but that his situation, when found by the *Flag,* was purely accidental, caused by the current and the disabled condition of his vessel, and that he was attempting to obtain relief from the blockading squadron. He made the point that he was attempting to accomplish this at the time he was discovered. His northeasterly course was given as proof of this intent as he and his crew were pulling away from the Stono "before the *Flag* was known to have any knowledge of the situation of his vessel."[4] This is an interesting statement by Carlin. He was trying to prove that he was already seeking help from the blockading squadron before he knew that the *Alert* had been seen by the *Flag.* Maybe the very name of his little ship gave the game away.

Carlin stated later, "At 7 o'clock I was boarded by the *Flag's* boats. But in running in had no design of breaking the blockade, unless none existed, when from the condition of my vessel I felt justified making for the nearest harbour."[5] He was already aware of the legal aspects of blockade-running at this early point in the conflict and was exasperated by his capture. He told the boarding party that, as he was an Englishman, he had perfect immunity and could fly any flag he liked.

Charles Robert Carlin in about 1861.
Courtesy of the Loxahatchee River Historical Society.

That is the story of the *Alert,* according to James Carlin, his brother Charles, and his loyal mate Robert Roberts.[6] Their statements, combined with Carlin's comments to the newspaper correspondent and the reports of the Union naval officers involved, give a vivid picture of events, but they do not tell the whole story.

The *Alert* followed a line of approach that was to become the classic blockade-runner's tactic. First, they kept well out to sea on the regular route beyond the outer Union navy's cordon. Then as night fell, they turned westwards and slipped through the widely scattered Union squadrons, taking soundings as they hit the shallow waters over the continental shelf. They would have planned to arrive well inshore at dawn but just clear of the surf line. In first light, with haze from the surf as cover and any dawn breeze, the *Alert* would have slipped across the Stono Bar and made its way up the creek and cuts to Charleston.

Carlin is reported as having flown both the palmetto flag of South Carolina and the Confederate flag while in harbor in Nassau, and as flying the "Secessionist" flag when discovered by the Union navy that morning, becalmed off Stono Inlet. He wanted to ensure that the Confederate batteries on the shore recognized him and did not fire. He quickly ran up the Red Ensign when he realized that the blockading squadron had seen him. He hauled this down, and ran it up again upside down, with the Union Jack in the down position that was internationally recognized as a distress signal.

We can imagine Carlin's dismay when the onshore morning breeze failed and he found his vessel becalmed on the surf line, with an incoming tide setting him toward the shore and enemy warships within sight. Carlin would develop a very considerable reputation for coolness in these situations, so it is interesting to observe his reactions in his first experience of having to think on his feet under gunfire.

Evidence of his state of mind in this crisis moment comes from reports about the flying of the Union Jack. James Carlin did not expect to find the Union navy well inshore within sighting distance of the Confederate flag he was flying for the benefit of the shore batteries. But the story about the damage to the *Alert* seemed well rehearsed, at least with the mate Robert Roberts and with Charles Carlin. The crew ran the British flag up quickly enough when the *Flag* approached to prevent further shots from the U.S. gunboat. The Union navy would not have readily fired shots aimed to hit a ship flying the British ensign, whatever their suspicions about its real purpose. Similarly, the ruse of hauling down the British ensign and sending it back up the mast in the reversed position to signify a vessel in distress may have been preplanned, but seems more likely to be quick thinking on Carlin's part. He then used in his defense the fact that the northeasterly course his boats were rowing when discovered took them directly toward the blockaders. We shall never know whether this was happy circumstance as his tiny crew labored to escape from the breakers or whether it was deliberate calculation.

However, Commander Sartori was withering in his assessment of the damaged sustained by the *Alert* during its passage north from the West Indies. He stated that he "could see no damage, but what could be remedied by any seaman in a half hour with material on board." But the *Alert* was in danger off Stono inlet; it was being set onto the surf by a flood tide and was not underway in becalmed conditions. In fact, the *Alert* was being towed by its ship boat. Given that there were only three men and a boy trying to haul the vessel out to sea lends credence to Carlin's plea that it was in distress and needed assistance of some kind. It is also likely that while the starting of the chains might seem minor in becalmed conditions, that damage would feel very different out at sea in a fresh gale.

Captain John Marsden reported that as the party from the *Flag* came on board, the mate Roberts was seen hiding something in the transom.[7] When they searched that portion of the ship, they found Confederate and palmetto flags. He also reported a statement by the Peruvian cook, who said that Roberts came into the galley to burn a bundle of papers as soon as it became obvious that the vessel would be captured. Marsden pointed out that the papers he sent on to Commodore Louis M. Goldsborough were all new, "as though got up for the occasion,"[8] and that they were all dated 21 September, the date before the *Alert* sailed. This indicates the care with which Carlin prepared his cover story and suggests that his actions were carefully calculated to take advantage of whatever happenstance produced.

While Captain Marsden admitted that while Carlin claimed to be English and that his papers, such as they were, confirmed his statement, there was so much evidence to the contrary that he decided to send the vessel to the naval base at Hampton Roads, Virginia. We have to conclude, as did the court in Baltimore, that Carlin and his crew were running the blockade but that there was indeed substantive damage to the vessel and that it was in some danger off the Stono Bar that morning in September 1861.

After their capture, Carlin and crew were taken to Hampton Roads, where Rear Admiral L. M. Goldsborough was commanding the North Atlantic Blockading Squadron from the U.S. flagship *Minnesota*. One the 23 October 1861 he wrote to Major General John E. Wool, commanding the Department of Virginia at Fortress Monroe, requesting that a free rail passage be given to the crew of the British schooner *Alert* to enable them to go to Baltimore to attend the trial of the *Alert*.

This note confirms that Charles Robert Carlin was detained with his older brother and released for the trial. For a lad of eighteen this must have been a lively experience. The rest of the crew were a makeshift bunch. Their background and characters are partly revealed by the Prize Court process.

The trial took the form of an inquiry based on a series of preset questions, or standing interrogations. It was conducted at 41 St. Paul Street, Baltimore, the office of the prize commissioner, Andrew S. Ridley, under the authority of the District Court of Maryland. Each crewmember was asked the same questions, and the commissioner then compared the answers and made a judgment. This was a prize court, not a criminal trial. The commissioner had to decide on the fate of the vessel and its cargo, not that of its master. The crew appeared to be free to return to the South at the end of the trial.

Joseph Dillman, who shipped in Nassau, was an able seaman on board the *Alert*. He stated under oath that he was born in Germany but was a naturalized British subject residing in Wallace, Nova Scotia, British North America.

He told an interesting tale. He said that he had heard that there were "good times at Nassau among the wreckers."[9] Today this term implies a deliberate act akin to piracy, of setting out to lure a vessel to its doom, perhaps by placing misleading lights or giving false information. While there were elements of this lawlessness, especially in the early days, the Bahamas lived by wrecking for many centuries, and the trade can be seen more as a legitimate salvage industry than as piracy. It is an indication of the danger of local navigation that by 1856 there were 302 ships licensed for salvage and 2,679 Bahamians held government wrecking licenses. Over two-thirds of exports from the islands comprised salvaged goods that had been sold through the Admiralty Vice Court at Nassau. Doubtless Dillman found that the Bahamians had the business all sewn up.[10]

Dillman had left Halifax the previous spring to go down to the West Indies. He stated that he shipped on board the *Alert* as a convenient way of returning home, there being no wrecking business at Nassau, and going to Brunswick was a "handy way to get there." This shows that Carlin may have had some intention of going to St. John, New Brunswick, or that if he planned on going to Charleston, he did not tell all the crewmembers. Dillman complained of being kept on board the *Roanoke* for ten days with additional time on the USS *Vandalia*. He said that the *Flag* fired three guns at the *Alert,* but that the shots fell short and that guns were also fired at the *Alert* from the shore batteries on the bar before the *Flag* fired. They, too, fell short.

Another witness, a foremast hand named W. Henry Relyea, confirmed that he had been with the ship for a year or more and that, as the *Mary Adelaide,* it had run the blockade out of Charleston on its voyage to Nassau under the command of Captain Carlin. He said that it had been wrecked on that trip and sold in Nassau. He thought that Joseph Roberts, an English resident of Nassau, had bought the schooner at auction for $600. Captain Marsden regarded Relyea as a "very intelligent lad," who told him that "he shipped under English papers, but not under the English flag," and that he shipped for St. John, New Brunswick, but now knew that the ship was headed for Charleston, South Carolina. Relyea had spent most of his life at sea and was a native of Staten Island, New York, and thus a United States citizen. He stated that he shipped for St. John's, Newfoundland, a point that is heavily underlined in his disposition, indicating that someone had seen the inconsistency between St. John, in the Canadian Province of New Brunswick, and what was then the separate British colony of Newfoundland.

He also said that he happened to take hold of the lead when they were some days north of the West Indies and observed from the soundings, "soil and stuff," that they were off the coast of the Carolinas, which he knew well from fishing trips. He mentioned this to the cook and said that this was their first indication of the ship's position. He then asked the captain what they were doing near the Carolinas and was told that they were heading into the blockading fleet, as their pumps "were mighty out of order." He confirmed that the ship was leaking and that the chain plates had drawn through the planking.[11] Following the court hearing, Relyea and the Peruvian cook were sent back to the *Alert*, now under the command of Midshipman John Weidman, U.S. Navy.

Charles Carlin was obviously under orders to say as little as possible and answered most questions with a "don't know." He confirmed that the rigging was in bad condition and that the ship was leaking badly. It had to be pumped every two hours, and the men were complaining of a "want of sleep." He also made the significant statement that "Stono Bar is at the mouth of a creek or bay leading to Charleston, the channel is about II foot deep."[12]

Captain Marsden ordered Captain Matthew C. Perry[13] of the USS *Vandalia* to take James Carlin, the mate Roberts, Charles Carlin, and Dillman to Hampton Roads. Marsden then pointed out to Captain Perry that "Captain Carlin claims the ownership of a part of the schooner; and being a naturalized citizen of South Carolina renders his portion liable to confiscation."[14] This is first occasion on which the Union navy raised the question of Carlin's nationality. Marsden or his crew must have recognized Carlin and knew of his service with the Coast Survey Department and assumed that he had been naturalized.

The *Alert* was brought into Baltimore under the charge of Midshipman Weidman. He inspected the cargo and found that the fruit was in a perishable condition due to the "closeness of the vessel." He ordered that the hatch covers be removed, then appointed a guard and told him to find an assistant to aid him with pumping. This cost the court twenty-five dollars for four days' work, night and day. He reported that the ship needed constant pumping as it was "in a very leaky and bad condition."[15] On 21 October the Prize Court ordered that the cargo be auctioned as soon as possible to prevent further damage, such a rapid sale being to the benefit of all parties.

During his time in Baltimore, Carlin would have been well aware of the excitement raised by the *Trent* Affair. On 8 November Captain Charles Wilkes of the USS *San Jacinto* stopped the British mail steamer *Trent* in the Old Bahama Channel, arresting the Confederate commissioners James Mason and John Slidell, who were on their way to Europe to conduct high-level Confederate diplomacy. This was seen as a sensational breach of international law. Captain Wilkes was initially lauded in the North for his initiative. Later, as the serious diplomatic fallout developed, Washington moved to disown his highhanded actions. Wilkes had been encouraged by the anti-British U.S. consul general in Havana, Robert W. Shufeldt, and had the tacit support of Secretary of State Seward.[16]

The Union authorities eventually released both commissioners after vigorous protests from the British that almost came to a declaration of war. The pair had planned to take a vessel from Nassau directly to Europe but had continued on to Havana when they found that that the onward steamer to Liverpool from Nassau was due to call at New York. While they were in Cuba, Confederate supporters welcomed them with enthusiasm, showing great support for their cause.

This incident would have further ramifications in the fallout from the capture of the British steamer *Memphis* and the struggle to have James Carlin released from prison. It showed the American leadership that Britain was serious about defending its maritime interests and its subjects from unlawful actions by foreign powers.

The Prize Court in Baltimore ruled on 14 November that the *Alert* was to be forfeited. On 30 December 1861 the Maryland District Court assessed the value of the cargoes as $1,567.17. The gross proceeds of the sale of the vessel and the cargo were $1,805.50. The value of the condemned schooner itself was assessed at $314.13, making a net total of $1,881.30, half of which went to the account of the court and half to the treasury of the United States. The *Alert* and the investment in its last cargo had been a total loss, although Carlin would have done well enough out of his earlier exploits with the vessel.[17]

The *Charleston Mercury* of 23 October 1861 recorded that J. Carlin had been liberated from the military prison in Washington on 10 October and was among the fifty-seven prisoners exchanged for the return of fifty-seven wounded Yankees. The men took an oath not to engage in the war against the United States. The *Mercury* also reported that "at the solicitation of friends of Yankee captives now in our hands, Lincoln has consented to a partial exchange of prisoners."

It is clear that James Carlin felt that this oath was given under some duress and referred to acts of war, not commercial enterprise. He took no notice of it, returning immediately to running the blockade. Charles Carlin may well have heeded his oath, for we have no record of any further involvement with the Confederate cause.

Charles Carlin entered the British Royal Navy as a "second-class" boy in about 1857.[18] The records of the Admiralty in London show that he left the Royal Navy by "purchase" in October 1864. This suggests that his brother James bought him out of the Navy. So what was he doing with James aboard the *Alert* in September 1861? British warships on the West Indies Station suffered heavy desertions during the Civil War, but there is no suggestion that Charles Carlin was one of them. Senior British naval officers took leaves of absence to make money running the blockade. This may be a unique case of a boy sailor doing the same thing.

British records suggest that Charles was serving with the Royal Navy in the West Indies and North America Squadron. He must have met up with his older brother while stationed in Nassau in the Bahamas. We can imagine Charles wangling a week's shore leave to spend time with his brother. He then accepted his brother's invitation to join the run to Charleston and found himself caught up in the capture and subsequent court case in Baltimore. Quite how he explained his delayed return to his commanding officer would itself make a good story.

While James Carlin was busy with the last voyage of the *Alert* and the court case in Baltimore, major changes were being planned for the way the Confederacy would be supplied with munitions and essential imports. This marked the end of the first phase of small-scale private ventures. Sailing vessels unable to outrun the steam warships waiting for them beyond the bar gave way to fast, shallow-draft steamers that could cope with adverse sea conditions. Blockade-running was becoming better organized as the Confederate government took control of vital imports and exports.

Chapter 9

# The Confederacy Confronts the Blockade
## The Business of Blockade-Running, 1861–1862

• • •

In the early stages of the war, the secession states hoped that the European powers would come to their aid. They thought that Europe would be greatly alarmed by the loss of Southern cotton, leading to the closure of their mills and the prospect of riot or worse from millworkers. As a consequence, the South was convinced that England and France would declare war on the North, or at least support its cause with essential military supplies.

In any event, British textile workers were laid off or put on short time, and by late 1862 only about a third of Manchester mills had sufficient cotton for full production, and 15 percent of workers were out of work. The situation was similar in France.[1] By 1864 cotton started to arrive from East India and Egypt, and the situation eased. The cotton mills of the Union states also brought in Indian cotton to supplement supplies smuggled or purchased from the South.

Southern planter interests had ensured that they would continue to sell cotton over the land border to the Northern mills. This trade is estimated to have supplied some two-thirds of the cotton used in the North during the war, providing a useful source of U.S. currency to the Confederate economy.[2]

Lord Palmerston, the British prime minister, and Lord Russell, his foreign secretary, were wary and piloted a cautious route between the conflicting interests of the warring states. Conscious that the Americans had not come to Britain's aid during the Crimean War and suspicious of "devious Yankees" and their intentions in British Canada, Britain was not about to go to war to aid either side. Palmerston declared a policy of strict neutrality and recognized the two warring sides as belligerents, arguing that Britain's neutral status permitted its merchants to trade with both sides. Over the course of the next few years, this interpretation would be tested in numerous court actions that upheld the British view but did not ease relations with the United States government.[3]

The South consequently withheld cotton exports in an attempt to put pressure on Britain and France to come to their aid. This misjudgment cost the Confederacy a valuable three months, during which the Union was only able to impose a paper blockade. The remains of the 1860 cotton crop might have been gathered up from plantations, railway sidings, and warehouses and exported to Europe, and munitions could have been accumulated before the Union navy gathered their forces and tightened the noose. The Blockade Board and the navy, appreciating the way the sea war was to develop, set about organizing an effective cordon using all the resources of the industrial North.

The South, in its initial naivety, expected to be able to continue purchasing industrial goods from the Northern states. Shipping records from New York and Bermuda show that Northern merchants indeed found ways to circumvent the blockade and continue their sales to the South.

Some blockade-runners were even owned or financed by Northern interests or had been purchased from Northern owners. Faced with the rapid buildup of the Union navy and the tightening net around the Southern coasts, these supplies dried up, and the Confederate government soon realized that it could not rely on contraband goods from Northern manufacturers. Alternative supplies from Europe had to be organized.[4]

Stephen Mallory, the Confederate secretary of the navy, took steps to rectify the situation by appointing commercial firms to find ways to evade the blockading squadrons. These arrangements were to be financed by the export trade in cotton and other Southern agricultural products, including rice, distilled turpentine and pine rosin, and tobacco.

The Confederacy had hoped to set up a joint merchant-shipping fleet staffed by Southern naval officers. Carlin's enrollment in Savannah as a pilot in the Confederates States Navy came at this point. The intention was to guarantee that the full value of the Southern cotton crop was realized on the European exchanges and that return cargoes were devoted to the needs of the military.

This was not to be, and much of the potential value of the South's monopoly on cotton was lost. The government shipping scheme proved impossible. Southern politicians did not believe that they should run shipping and exporting companies, so commercial interests had to be relied on to maintain the import-export trade. However, government agents were sent to England and France to purchase military and naval supplies, using established trading houses for financing, customs clearing, forwarding, and shipping.

The prospect of quick profits and endless opportunities for speculation of all kinds, combined with high adventure, brought investors from far afield. Cases heard in the New York Prize Court show that ships were being dispatched from the United Kingdom and its colonies in the West Indies, from Canada, and also from Texas and the northeastern states of the Union. There were also vessels whose ports of registration were Havana, Honduras, Mexico, and beyond. The English vessel *Saxon* was registered in Cape Town, far across the South Atlantic. It had been captured by the USS *Vanderbilt* on suspicion of belonging to Confederates while in the harbor of Angra Pequena, later renamed Lüderitz Bay, in German South West Africa (now Namibia).[5] Unsurprisingly, the Prize Court released the vessel. Brazilian, Spanish, Danish, Dutch, and Prussian ship owners were also drawn by the excitement and profits on offer.[6]

Substantial financial returns were on offer to those with the capital to buy suitable ships and hire experienced captains. Some analyses of the figures show that for many the rewards did not outweigh the risks. Economist Stanley Lebergott argues that a large proportion, perhaps up to 90 percent, of the vessels arriving and departing Southern ports during the war made only one voyage.[7]

There are also uncertainties over figures relating to the profitability of blockade-running. Lebergott analyzed Marcus Price's listings and raised the paradoxical question: "If smuggling [i.e. blockade running] yielded spectacular profit rates, why did so few successful investors try a second time?"[8] Bruce W. Hetherington and Peter J. Kower reworked the numbers from Marcus Price and also from Stephen Wise and came up with "startlingly different results." Their conclusion is that the number of blockade-runners who chose to try again after an initial success was much higher than the 10 percent rate reported by Lebergott. They conclude that "our estimated rate of multiple attempts is more consistent with findings that successful blockade runs offered high profits." [9]

Clearly successful captains were those who knew their business, had luck on their side, and were able to obtain suitable vessels with access to readily available cotton. Only then were the net profits sufficient to outweigh the risk of ships captured and cargoes lost.

Fraser, Trenholm and Company of Liverpool, along with its associate John Fraser and Company of Charleston, was the leading trading house appointed by the Confederate government to conduct trade on its behalf. John Augustus Fraser and George Alfred Trenholm were the principal partners in the company formed by Fraser's grandfather.[10] The Liverpool branch was to act as a financial clearinghouse for the purchasing agents the Confederate government had sent to ensure military and naval supplies. At the beginning of the war, the firm had very large warehouses and extensive offices at the river end of Cumberland Street at North Central Wharf in Charleston. These facilities could handle twenty thousand bales of cotton in a morning.

Most of Fraser, Trenholm's inward freight was allocated to munitions for the Confederacy, rather than more profitable items for the luxury trade in Charleston. This suggests a real commitment to the Confederate cause. Profits were invested in Confederate bonds, strengthening the finances of the South. The company's pilots and captains were especially well rewarded, and their success rate was relatively high.[11]

Henry Adderley and Company were Fraser, Trenholm's ship-handling agents in Nassau until 1862, when John Baptist Lafitte was sent from Charleston to handle the company's increasing business in Nassau. Lafitte was acknowledged as the "King's Conch" and more important than the British governor—in the eyes of the Americans, at least. Mrs. Lafitte entertained Confederate visitors on a lavish scale in her large house. As James Carlin's reputation grew, he would have moved nearer the top of her invitation list, surely "entitled to a seat at the festive board" during his visits to the colony.[12]

At the start of the second, more organized phase of the blockade-running operations, the Liverpool branch of Fraser, Trenholm dispatched the *Bermuda* to a Southern port with a large cargo of general military supplies, including arms. Its explicit purpose was to demonstrate that the blockade was ineffective. Confederate representatives in Europe tried to make the case that their vessels' frequent breaches of the Union navy's cordon proved that it was ineffective and thus void.[13] They also argued that the blockade "violated the neutral rights of their primary trading partners," according to historian Kevin Weddle. "But they failed to persuade Great Britain, which formally recognized the blockade in February 1862."[14]

Fraser, Trenholm hoped to make a good commercial yield, but they also planned to show others that the enterprise was worthwhile and so encourage more runners to aid the war effort. The *Bermuda* made a fast run into Savannah on 18

View of Nassau, in the British West Indies, the depot for the blockade-running trade. Courtesy of "The Civil War in America from the *Illustrated London News*." A joint project by Sandra J. Still, Emily E. Katt, Collection Management, and the Beck Center of Emory University.

September under the command of Captain Eugene L. Tessier with Captain "Fenn" Ferdinand Peck as the pilot. It returned to Liverpool filled with cotton.

The *Gladiator* was the next large vessel to be dispatched, clearing from the Port of London on 9 November 1861. It was loaded with a million dollars' worth of munitions, including more than twenty thousand Enfield rifles. Its movements had been closely monitored by the U.S. consul in London and by Commander J. B. Marchand of the USS *James Adger*, who was ordered to intercept the vessel in the English Channel. Marchand admitted that the capture of the *Gladiator* would have "caused a rupture between the Government of England and the United States by which they [the Confederates] would ultimately benefit."[15] He hoped to find that the *Gladiator* was diverting from its legal destination, Nassau, and thus have an excuse to detain the ship. He was determined to stop it in any event.

However, the USS *James Adger* was delayed by bad weather and failed to find the *Gladiator* in the Channel. Marchand then searched the Azores and the Atlantic coaling station of Funchal on the island of Madeira. The U.S. Navy then trailed it across the Atlantic without coming up on the vessel.

The *Gladiator* arrived safely in Nassau. From there it was to run straight into one of the Confederate states. The ship's charter conditions stipulated that its cargo had to be delivered into a Southern port. Neither supplier nor shipper could be paid until the consignment was correctly documented as delivered to its final destination. But there were fast Union steam warships in the vicinity, and the *Gladiator* was heavily laden. It drew too much water and was too slow to outpace the U.S. Navy cruisers.

Up to this point, Charles Helm had run Confederate government affairs in Nassau from the larger consulate in Havana. He contracted various commercial shipping firms and bought shipping space on behalf of the government to ensure that military supplies got through. With the arrival of increasing amounts of War Department consignments, Louis C. Hetlinger was sent out on the *Theodore* to oversee Confederate business in the tiny British colony. He found the *Gladiator* and its vital cargo marooned in Nassau, with the captain threatening to break his contract and return the ship and its cargo to England.

To stop this, Hetlinger had to buy the *Gladiator* for the Confederate government. When George Trenholm in Charleston heard of these difficulties, he offered to make the John Fraser Company vessels *Cecile* and the *Carolina* (later the *Kate*) available to the government so that these smaller, faster ships could run the *Gladiator*'s cargo into the Confederacy. In December 1861 the Confederate government agreed to pay the company $65,000 for each safe arrival of the *Kate* and *Cecile*.[16]

The success of these smaller vessels in landing the *Gladiator*'s cargo led the way to a new, more strategic approach to blockade-running. Deep-hulled, oceangoing vessels were to be used for the transatlantic routes with onward transshipment at neutral ports such as Nassau, Bermuda, and Havana. Small, more nimble vessels with shallow drafts were then to dash through the Union navy and run down the surf line until they reached the harbor entrance.

This policy of transshipping from ocean to coastal vessels was dictated by practical matters of economy, but a principle of international law lay behind the initial thinking. British ship owners must have had in mind the international regulations laid out by the Declaration of Paris. They hoped to argue that, if stopped and inspected by the United States Navy on the open ocean, the captains of their vessels could claim that their ships' manifests showed that articles of war in their cargoes were being delivered to a neutral destination such as Cuba, Nassau, Bermuda, or Mexico and not directly to the Confederates.

The declaration stated that neutral ships could carry any goods from one neutral port to another, including "contraband of war," if intended for actual delivery at the port of destination to become part of the "common stock" of that country or port. It was for Union officials to prove their case if they thought otherwise, for the declaration also stated that if the intention was to transfer the contraband to a belligerent state whether by ship or overland, as was the case on the Mexican border, then the contraband became liable to seizure.

On 18 August 1862 Gideon Welles issued a further circular to the flag officers commanding squadrons and officers commanding cruisers. In the context of recent captures, he repeated his instructions on how the navy should handle the blockade. He was adamant that the United States government should uphold its own rights and act with firmness but that it should "scrupulously regard the rights of others." He emphasized that they were not authorized to "chase or fire at a foreign vessel without showing their colors" and giving notice that they wished to come aboard or "talk." He also instructed that no official seals were to be broken on any pretext on letters of foreign authorities found on board, but that such letters must be handed to the district judge conducting the case.[17]

These were the rules of the game, which both sides tried to exploit to their advantage.

The *Kate* and *Cecile* had been operated by the Florida Steam Packet Line before the war, when they made regular runs from Charleston to the ports of eastern Florida under Captains Thomas Lockwood and Ferdinand Peck. Ports of call included Fernandina and intermediate landings on St. Johns River.[18] Some reports connect James Carlin to this company in the period after he left the Survey, and he is credited with being in command of the *Cecile* in this prewar coastal trade.[19] He was also said to be associated with the Ravenal brothers' vessel *Mackinaw*, a 1,095-ton sailing ship that was on the prewar Savannah run but that appears to have been marooned alongside Vanderhorst's Wharf in Charleston during 1861 and 1862.[20]

# Chapter 10

# Running through the Blockade for Trenholm and Company, 1861–1862

. . .

Following the end of the trial in Baltimore in November 1861, James Carlin was free of the affairs of the *Alert* and returned home to Charleston. He would have heard with dismay of the capture of Port Royal on 8 November 1861 by Post Captain Samuel Du Pont. This gave the U.S. Navy effective command of all the sea islands and inland waterways on the coast and threatened Charleston itself. The South Atlantic Blockading Squadron now had a secure operating base to control the offshore waters as instructed by the Blockade Strategy Board in Washington. This base also eased their resupply difficulties, and they were able to keep more vessels at sea.

Carlin was soon in Nassau. There he sought out his old shipmate and commander, John Newland Maffitt, who had been sent by the Confederate States Department of the Navy to organize the transshipment of the *Gladiator's* cargo.[1] By the spring of 1862, Carlin was employed by John Fraser Company as first officer on the steamer *Kate*, commanded by Captain Thomas Lockwood. The *Kate*, which ran the blockade to Florida, was renamed for the wife of George A. Trenholm.[2] It had been built as the *Carolina* in Green Point, New York, in 1852 and was 165 feet long, with a beam of just under 30 feet. Its side paddles were driven by one 320-horsepower engine. Built for the packet trade, the ship had 27 staterooms and could carry 150 deck passengers, or some 330 bales of cotton. In January 1862 the *Kate* was registered to Augustus John Adderley of Nassau to gain British registry, although Fraser, Trenholm and Company was its actual owner by then.[3]

After complex negotiations between all the parties, a deal was agreed to and arrangements made to transship the *Gladiator's* cargo using the *Kate*, *Cecile*, and the *Ella Worley*. It was then a question of where to land the munitions. Judah P. Benjamin, then the Confederate secretary of war, suggested Wilmington, Georgetown, or Brunswick, Ga. George Trenholm was anxious that his ships should be well managed during this hazardous operation and had recommended that

Commander Maffitt be given leave from the navy to take charge of all blockade-running out of Nassau.

In the later part of the war, Maffitt was captain of the armed raider CSS *Florida* and caused havoc among American shipping around the world. He rivaled the exploits of the CSS *Alabama* under Captain Semmes, who was celebrated as far afield as South Africa. There, school choirs still sing the traditional Afrikaans folk-song "Daar Kom Die Alabama," a response by the Afrikaner settlers to the British government's prohibition of slavery in Cape Colony some thirty years earlier. The volume of U.S. shipping destroyed by the CSS *Alabama* and other Confederate cruisers was so great that it led to protracted postwar legal proceedings known as the Alabama Claims. The United States initially demanded $2 billion or much of Canada, but in 1871 Britain eventually paid $14 million to settle claims for reparations.

Maffitt chose to deliver the *Gladiator*'s cargo to Mosquito Inlet, now Ponce de Leon Inlet near New Smyrna on the northeast coast of Florida. This apparently remote point had secure, if laborious, connections to the interior and gave access to the coastal rivers system. He argued for the Florida coast on the basis that it was only two days' sailing from Nassau. Additionally, the *Kate* and *Cecile* would have the advantage of the north-setting Gulf Stream speeding them on their way. This course would escape the danger of meeting a southbound warship of the blockading squadron tracking to the east of the Gulf Stream to skirt the northerly current.[4] While these arrangements were being finalized, Thomas Lockwood brought the *Kate* into Nassau Harbor to load part of the *Gladiator*'s cargo. It had been hoped to lighten the larger ship sufficiently to allow it to run the rest of the munitions directly into a main Southern port. Meanwhile, the Confederate general Robert E. Lee ordered the fortification of the harbor at Mosquito Inlet with earthworks, mounting two guns in preparation for the arrival of the munitions.[5]

On 7 March 1862 the *Kate*, under Peck with James Carlin as mate, cleared outward bound from Nassau to St. John, New Brunswick. In fact, the ship was headed for New Smyrna, Florida. The *Kate* made an easy twenty-hour run to the unblockaded Florida coast, with some six thousand Enfield rifles and other military supplies. These were loaded onto wagons and carried to the St. Johns River, where river steamers took them to the terminus of the Cedar Keys Railroad at Fernandina, just north of Jacksonville, for onward consignment to the forces of the Confederacy. Under the supervision of Maffitt, the *Cecile* and the *Kate*, running a few days apart, quickly completed the transfer of the *Gladiator*'s cargo to the Florida coast, sometimes picking up cargo from Charleston for the return trip.[6] The *Gladiator* returned to Britain with a large consignment of cotton bales, its mission completed.

These activities prompted the Union forces on the ground in northern Florida to counterattack and occupy the area. The closure of this lightly blockaded route, with its wagon and riverboat connections, led the runners to concentrate on Charleston and Wilmington, both of which also had direct connections to the railroad system.

After his trips in the *Kate,* James Carlin commanded the *Cecile* for at least one of its voyages to Florida in March 1862. The *Cecile* had been built in Wilmington, Delaware, in 1857 as a side-wheel packet steamer with a rounded stern and had been converted to a blockade-runner in 1861.[7] The ship was 156.5 feet in length, its beam was 29 feet, and its depth 8.5 feet, with 27 staterooms. The side wheels were powered by one low-pressure boiler. Fully laden, the *Cecile* took 250 bales but was usually limited to 125–50 bales to maintain its speed.[8]

Ferdinand Peck and James Carlin made multiple trips between Charleston and Nassau in the spring of 1862 and invested some of their earnings in the John Fraser Company.[9] On 15 February the *Kate* brought out a cargo of cotton. Peck in the *Cecile* arrived a week later. The *Cecile* made another trip to Charleston, returning to Nassau on 8 March with more cotton. Carlin then took the *Kate* into Charleston, arriving in Nassau with further cotton on 11 March.

Peck, Lockwood, and Carlin changed ships and responsibilities as the occasion demanded. The *Cecile* was well known from its days as a packet. Although it was regarded as slow, Carlin enhanced his reputation as its commander, and author Dave Horner credits the ship with making twelve successful runs through the blockade.[10]

On 16 April James Carlin was in Nassau Harbor, having the boilers of the *Cecile* repaired, when the large British mail steamer RMS *Karnak* tried to run into the main harbor despite heavy surf on the bar. This fine screw steamer of 7,931 tons had been built in 1852 by William Denny and Sons of Dumbarton and was en route from Havana with some sixty passengers, about half of whom were women and children. The captain, le Messurier, had raised objections, but Mr. Cooke, the local pilot, had assured him that conditions were the same as during its March trip, when they had come though South West Bay. The pilot was wrong: the ship struck the bar heavily and was thrown onto the coral reef. Although the engines were working perfectly, it proved impossible to get the vessel off the reef.

The *Nassau Guardian* commended James Carlin for doing "all he could to facilitate the repairs to the *Cecile*'s boilers," but the ship was unable to get steam up in under six hours. We can imagine the frustrated captain with the glint of salvage in his eyes, urging on the engineers in the boiler room. The other steamers in the harbor, including the blockade-runners *Thomas L. Wagg* and *Gladiator,* were also unable to help, being out of coal or restricted by the reefs. The *Karnak* was soon "rolling heavily from side to side and presenting her starboard side to the breakers, thumping awfully at every turn and began to leak." Boats and men rushed to help. The ship's surgeon, Dr. Linquist, risked his life passing the women and children into the local craft milling around the ship's gangway. The *Karnak* was soon boarded by Nassau's wreckers, some of whom were injured by shifting boxes of sugar in the holds. A Royal Navy diver from HMS *Bulldog* reported that the starboard amidships compartment was stove in.[11] This incident highlighted the need for urgent improvements to Nassau Harbor to accommodate the large vessels then flocking to the island.[12]

During April and May 1862, fifteen blockade-runners evaded the Union navy lying off the Charleston bar and slipped into the harbor. Twenty-one runners were able to depart carrying more than ten thousand bales of cotton.

Carlin made big money on these trips. In the spring of 1862 he purchased shares in the Importing and Exporting Company of South Carolina (I&E Company, also known as the Bee Company after William Bee, the chairman). He was also paid in shares, which he probably accepted in lieu of Confederate dollars. He certainly made good use of the tricks of blockade-running he had developed with Captain Thomas J. Lockwood. However, there is no suggestion that Carlin used Lockwood's approach. According to the U.S. Liverpool consul Thomas Haines Dudley, Lockwood used to boast of his "arrangements" with U.S. naval officers to let him by.[13]

Lockwood was to end the war as a prisoner in Fort Lafayette. He had run the blockade once too often and had been caught and released too many times for the Yankees to let him try his luck yet again.

Some British blockade-running captains had brought their wives out to the West Indies. These women were quick to take advantage of the needs of their counterparts in the South. They entrusted small packages of luxuries to their favorite captains to take to the cities of the Confederacy and made useful additions to their "pin money" (the allowances they received from their husbands) in the process. One such woman earned enormous profits from her consignments of yellow soap.[14]

The *Kate* was the first runner to be painted a dull grey, and family legend credits James Carlin with initiating the camouflaging of warships by painting them the very light shade of blue grey that was later known in British naval circles as "Battleship Grey." Previously, runners had been painted black to blend into the night, but it became clear that the most dangerous times were at sunset and sunrise. This color was a well-judged, very pale off-white that enabled the ships to blend into the haze or fade into the early morning mists or the loom of land.

By the end of the war, this tactic had developed so that the runners were barely perceptible, in a misty dawn light, from a hundred or so yards. From the blockading squadron to seaward, looking toward the spray of the surf line and the pale dunes, the ships became almost invisible. The runners also had other ploys that were used to slip through the Union blockaders. Spars and as much standing rigging as possible would be lowered, and the masts and funnels were unshipped, or hinged, so that they could be stowed on deck. Even the ship's boats would be dropped in their davits to reduce the height and profile of the vessels. All lights were extinguished, and the binnacle light was heavily shaded so that the helmsman had to peer at the compass through the barest slit. Smoking was prohibited and silence enforced. Some captains insisted on the crew wearing white at night so that no hint of black appeared above the horizon line. No detail was overlooked: cockerels were banned on board to ensure that their dawn chorus would not alert the early watch as the runners slipped through a sleepy Union blockade.

Excess boiler pressure was blown off under the waterline, and the edges of paddle wheels were feathered with canvas to reducing their characteristic splashing rhythm. The paddle wheels' boxes were also muffled to reduce the giveaway *clack, clack* sound as the blades of the paddles churned the passing water. Frank Bonneau later claimed to have draped weighted cloth covers over the paddle boxes to help reduce the noise of their splashing.[15] Runners preferred paddle wheelers to screw-driven vessels as the side-wheelers could accelerate faster, raising the chances of a speedy getaway. They were also highly maneuverable and could turn very sharply by reversing one paddle. They also favored the side-wheelers, as they could literally rock the ship off the sands by working the paddles in a rocking motion in alternate directions, breaking the suction of the hull on the bottom and creating a groove in the sea bed to ease a way through. Captain Augustus Hobart-Hampden of the Royal Navy praised his runner's "Symon's twin screws" that enabled one engine to be reversed, thus turning his vessel like a "tee totem."[16]

Blockade-runners only sailed on moonless nights or took advantage of late or early moon risings for their ventures. The captains tried to "save their dark" and ensure that the ship-handling agents maximized the best operating period to avoid a costly two-week delay in Nassau, with port charges and crew costs mounting. The nights of the full moon were spent enjoying the hospitality on offer in Nassau to those with money in their pockets and little to do until the next adrenalin-fueled adventure.

The *Kate* carried anthracite coal, which was favored because it burned without leaving a telltale trail of smoke. Alternatively, a cheaper, dirtier type of coal dust would be burned for a few minutes to put down a heavy black screen into which the runner would disappear, only to emerge on a different course a few minutes later burning clean coal, thus tricking the pursuing naval vessels. A different tactic that worked in the early days of the blockade was for the *Kate* to fly a United States flag and loiter among the blockading fleet during the day and then slip away through the fleet during the hours of darkness.

Post Captain Augustus Hobart-Hampden was one of the half-pay Royal Naval officers who joined in the excitement of running through the U.S. Navy's blockading fleet. He was later an admiral in the Turkish navy with the title of pasha and a

Royal Navy vice-admiral. He told of creeping very close inshore and anchoring for the moonlit hours and even in daylight, without being seen by U.S. Navy patrol vessels passing by farther out to sea. Hobart-Hampden was a bluff and forthright character who was struck off the British Navy list on two occasions for contravening the British Foreign Enlistment Act. He carried on regardless.[17]

Tactics on the outward trip became equally well developed. Captains and their pilots would go down to the entrance of the port on the eve of departure and take careful bearings on those ships of the blockading fleet that were visible from the shore. Then a course would be plotted to pass safely out of the harbor mouth and through the first cordon. The second offshore cordon was always more difficult and had to be risked as it could not be observed from the shore. These offshore ships were more dispersed, and with luck and good judgment, a runner could slip through unseen.

Outward-bound runners had an inherent advantage. With full steam and the engine going full pelt, they could run through the Union navy line before their engineers could fire up the boilers, raise steam, haul anchor, and give chase. The blockading squadrons needed some three thousand tons of anthracite a week by 1863 and were limited by difficulties over coal supplies.[18] This restricted their range and made them dependent on the captured ports of Port Royal, Key West, and Hampton Roads to the north.

Sometimes the runner would have to make maximum steam to escape. If fast steaming went on too long, there was the risk of running out of coal on the return voyage. One trick that could be used on a dark night was to make a ninety-degree turn in an unexpected direction and steam on for a short distance before stopping and lying quiet for a while. The runner would then resume its original course on a parallel line, its commander hoping that the warship would be out of sight at sunup.[19]

Lockwood stayed with John Fraser Company in command of the *Kate*. He made many more runs while Carlin transferred to the I&E Company when William Bee bought the *Cecile* from Fraser's, whose officials had thought it too small for their purposes.[20] On 5 April 1862 the *Cecile* made its first run out of Charleston for the I&E Company with 257 bales of cotton valued at $13,358. These sold in Nassau for some $25,900 in Confederate currency. The profits on the return trip into Charleston were even better. Six dozen ladies' spring skirts bought for $10 a dozen sold at auction for $72 per dozen.[21]

A ship's captain had many and varied duties, including taking responsibility for the cargo and ensuring its safe delivery to the consignees so that bills of lading could be signed off and payments collected. Carlin found himself with another task. As the following letter suggests, urgent domestic needs combined with serious shipping matters to make a blockade captain's life a busy one on shore and at sea.

Charleston 3 May 1862
Captain J Carlin, Steamer Cecile
Dear Captain,
We have written to Messrs H. Adderly & Co. fully as to the disposition of
the cargo for Cecile which letter conforms with the understanding we had
with you— The Invoice and B/Lading we have enclosed in a separate package so marked.

We have also written to Mr. Lafitte and explained the circumstances of
the change of consignees which you can do like with.

We have merely to request that you can purchase for us two hoop skirts,
long but of narrow circumference, a dozen of Cambric pocket handkerchiefs,
three dozen cakes of Windsor Soap and a dozen tooth brushes of best quality
. . . do so.

Wishing you most sincerely and heartily a safe and prosperous voyage
out and home again.
Yours Truly
M. C. Bee. & Co.[22]

The *Cecile* is credited with making a dozen safe runs between April and June,
but the ship came to an end on a dark night on the banks of the Bahamas, dashed
on a reef by conflicting currents. The steamer left Nassau on 18 or 22 June, bound
for Charleston with a cargo of munitions intended to replenish the losses suffered
by the army of the ill-fated General Arthur Sidney Johnson after his defeat at
Shiloh on 6–7 April 1862. The vessel carried 2,000 rifles; a battery of 8 brass cannons, with ammunition wagons and harness together worth $60,000; 400 barrels
of gunpowder; and assorted equipment. It also carried medical supplies including
quinine and opium.

Leaving behind Northeast Providence Channel, the *Cecile* was working to get a
fix on Abaco light, when it was caught by the set of the current and swept onto the
dreaded Abaco reefs. In Dave Horner's graphic description, the *Cecile* "bumped
lightly at first, rolled and groaned, then struck hard as her heavily weighted hull
crashed into a large coral pinnacle. *Cecile's* entire bottom was gored open and she
sank in ten minutes. Not a single item was saved."[23] The crew only just got away
in the ship's boats. Carlin's name is not linked to this event, and he appears not to
have been on board at the time.

The *Cecile* had gone down in eight fathoms and most of the cargo was completely ruined. Bahamian salvagers managed to recover the brass cannons and some
small arms.[24] These were bought by John B. Lafitte of Henry Adderley and Co.
and sold at cost price to the Confederate War Department. The cannons fetched
$125.00 each and the small arms $1.50 to $3.00 each.[25]

As the blockade-runners adapted their tactics, so too did the U.S. Navy. When large neutral ships were used to carry cargoes across the Atlantic to Nassau, Havana, and Hamilton in Bermuda, so the U.S. Navy moved farther offshore and ran down these larger vessels wherever they found them. The U.S. Navy held the Port of Nassau under virtual siege, and the British stationed two powerful warships off the Bahamas as a warning to the authorities in Washington.

On leaving Nassau, British-owned and -flagged blockade-runners would keep close inshore for as long as possible. If they were challenged by the lurking Union warships, they could claim to be British vessels in British territorial waters. The U.S. Navy even stopped ships off the coast of Madeira, over two thousand miles from the Southern states in apparent contravention of the Paris Declaration, which prohibited interference with neutral vessels running between neutral ports. This exasperated the British authorities and tensions ran high. The U.S. Navy was beginning to exert its increased strength in areas that had hitherto been the dominion of the British Royal Navy.

# Chapter 11

# The *Memphis* Affair,
# July 31–August 1, 1862

. . .

Look Out For Squalls. John Bull: "You do what's right my son, or
I will blow you out of the water." *Punch,* 7 December 1861.
Courtesy of Bristol Record Office.

The case of James Carlin and his involvement with the British steamer *Memphis* comes to us from the leather-bound volume found in the British National Archives, supplemented by transcripts of the New York Prize Court, British Consular Records, and the reports of his jubilant captor, Acting (volunteer) Lieutenant William Budd, who had just made his fortune.

While James Carlin was supposedly only a passenger on the *Memphis,* the events that followed its capture were to affect him deeply. The extensive documentation on the capture, trial, and his eventual release allow for a detailed examination of a notable event in the history of blockade-running during the Civil War. They show that numerous parties had varied and contradictory interests in the ship and its cargo, as well as conflicting motives and loyalties.

Letters found on the captured *Memphis* reveal the inside story of ship owning, seaborne trade, and blockade-running in the middle of the nineteenth century. The vessel was built in Scotland to the order of Peter Denny and Thomas Sterling Begbie. Denny was a partner in the Clydeside shipbuilders of William Denny and Sons. Thomas Begbie, a "London Scot," was a ship owner and broker who conducted business from premises in both the City of London and Glasgow.[1]

Following usual shipping practice, ownership of the *Memphis* was spread among a number of parties. Begbie, as managing owner, had thirty-two shares, as did Peter Denny. Denny and Company of Clydeside took fifteen shares. An undisclosed "WDB" had eleven shares, and James Denny had six shares. The vessel cost £17,441 ready and complete for sea. The engines, boilers, and winches cost an extra £6,114, making a total cost of £23,556.

On 9 March 1862 Begbie arranged a three-month charter for the *Memphis* with the armaments dealers Zollinger, Andreas and Company of Manchester. The rate was £2,500 per month, plus a 40 percent premium on the insurance value of £26,000 to cover all risks, including seizure on the voyage from Liverpool to Charleston and back.[2]

Begbie had been encouraged by the money he had made from the *Bermuda's* run into Savannah and was keen to repeat this success. He was well aware of the risks and sought to set them off as widely as possible.

Union consuls and agents were keeping a sharp watch on the new vessel. In a dispatch dated 30 April, Thomas H. Dudley, the U.S. consul in Liverpool, reported:

A new screw steamer called the *Memphis,* arrived at this port last week from the Clyde . . . to load for Havana. She is 791 tons burden, commanded by Captain Cruikshank, her consignees are Dunkerley & Steinmann.

This vessel has been purchased by southern agents and will be loaded and attempt to run the blockade. Will send a description of her in my next.

He describes another steamer and then comments,

> The last two vessels will clear [Liverpool customs] as British vessels and sail under that flag when they leave here. They had a mock sale and pretend that that they have been purchased by an Englishman.[3]

These notices were widely distributed to U.S. consuls and to the Union navy with exhortations for all concerned to keep a sharp eye out for the named vessels and prevent their blockade-running activities.

Meanwhile, in Brussels others were also attempting to make money out of the enterprise. On 1 April, H. S. Sanford, the United States consul at the U.S. Legation in Belgium, sent a confidential dispatch to Secretary of State William H. Seward. It read in part:

> SIR: With reference to my dispatch of the 20th March, I have to report that an offer has been made by the owners of the new steamer *Memphis* to leave Liverpool 20th instant with a cargo of 1,100 tons, consisting of blankets, shoes, cloth, powder, etc., which cost £65,000, and with the ship valued at £90,000, to run her into the hands of our blockading squadron or aground so that she can be secured, for £53,000.[4]

This is a curious incident. Who was double-dealing on 1 April and why? The implication is that the ship's owners, Begbie and perhaps Denny and the others, were conspiring to instruct the ship's master, Captain Donald Cruikshank, to hand over the *Memphis* to the Union navy, thus defrauding the owners of the cargo and also the insurers who underwrote the whole enterprise. Combined with the insurance payout, the "owners" would have tripled their original outlay on the vessel.

Thomas Begbie was known to be ambivalent in his support of the Confederate cause. He feared the consequences of a decisive Union victory, and he may well have been trying to hedge his bets, both politically and financially, by making the offer to the Union official in Belgium and inflating his prices into the bargain. Begbie could have been trying to build a fallback position in case the Union navy seized the *Memphis*. It is unlikely that the New York Prize Court would have accepted that any such capture was deliberately contrived for the sake of a side deal arranged in Brussels without clear evidence of Washington's agreement.

Zollinger and Andreas were probably acting for Fraser, Trenholm and Company in Liverpool for this consignment.[5] While Trenholm would have been anxious to lay off their risks, they were not going to ruin their reputation with the Confederate authorities for the sake of one steamer and its cargo. As Lieutenant Budd commented in his report to Gideon Welles, efforts had been made to sink the *Memphis* when it had become obvious that it was about to be captured.[6] Someone on board the *Memphis* had the conditions of the insurance contract in mind rather than the Brussels offer.

Begbie was an astute financier and was anxious to cover the financial downside. Suspicion falls on him after the USS *Magnolia* captured the *Memphis* in international waters. In August, according to Eric Graham, "Begbie, being fully insured, sardonically reported her loss to the Scots shipbuilder John Scott: '*Memphis* taken, bless the Yankees! It is pleasant, very, to see them get such a steamer and so loaded!'"[7] His machinations paid off, and Begbie came out the financial winner.

The SS *Memphis*, "a most sightly vessel" in the eyes of the *Charleston Mercury*,[8] was a large, single-screw-propelled auxiliary passenger and cargo steamer and carried two square-rigged masts with cross spars or yards that required a relatively large crew. It was of 792 tons English measure and 230 feet in length with a beam of 30 feet. Its draft in the hold was some 19 feet, giving it a cargo capacity of 52,750 cubic feet, plus space for 204 tons of coal. The engine was direct-acting, inverted-surface condensing, with two cylinders providing 705 indicated horsepower and 141 nominal horsepower from two tubular boilers. This gave it a speed of 11.5 knots, using 23 tons of coal a day, and a top speed of 14 knots.[9]

The SS *Memphis* left Liverpool on 10 May and arrived in Nassau on 27 May. Given the ship's coal bunker capacity and daily usage, it probably stopped at Funchal en route to replenish supplies. It had been stopped en route to Nassau and boarded by sailors of the U.S. gunboat *Quaker City*, who had fired "four or five shots across her bows" as a signal that they meant business. The *Memphis* was allowed to continue to the British Bahamian port after an examination lasting merely half an hour. The owners had ensured that the ship's papers had been well prepared and with all the cargo consigned to British firms in Nassau.

In another twist to the tangled ownership, the vessel was then sold or perhaps just offered for sale by a Mr. T. F. Smith to the armament dealers Theodore Andreas and Ivan Chludow of Manchester. Later Begbie claimed that Smith had no authority to do this, although Begbie appears to have been ready to accept the transaction, provided he was paid what he considered to be the right price of £34,900. This Mr. Smith appears to be the Englishman who made the false sale referred to by Consul Dudley in Liverpool. After a month in Nassau, during which these negotiations appear not to have been concluded, the *Memphis* sailed for Charleston.

The run into Charleston had been carefully prepared. Stephen Wise states that the *Memphis* had been given a special red-light signal to show as it approached the entrance to the harbor. The Confederates answered these signals correctly, but before the ship could slip into the deeper water, it grounded on the sand banks of Sullivan's Island. In the darkness and confusion, the Confederate guard in Fort Sumter opened fire, but the red-light signal was shown again and the firing stopped.[10] Robert Bunch reported, "One blockading vessel fired a few shells at her, without effect, but no effort was made to capture her by means of boats, or indeed any disposition to incur the slightest risk."[11]

The troubles of the *Memphis* did not end there. The ship was still aground at daybreak of the twenty-third and in plain sight of the offshore blockading squadron, who opened fire at long range. This must have been disconcerting for the crew and passengers very conscious of the fifteen tons of gunpowder in the hold. From sunup the soldiers from Sullivan's Island spent a desperate day under gunfire removing the powder in barges. At 5:00 P.M. the lightened *Memphis* floated off, and the tugs *Marion* and *Etiwan* took the ship and the rest of its valuable cargo to a wharf in Charleston.[12]

Passenger certificate for the SS *Memphis* showing also Captain Cruikshank's masters' certificate number. Courtesy Columbia University in the City of New York, Law School Library, United States District Court, New York Case of the Memphis.

James Carlin was probably not on board the vessel on the trip from Nassau, as he is later named as a "Charleston pilot," the inference being that he and other pilots boarded it for the outward-bound voyage from Charleston. We can assume also that he would not have wanted to be an inward passenger when there was big money to be made piloting other vessels into Confederate ports, and there were ships in Nassau Harbor awaiting expert pilotage.

The remainder of the ship's cargo was unloaded, including 11,000 small arms, 1 million percussion caps, 25 tons of lead, 23 hundredweight of cartridges, 12,000 pairs of woolen blankets, 20 hundredweight of lead shot, some 4 tons of steel bars, medicines, and other items. Some 1,500 cotton bales were then loaded onto the *Memphis*. It is not clear how long this took, but the captain and crew waited for the next spell of dark nights at the end of July before risking the blockading squadron lined up and visible on the horizon. The *Memphis* made its escape from Charleston on the night of 30 July, only to be stopped in international waters by the USS *Magnolia*.[13]

C. M. Allen, the U.S. consul in Bermuda, reported on 19 August 1862 that the *Memphis* had been bound for Bermuda when it was captured in international waters. Bermuda was a coaling station, where the bunkers of the *Memphis* were to have been filled before the voyage across the Atlantic to Liverpool with the cargo of cotton and rosin. There was no stoking coal in Charleston, and the long stay there must have further depleted the ship's supplies. The consul also reported that the large British steamer *Peterhof* was still in port at Hamilton awaiting the arrival of the *Memphis*.

The Charleston pilot H. Lea was probably planning to bring in the *Peterhof,* while H. Smith or J. Murray may have been waiting for the arrival of the *Merrimac,* a Begbie steamer that was expected shortly. Carlin himself and also the second mate of the *Memphis* both stated that they were bound for Liverpool via Halifax, Nova Scotia, as the British consul, Robert Bunch, reported in his dispatch to Lord Russell.

William Budd's vivid account of the capture leads into the complexities of the events that followed. The account is drawn from his Official Report (see appendix 1). At 2:00 P.M. on 31 July 1862, the USS *Magnolia* was steaming in a southwesterly direction, making a passage to its station at Key West, Florida. The crew sighted Cape Lookout, North Carolina, some ten miles off to the north-northwest. By the end of that afternoon, the weather was looking squally, with strong winds from the northwest and north-northwest. The USS *Magnolia* was a former blockade-runner, which had been caught in February 1862 while trying to run cotton and rosin out of a port on the Gulf of Mexico. It was a wooden-hulled, side-wheel steamer built in 1854.

During that evening the officer of the watch had reported depths of between ten to nineteen fathoms. The engines were logged as working well. Lieutenant Budd took over the early morning watch and reported southwesterly winds and passing rain. William Budd was a tough character who had served as a civilian with the U.S. Coast Survey in a capacity similar to that of James Carlin. According to a history of the Survey by the National Oceanic and Atmospheric Administration, "The Coast Survey had its own Billy Budd. More properly speaking it had William Budd, Sailing Master. But as opposed to the hero of Hermann Melville's novel, this

William Budd was not a victim of circumstances. He was a man who made things happen. When they did happen, they usually happened in a way that William Budd was the better for them."[14]

Budd enjoyed a notable career in the United States Navy, rising to the rank of volunteer lieutenant commander and serving as captain of six ships in many varied theaters of war, including the great rivers of the interior. He was one of three named Coast Survey sailing masters who went on to "illustrious Civil War careers"; the others were a Robert Platt and James C. Carlin. Budd was in frequent correspondence with Secretary of the Navy Gideon Welles, and his familiar tone suggests that he knew him well. He certainly knew Dr. Bache of the Survey, who had singled him out for praise in his reports of 1858 and 1860.

At 5:30 A.M. on 1 August 1862, when the *Magnolia* was some forty miles south and west of Cape Romain, well off the coast of South Carolina, the ship's commander sighted a steamer six miles to the west, painted a cream color and steaming northeast by east with housed topmasts. It was the *Memphis*. It must have stood out very clearly, lit up by the low dawn sun against the dark western sea.[15]

At 6:00 A.M. the *Magnolia* changed course and gave chase. The *Memphis* crew immediately fired up the boilers and turned to the east so that the ship's fore and after sails were drawing to full advantage in the southwesterly wind.[16] The position of the *Memphis* at the time of its capture suggests that it was running on a course that would take it inside the outer ring of Federal warships standing off Charleston. The plan was to outflank the Union vessels to the north before turning east-southeast for Bermuda. But the triangulation of their respective courses and speeds did not work for the *Memphis*. At 8:00 A.M. the officers and crew of the *Magnolia,* having closed in on their quarry, left off the chase momentarily and fired a ball-shot from the bow gun that went between the two masts of the *Memphis* and splashed into the sea two hundred yards off. The steamer then showed English colors and made all the speed it could under sail and power, as wood was thrown overboard.

The wood was found to be southern pine, convincing proof of the vessel's visit to a Confederate port. Budd continued the chase, gaining on his quarry. He ordered another ball shot that landed alongside the *Memphis*. Budd then directed that an exploding shell be fired; it landed close to the starboard quarter, with fragments flying over the poop deck. This came too close for comfort. The engines of the *Memphis* were stopped and the flag hauled down to half-mast. After being chased for three hours, the *Memphis* was surrendered at 9:00 A.M. rather than risk more damaging shells. Budd logged that the gun crew on the forecastle of the USS *Magnolia* saw a quantity of papers that were clearly weighted for immediate sinking being thrown overboard from the *Memphis*. Lieutenant Budd himself boarded the *Memphis* and found that the ship's master could not produce a cargo manifest, port customs clearance, or ship's log. He then took possession of the *Memphis* and raised the American flag. Budd put fifteen U.S. sailors on board as a prize crew, under the command of Acting Master Charles Potter.

At this point Budd "exercised a little tact," not a trait, by all accounts, normally associated with his character. He managed to obtain some documents and letters that showed the real nature of his capture. The ship proved to be the SS *Memphis* of London, whose last port of call had been Charleston, laden with 1,534 bales of cotton and 500 barrels of rosin consigned by Fraser, Trenholm and Company in Charleston to their associate company in Liverpool. These documents later formed part of the evidence used during the trial that followed. Rosin or pine resin—widely used in sealing wax, soaps, and varnishes—was an important Southern export.

The USS *Memphis,* painted by Clement Drew, M2651.
Courtesy of the Peabody Essex Museum.

This was the point at which Budd, having been through the remaining documents of the *Memphis,* realized that his future was secure. He had just netted a very valuable prize, of which his share, as captain, would set him up for life. He was not going to let it slip away by undermanning the large steamer, or by allowing the crew or passengers of the *Memphis* to recapture it from a small prize party of Union sailors.

Budd had found a very large crew on the *Memphis,* some fifty men, not including officers and passengers, so he sent another boat's crew to reinforce his grip on the prize. He also took the precaution of transporting all the officers, crewmen, and passengers to the *Magnolia* and putting two additional prize masters on board. He had no intention of losing his trophy. At 4:00 P.M. that afternoon, all the Union sailors were armed with pistols and cutlasses and a guard placed over all the hatches and companionways leading to the wardrooms and cabins where the prisoners were confined.[17]

Budd also found time to scrutinize the passengers and found one whom he recognized as an old shipmate from his days in the Coast Survey. Some reports say that James Carlin tried to hide among the passengers. He or his associates tried rather disingenuously to disguise his name as Carlingford, the name of a large sea lough on the east coast of Northern Ireland, where James had lived as a boy at the Coast Guard station overlooking the inlet.

Budd spotted him and singled him out from the other passengers. He also recognized John C. Lea and another Charleston pilot. He ordered his master-at-arms to detain all three. Other passengers were Theodore Andreas and Ivan Chludow, a Russian, who appeared as partners on some of the shipping documents. These two are described as Germans or Russians from Moscow. Two further passengers were Edward Decker and George Adshead, who had been on board from the start of the voyage in Liverpool, and a Mr. Smith, presumably the pilot, and a Mr. Putnam. There were also three "stowaways" who had been traveling in steerage. While James Carlin and William Budd do not appear to have served on the same Survey schooner, they held similar rank, and their paths must have crossed at some point. In any event, Budd knew him when he saw him on the deck of the *Memphis* and knew that he had a coup to report to his "patron" Gideon Welles, secretary of the navy.

The *Magnolia*, unaided and out of sight of any other Union warship, had captured a fully laden blockade-runner and brought it safely into a Union port. Budd made $38,318.55, or some $900,000.00 in today's dollars.[18] This was the single largest award of prize money during the Civil War. The ordinary seamen on the *Magnolia* each received over $1,700.00.[19]

On 4 August, Budd telegraphed G. V. Fox, assistant secretary of the navy: "I arrived here last night with British steamer *Memphis*. Have captured her off Charleston; had to convoy her: too weak to send her. *Magnolia* requires some repairs. I have got important information; telegraph for me to come to Washington."[20] Budd's triumph was complete. He was not going to entrust his valuable booty to a prize crew to bring safely into port. He used the excuse of repairs to the *Magnolia* to justify his return to New York with the *Memphis* under armed escort and firmly under his control. Nor was he going to pass up the chance to flaunt his success in Washington, D.C. On arrival in New York, James Carlin and the other Charleston pilots and all the crew were "at once consigned to one of the City Jails, pending examination by the Court."[21]

The capture of the *Memphis* following that of the other large steamers, the *Bermuda* and *Columbia,* effectively stopped direct shipments from Europe into southern ports. Thereafter, smaller, faster, shallower-draft vessels came into their own, leaving the larger vessels to make the transatlantic voyage to the offshore transshipment points of Nassau, Havana, and Bermuda.

# Chapter 12

# The Trial of the *Memphis,*
# August–September 1862

. . .

Following normal procedure, the non-American passengers, officers, and crew were freed after several days' captivity in the House of Detention at Mulberry Street. This was a notoriously corrupt institution housed in an Egyptian-style building known locally as the Tombs. However, the four "Charleston pilots" stayed in detention. The other three pilots were H. Lea, J. Murray, and H. Smith, named by James Carlin as fellow captives with him in Fort Lafayette.

The proceedings in the Prize Court trial of the *Memphis* were of great concern to Carlin, although he had no financial interest in the vessel or the cargo.[1] His freedom was at stake, and he needed to establish the legal basis on which both passengers and crew had been taken from the *Memphis*. In particular he had to confirm why the authorities continued to hold him, an Englishman, when the other non-Americans were freed.

There is no evidence to suggest that he had a hand in the escape of the *Memphis* from Charleston, and Budd described him as a passenger. He may well have been on the bridge with the other pilots and helped in the decisions that enabled the vessel to break through the cordon of Union warships. The ship's officers made no admission that this was the case, and they specifically stated that the passengers exercised no control over the ship.

Carlin was a British passenger on a British ship and had been removed from that vessel by force of arms. What was his status? Could he be charged with some criminal offence, or was there a civil law case to answer? Was he a prisoner of war subject to transfer to the notorious prison camps where Southern troops suffered harsh conditions? No one in New York could prove that he was enrolled in the armed services of the Confederacy, although such proof existed in the records of the Confederate navy in Savannah, where he was listed as a pilot. Without sight of this document, no U.S. court could show that he was a legitimate prisoner of war.

It was not until 9 May 1864 that Gideon Welles tried to codify the rules concerning foreigners captured running the blockade. Bona fide foreigners captured on neutral ships were "not to be treated as prisoners of war unless guilty of belligerent acts" and were to be released immediately, unless required as witnesses. Bona fide foreign subjects captured on "ships without flag or papers," or caught on ships flying the rebel flag, or who were in the service of the insurgent government, or were officers or crew of the captured ship were to be detained as prisoners of war. But even "habitual blockade runners" could not be detained if found to be genuine passengers on neutral ships. If doubt existed as to whether they were foreign subjects, they were to be obliged to declare under oath that they had never been naturalized in the United States and were indeed foreign subjects.[2]

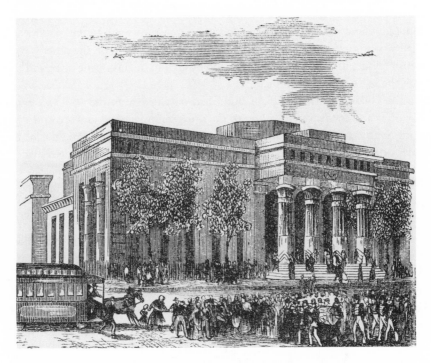

The first Tombs building in New York. 1880. Public domain.
Shutterstock©123RF.com.

Carlin's service with the Coast Survey led to a presumption that he had become a naturalized U.S. citizen. This was only an excuse to detain him and prevent him from using his skills as a blockade-runner. In fact, he was being held unlawfully as a prisoner of convenience. New York papers reporting the capture of the *Memphis* and the fate of the pilots on board linked him with the Coast Survey and called all of them "Americans."

The next issue was the legality of the U.S. Navy's capture of a British merchant ship in international waters. This was complicated by the question of the efficacy of the blockade. If, as the officers of the *Memphis* were careful to say, their entry and exit to Charleston was not challenged, then the defense could argue that they were not subject to the blockade restrictions. Both the chief officer and second mate admitted that the master of the vessel had received a general warning of the blockade of Charleston, but no written notice was entered in the ship's documents. If the defendants Theodore Andreas and his associates could prove their point in court, then technically at least the ship and all the passengers should be released immediately. A review of the evidence presented to the court shows that the ship's officers were aware of these aspects of international law and tried to phrase their answers accordingly.[3]

These questions were closely argued in the very extensive correspondence that took place between the British and American governments. On one side was the legality of stopping, searching, and detaining British vessels; on the other was the British failure, in U.S. eyes at least, to stop exports to the insurgent states and prohibit the sale of warships to them.

The documents that William Budd had obtained from the *Memphis* by the "use of tact" were delivered by him to the prize commissioners and are in the files of the Southern District Court of New York.[4] Their details range from the loading labels on some of the bales of cotton to lists of advances against wages made to the crew while laying up in Charleston and personal letters and numerous bills of exchange drawn on individuals, trading houses, and banks, including Baring Brothers in the City of London and Liverpool.

One of the most telling papers was a list of crew members who had signed up and agreed to proceed to any port in the Confederate States of America, blockaded or not, in consideration of a bounty of fifteen pounds sterling for each man: five pounds to be paid before starting and another five pounds to be paid for the vessel's safe arrival in a Confederate port, with the remaining five pounds to be paid on the safe arrival at any English port from any Confederate port. There were twenty-three signatures. A further three men signed on for ten guineas each. While some men had joined in Charleston, this list showed that others were not due the bounty and presumably had not signed up for the excitements of being shelled and captured by a fully armed warship.

The *Memphis* had been authorized to carry sixty-five passengers and examined by the Port of London authorities to ensure that it had adequate safety equipment, including blue flares, a signal gun, and eight lifeboats, plus safety valves on each of the boilers and fire-hoses. T. S. Begbie, Esquire, of 4, Mansion House Place, London, paid four pounds, nineteen shillings, and sixpence for this certificate.

The case of *The United States v. the Steamer* Memphis, the ship's tackle and cargo held "in prize," was heard before E. Delafield Smith, U.S. district attorney, with J. N. Upton for the captors and Charles Edwards as counsel for the owners of the vessel and cargo.[5]

A motion to put aside this order was made to the court on 13 August. The case received a mention in court on 26 August. On 2 September, Peter Denny, Thomas Sterling Begbie, and Theodore Andreas, who was representing the interests of his company, the charter party, and owners of most of the cargo, all filed claims.

During the formal interrogation section of the court hearing, Captain Donald Cruikshank confirmed that the vessel had been about eighty-five miles east of Charleston when captured and that the *Memphis* had no commission or authority to make prizes and thus was not a privateer. He admitted that the ship's owners had signed him on "I suppose because they imagined I had run the blockade" and pointed out that the vessel sailed under English colors and that it had no other country's colors on board. He stated that the vessel was bound for Halifax and made no mention of Bermuda, where the U.S. consul had reported it was expected daily.

The cargo that the *Memphis* carried from England included, as the captain said, "a little of everything": blankets, boots and shoes, leather, steel, iron, lead, copper, and nails. A portion of this shipment was discharged in Nassau, where the ship also took on some twelve cases of medicine, probably quinine. Cruikshank made no mention of gunpowder. He stated that he "never held any legal authority to sell the vessel," but that he thought that there was "an agreement entered into to purchase at Nassau." He never saw it, so could not swear who the parties were, but he thought it was "to sell the vessel for £26,000 Sterling, the same as she cost." He was certain that it was not to be sold to any person connected with the Confederate government.

He also declared that he would suffer personal loss from the capture of the vessel and confiscation of all documents if his personal possessions were not returned. These included his nautical instruments and clothing, and a draft of £1,000 drawn by the Bank of Charleston on the Bank of Liverpool, payable to the order of Mr. W. F. McRae, Esquire, no. 7 Great Winchester Street, London, and a draft for £500 drawn by John Fraser and Company of Charleston on Fraser, Trenholm and Company of Liverpool. The smaller bill was a bonus payment and was accompanied by a letter:

> Accept enclosed Bill on England drawn by Messrs. Fraser upon their house
> in Liverpool for £500. as some acknowledgement on behalf of Messrs. Jones
> & North of your courage and undaunted perseverance in conducting your
> steamer with their goods safely to this port, having run the gauntlet against
> as strong a blockading fleet as never previously experienced, so much less,
> accomplished its circumvention.
>
> With every wish for a safe voyage to England
> Believe me, dear Sir, yours sincerely Wm. North, Jr.[6]

His items were not indemnified by anyone for loss. He also made the point that none of the passengers had held any executive role or commission on the ship; nor, so far as he knew, were any acting as agents.

The chief officer, Henry May, then answered the same set of questions. He had been on board the *Memphis* since its commissioning at Dumbarton. He recalled that the vessel had left Nassau on 19 June, passing through the blockading squadron and arriving in Charleston on the morning of the twenty-third. He had been promised one hundred pounds sterling if the voyage was successful. He admitted that there was "a like understanding with the remainder of those on board."[7] However, he remarked that when they "went into Charleston from Nassau, we passed several Vessels of War lying off that port, which however took no measures to prevent our entering." He also stated that the master had a general warning but met no opposition as the ship ran into Charleston. Nor had any such warning been endorsed on the ship's papers.

His most revealing comments concerned the passengers. He said that no passengers "were hid on board," implying that the questioner had asked him about the stowaways or, more probably, the Charleston pilots and James Carlingford, a.k.a. James Carlin. James Philips, the second mate, was candid in answering the same questions. He admitted that the *Memphis* carried eighty tons of powder into Charleston. Philips was of the opinion that the ship was about "40 miles to the Northward and Eastward of the entrance of Charleston harbour" when it was captured. His bonus for a successful voyage was to be fifty pounds sterling. Philips confirmed the names of the pilots and said that Mr. Smith came on board in Nassau.

Theodore Andreas's testimony followed similar lines. He had been born in Germany, had lived for the past nine or ten years in Manchester, England, and was a British subject. He also confirmed that no "resistance was made at the time of capture" and that "some schooners were in sight—but no vessels of war." He disclaimed an interest in the ownership of the vessel or knowledge of the owners other than Thomas Begbie. He admitted that Zollinger, Andrea and Company had an interest in the cotton that he reckoned to be worth about the cash price of $60,000, meaning the price in Charleston. But he was unable to be more exact.

Theodore Andreas seemed anxious to add the following statement: "When we had arrived in Nassau I made an offer to purchase the Steamer to the agent of the owners at that place, a Mr. T. F. Smith, upon certain terms as to the price, but not having heard from England since, I don't know whether my offer has been accepted." He had not received a bill of sale for the vessel. He also stated that Zollinger, Andreas and Company, the York Irish Flax Spinning Company of Belfast, and Jones and North of Leeds owned the cargo loaded at Liverpool. A portion was "on freight for Parties in Charleston." He added Enfield rifles and ammunition to the list of goods on the outward cargo, as well as flannel, felt, and straw hats.

William Budd and the officers and crew of the USS *Magnolia* also petitioned the court. They acted to establish their claim and ensure that they secured their rich prize. They wanted to show that they were the sole captors of the *Memphis* and earnestly prayed that the captured property be condemned as a lawful prize of war and sold forthwith. There were others associated with the court who were particularly anxious that the most valuable prize yet to come into their hands should not slip beyond their grasp through some legal technicality.

On the detention of his crew in New York, Captain Cruikshank is said to have made an immediate application for their discharge, although court officials disputed this. Charles Edwards, acting also as the legal counsel for the British consul in New York, reported to London that one of the New York prize commissioners had told Cruikshank that if he agreed to the confiscation of the vessel and her cargo, he and his men would be released. Edwards commented, "I need not enlarge upon the nature of such a proposition by an officer so deeply interested in obtaining the condemnation [or forfeiture] of delinquent vessels. I cite it only as an instance of the profound corruption which pervades the Court in question."[8]

A year later, there was a full-scale investigation into the practices of this court and the prize commissioners who handled the process of securing the cargoes, arranging the auctions, and disposing of the vessels. There were allegations that they were in collusion with certain prospective purchasers who received favorable treatment not available to others. The New York newspapers took up the story and assertions flew around and rumors spread. The end result was that the naval captors of blockading runners no longer sent their prizes to New York for disposal, but favored Boston, Philadelphia, Key West, Baltimore, and Washington.

Madeline Russell Robinton gives some revealing figures. Of 367 cases sent to the prize courts by February 1863, 141 went to New York for adjudication. In the next two years, only fifty-four cases were sent to New York, a "Tomb of Capulets," in the words of the journalist investigating the affair for the *New York Express*.[9] Yet total captures had risen to a total of over a thousand for the four years of the blockade. The terms of reference of the inquiry were to investigate charges of "irregularities in the custody and deposition of prize property."[10] The hearings into the activities of the Prize Court continued for some five years. It concluded that there was no evidence of serious offences or breaches in correct procedure, although there were some lapses due to carelessness. Robinton noted that regardless of the validity of the investigator's conclusions, New York's share in the number of the prize cases decreased tremendously after the investigation started.[11] These allegations were to have more international ramifications in the events that followed.

The sale of the cargo raised $440,495.12. The *Memphis* was assessed at $103,000.00, making a total of $543,495.12, from which $2,717.48 in court costs were deducted by the Southern District of New York. Although the owners appealed to the Circuit Court, the District Court's verdict was upheld, and the ship and the cargo of 1,521 bales of cotton and 500 barrels of rosin was forfeited. This was said to be the most cotton found on any prize vessel and the most valuable prize taken during the course of the war. William Budd was indeed a lucky man.[12]

As for the *Memphis,* the ship was purchased by the U.S. Navy after its value had been appraised by expert assessors, and it was converted to naval use. In October 1862 it captured another Begbie-owned steamer, the *Ouachita.* Begbie was indeed playing his part on both sides of the conflict.

# Chapter 13

# Recriminations and Fallout,
# September 1862

$\cdots$

The extensive diplomatic correspondence provoked by these events started with a spat between the British consul in New York and the prize commissioners over Captain Cruikshank's allegations that they offered to release the crew in exchange for his agreement to the confiscation of the *Memphis* and its cargo. At this stage these events concerned the British Foreign Office more than the fate of James Carlin.

The playing out of the *Memphis* affair reveals how a background of mistrust and dishonesty influenced the events. Acting consul Charles Edwards had reported the corruption directly to London, which had forwarded his letters to the British Embassy in Washington. Once they had confirmed that the prize commissioner in question was Henry A. Elliott, the British minister (that is, the ambassador) took up the matter with U.S. Secretary of State Seward, who replied by stating that Elliott emphatically denied these allegations.

Edwards managed to obtain sworn statements from Theodore Andreas and Donald Cruikshank before they left New York on the first available steamer to England.[1] In Edwards's view, their statements showed that Elliott was guilty of corruption. This incident set the tone for the subsequent lengthy negotiations for James Carlin's release and revealed British attitudes toward dealing with the New York officials.

After the *Memphis* was escorted to the Brooklyn Navy Yard, U.S. Marshal Robert Murray took the crew and passengers to the offices of the prize commissioners. Here, in the grand jury room, Captain Cruikshank was stripped of all his outer clothing and searched, even to his undergarments and shirt. This was a serious affront to his rank and nationality and was taken up by the British Consulate.

Murray wrote to the British consul on 19 August, denying that he had ordered the search and blamed Lieutenant William Budd, stating that the naval officer had ordered the intimate search to find incriminating letters to Confederate agents and documents that might affect the outcome of the trial of the vessel.

Whatever the actual truth of this accusation and counterclaim, Robert Murray was obliged to write to Secretary of State Seward, refuting the protest in strong and finely tuned terms: "I have instituted the requisite inquiry, and respectfully report to you that the several allegations referred to have no foundation whatever, but are fabrications of a tendency so mischievous, and made with a design so manifestly nefarious, that those whom the charges seek to inculpate, earnestly hope that fit and proper measures may be adopted to the end that their author may at last be deprived of all capacity to practice future mischief."[2]

Marshal Murray included eight affidavits designed to counter these allegations. These depositions were taken in the District Court, but full transcripts appear in the British Foreign Office files in London. The British consul must have attended the hearings and taken verbatim records. The survival of these records underlines their importance and confirms the view that there was such widespread suspicion of the whole process that the transcripts were viewed as potential evidence in any subsequent action.

The court officers were clearly furious that their probity had been questioned so publicly and that the allegations had reached as far as Seward in Washington. They took vigorous measures to refute Cruikshank's allegations. The impression left to today's reader is that they protested too much and appeared rehearsed.

Henry Elliot, the New York prize commissioner, stated under oath that Lieutenant Budd had told him that the captured crew aboard the USS *Magnolia* had attempted to set fire to his ship. Budd thought that this fire was designed to allow the master and crew to return to the *Memphis* to recapture the vessel or to hide or dispose of important documents. All present decided that none of the *Memphis* crew should be allowed back on board, except under strict supervision.

The one person who emerges well from this murky world is Stewart L. Woodford, the Assistant District Attorney in E. Delafield Smith's office. Either he was playing a particularly devious game or else he was the one honest person there. Did he catch wind of a scheme to cash in Cruikshank's bills of exchange and decide to put an end to it by pointing out that they were second or third copies of exchange? He meant that they were probably uncashable as the first could be well on its way to England for payment (the first bill to be presented for payment automatically cancelled the other bills in the set.) Woodford's straightforward testimony seems above board and clear. All the others scrambled to clear their names, while trying to ensure that their rich prize did not slip though their hands.

E. Delafield Smith already had his suspicions of Robert Murray and wrote to him on 26 September 1862, asking for assurances that the large commissions allowed to auctioneers were paid in "good faith, without any bargains or arrangements for sharing."[3]

In his deposition, U.S. Marshal Robert Murray told a tale of the desperate characters among the crew who had tried to set fire to the ship on the way to New

York. He also stated that the crew (and presumably the passengers, minus the Charleston pilots) were not detained in the city jails but sent to the House of Detention for Witnesses, "a comfortable place where they were provided for and kindly treated, and from where they were released the following day."

The use of the word "kindly" surely begs the question. Murray's main allegation was that Captain Cruikshank seemed perfectly content with his treatment and the manner in which he was searched until he "fell into the hands of the Legal Counsel and Proctor for the British Consul, Mr Charles Edwards before whom and by whom he was subsequently induced to make a protest."[4] In an attempt to deflect criticism, Murray accused Charles Edwards of delaying proceedings unnecessarily by engaging in long and technical legal arguments.

There are no marginal comments on these court transcripts in the British Foreign Office archives to hint at the British attitude to all this, but the fact that they are bound in the same leather and marble covers as the correspondence about James Carlin's release shows that they were thought to have a bearing on the matter.

While the opinions of true-blue, anti-British Yankees may well be reflected by the stance of U.S. Marshal Robert Murray, there were others, including those in the New York District Attorney's Office, who had a more skeptical view of the operations of this court. The British Consulate in New York shared this skepticism, as did the Foreign Office in London, while the British Legation in Washington took a more calculatedly neutral line.

Cruikshank and Andreas, and probably the rest of the crew and the other passengers, caught the earliest steamer out of New York that was available. The officials of the Prize Court and their associates, the auctioneers, and other hangers-on got their commissions; Manchester and Glasgow claimed their insurance money. Imprisoned in Fort Lafayette, James Carlin set about obtaining his release.

# Chapter 14

# Fort Lafayette

### Anglo-American Diplomatic Exchanges and James Carlin's Struggle for Release, August–December 1862

. . .

Fort Lafayette, New York, Seth Eastman, oil on canvas,
Collection of the U.S. House of Representatives.

I f the legitimate passengers and crew of the *Memphis* were confined in common prisons in New York, we can assume that James Carlin and the pilots Lee,
Smith, and Murray received rougher treatment. Separated from the others, they
were also detained in the city's New Prison before being moved to Fort Lafayette. New York papers reported with glee that the rebel pilots had been "steered"

across the harbor to captivity in a neat reversal of their usual role. Marshal Robert Murray took them to Fort Hamilton, where they were handed over to Colonel Martin "Tyrant" Burke, the commander of Fort Lafayette.

Their five-man guard had fixed bayonets as the prisoners sat in a small boat for the three-hundred-yard row over to the Bastille landing, where they were escorted under guard to the presence of Lieutenant C. O. Wood, a former railroad conductor. After a roll call, their watches and money were removed, and they were searched by a sergeant. From this "unpleasant ceremony," they were taken to Casement Six, a battery embrasure on the lower tier on the fort's west side that mounted five 35-pounder guns.

A casement in Fort Lafayette. Courtesy of "The Civil War in America from the *Illustrated London News.*" A Joint Project by Sandra J. Still, Emily E. Katt, Collection Management, and the Beck Center of Emory University.

Carlin was held as a civilian prisoner of war in the grim fortress of Fort Lafayette for five months. The casements each held twelve men, crammed into a space measuring fifteen by eleven feet. They had a small table, a washbasin, and a single bucket; the men slept in hammocks slung from nails in the roof. The conditions were, by most accounts, harsh.[1] Other reports indicate somewhat more tolerable conditions.

This large diamond-shaped citadel protected the entrance to New York Harbor and thus access to the water route inland up the Hudson River. The building was demolished in 1960, and the remains lie beneath a supporting tower of the huge bridge that now spans the Verrazano Narrows at the entrance to the harbor. The fort was built on Hendricks Reef, some two hundred yards from the Brooklyn shoreline opposite Fort Hamilton. From his casement Carlin and the other captains may well have seen further vessels brought in as prizes by Union warships and would later have news of the blockade when more captives were brought to the fort.

Construction on the fort had begun during the War of 1812. Originally named Fort Diamond, it was renamed in 1823 to honor the last visit to America of the Marquis de Lafayette, the French marshal who had aided the American revolutionary forces during the war to gain independence from Great Britain. This massive stone construction was also known as the "Brooklyn Bastille" and in the South as the "Northern Bastille." It covered some two and a half acres and consisted of three tiers of casements accommodating seventy-three guns. During the Civil War, high-ranking prisoners of war and important civilian detainees were confined in the gun casements.

Among Carlin's first actions once he was imprisoned at Fort Lafayette was to begin writing letters in hopes of obtaining his release. He wrote to his father in Ireland, and also the following letter to Her Majesty's Minister at the British Legation in Washington:

Fort Lafayette
12th August 1862
Sir,
I beg leave to inform you of my detention as a prisoner of war.

I was a passenger on board the British Steamship "Memphis" having run the blockade of the Port of Charleston. The Captain, Crew and Passengers have been released, and from all I can understand I am detained upon the supposition that I am a citizen of this country I having been in the coastal survey Service of the United States for a short time previous to the War which has led to this misunderstanding.

I have never become a Citizen of this Country and now respectfully claim your attention to my case. My father has been in H.M. service for thirty-five years, and not having heard of him for some months, I was on my way to see him.

I have written to his last address (which was when I last Heard from him Carrickfergus Co. Antrim Ireland) informing of the particulars, and requesting his immediate interference. He is in the Coast Guard Service and liable to removal at any time so my communication may not reach him for a considerable time—I may be subjected to long and unjust imprisonment. And will be much obliged if you will attend to my case at your earliest convenience.

I remain (signed) James Carlin

P.S. I commanded a steamer in which I ran the blockade a few times but cannot see why I should be made an exception to the general rule, of allowing men so engaged to go free shortly after capture.—(signed) J.C.[2]

This was no straightforward matter. Carlin was a prized prisoner. In the eyes of the North, his detention could reduce the volume of munitions that reached the Confederate forces. From the perspective of James Carlin, his family, and British authorities, the rights of a British subject were at stake, and Carlin's life was in danger, too.

Despite his son's fears that his father had been transferred from Carrickfergus, news of his plight arrived there safely and immediate action was taken. Notwithstanding his modest rank in the British Coast Guard Service, Carlin's father mobilized the greatest in the land to come to the aid of his son. Carlin family sources in Florida are adamant that Charles Robert Carlin went to Paris and then on to England to secure his brother's release. Perhaps Ella Rosa, with her Montijo connection, wanted the Confederate delegation in Paris to ask the Empress Eugénie for help.

Doubtless following advice from his son, and with the help of Charles, James Carlin Sr. contacted Weir Anderson, a Liverpool solicitor, trustee commissioner, and political agent of the Liverpool Conservative Party. Both Anderson and his wife, Margaret Weir, had been born in Jamaica. He had been in practice in Liverpool since at least 1845, around the time when he first met Charles Turner, M.P., who was to become one of the three local members of Parliament for South Lancashire.

In his letter to Anderson, James Carlin Sr. made a heartfelt plea for aid in ending his son's imprisonment:

Coast Guard Station, Port Muck

September 4th 1862

Weir Anderson Esq.

Liverpool

Sir

On the 30th July last, my son James Carlin sailed from the Port of Charleston, South Carolina, as a passenger on board the British Steamer "Memphis" on his way home to visit me. On the morning of the 31st July the above steamer was captured by the United States Gunboat "Magnolia" Lieut. Budd commanding and taken to New York along with her passengers and Crew.

After several days confinement in the House of Detention in Mulberry Street New York the passengers, officers and Crew were all released excepting my Son James Carlin and three other passengers, who were detained.

And I have reason to believe are now imprisoned in Fort Lafayette or some other Prison in the United States. My son is a British subject, he was born in Hunstanton in the county of Norfolk as is evidenced by the accompanying Certificates of his birth and apprenticeship, whilst in America he had at one time been employed in the "Coast survey" Service of the United States but he never became naturalized nor took the Oath of allegiance to the United States government, nor did he ever vote, or in anyway compromise his rights and privileges as a British Subject— My object in writing you is to beg that you will have attention called to his case, as he had no friends in America to look after him and to solicit your efforts on his behalf to obtain his release from a most unjust imprisonment.

I remain Sir, Yours very respectfully
Samuel [James][3] Carlin, Commissioned Boatman Coast Guard Service[4]

Weir Anderson contacted his acquaintance Charles Turner, who wrote to Earl Russell, the British foreign secretary, on 8 September 1862.

From Dingle Head, Liverpool.
My Lord,
At the request of one of my constituents, I have the honour to forward to your lordship the enclosed letter. The writer I am informed is a very respectable man and this letter as stated appears to be one of hardship and affliction on the part of the Government of the United States.
May I by the favour of your [illegible] and [request] that your lordship will take such steps to obtain the release of Captain Carlin as your ministry [thinks necessary.]
I am your faithful and obedient servant Charles Turner.[5]

Charles Turner was a man of influence and his voice counted in London. Starting as a merchant in the East India Company, he had been chairman of the British Ship Owners Association. In 1861 he was chairman of the Mersey Dock and Harbour Board, deputy lieutenant of the county, and a director of numerous other concerns, including the Great Northern Railway.

The diplomatic exchange that followed shows the muscle of the British Foreign Office in the 1860s. "While Her Majesty's government insisted that it would not interfere with the blockade, the United States could legally subject neutral blockade violators to no punitive measures beyond condemnation of offending property. Earl Russell made far less clear exactly how far he intended to go in defending that position if necessary."[6] The tacit threat of British action, even leading to outright war, was the ever-present, if unstated, current behind the events that followed.

Foreign Secretary Russell and his clerks acted immediately on Turner's letter. By 13 September a copy, together with the letter from James Carlin Sr., was on its way to the British Embassy in Washington, with Russell's request for clarification as to whether James Carlin and the other passengers had been released with the rest of the crew of the *Memphis*.

Charles Turner, M.P., first chairman of the Mersey Docks and Harbour Board, 1803–1875. Courtesy of Liverpool *Town Crier* Album.

The resulting extensive correspondence makes it clear that James was sent to Fort Lafayette at the request of Provost Marshal Robert Murray, who was determined to take a hard line and follow government policy to detain all those with knowledge of the Southern coasts. Murray followed Budd's lead in insisting that James Carlin must be an American citizen. Murray's letter of 5 September 1862 to Her Majesty's Consul Edward M. Archibald in New York reflects this view. He informed Archibald that Carlin was detained as a prisoner of war because he was formerly an officer in the Coast Survey and as such, took an oath of allegiance to this [the U.S.] Government."

John Russell, 1st Earl Russell, British secretary of state for foreign affairs between 1859–1865.
© National Portrait Gallery, London.

Murray then stated that Carlin "deserted into rebel service, and having broken his oath, is amenable to a traitor's punishment." He repeated Budd's allegations about Carlin's naturalization and use of the name Carlingford when captured. Budd was also reported to have said that Carlin was in command of the *Memphis,* although this may be just malice or an attempt to strengthen his case by suggesting that Carlin had piloted the *Memphis* out of Charleston and through the blockading squadron that night. However, there is no other testimony to that effect.

Murray also asserted that an intercepted letter from one of the passengers on the *Memphis* to a rebel agent in Nassau proved beyond doubt that "Carlin's pretence to be a British subject is merely a subterfuge."[7] He asserted that he anticipated some such step by James, and had thus placed this letter and other proof of James's citizenship on file in the State Department in Washington. No sign of this file has emerged since. Murray then overstated his case by commenting that he had proof of several passengers and crew on captured vessels declaring under oath that they were British subjects, only to boast of their America citizenship once they were released.

Some 76 percent of the foreigners arrested for anti-Union activities were British, so Consul Archibald had to deal with a large number of cases. It took five and a half hours to travel to Fort Lafayette from New York City before the laborious process of determining the prisoner's citizenship, reasons for arrest, and degree of guilt. Although he was generally a Union sympathizer, Archibald was particularly concerned about the treatment of the prisoners. He complained that "the feeding of them is jobbed at 43 cents a day, but not more than 10 cents worth, I am afraid, reaches the prisoners."[8]

Much of the nuance of what follows stems from the previous history of the main figures involved in "The Case of James Carlin." The letters themselves are in formal diplomatic language, which makes assumptions not always obvious today, but reflects the fallout from the *Trent* Affair and other tests of strength between the British and the U.S. governments.

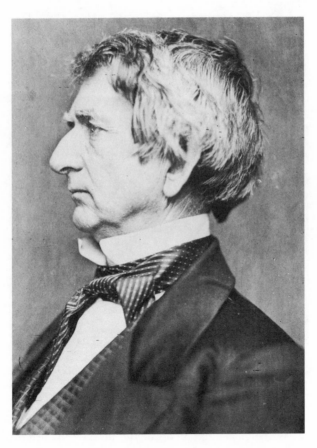

William Henry Seward, U.S. secretary of state between 1861 and 1867.
Courtesy of Library of Congress.

The question of James Carlin's nationality formed the basis of the first round of exchanges between Secretary of State William Henry Seward and the British legation in Washington and through them to the Foreign Office in London. Russell was anxious to protect the rights of British subjects abroad and urged a more forceful response from his legation in Washington. However, Lyons was circumspect in his dealings with Seward on British subjects detained by the Union for pro-Confederate activities and took each on a case-by-case basis.

Richard Lyons, 1st Viscount Lyons, British minister, Washington Legation, 1862 and 1863. Courtesy of Library of Congress.

Seward was a formidable force in Abraham Lincoln's administration. He was to survive an assassination attempt on the night Lincoln was killed by John Wilkes Booth. He is known for his support of the concept of Manifest Destiny that led to the purchase of Alaska from the Russians in 1867—a purchase dubbed "Seward's

Icebox" or "Seward's Folly." By 1870 Seward was planning to gain American control of the whole Pacific Northwest. This was to be achieved by outright annexation, British Columbian secession from Canada, or as compensation for the damage caused by Britain's alleged violation of the Neutrality Act in permitting the construction of armed raiders for the Confederate cause.

Seward was well known to Richard Lyons, the British minister in Washington. Together they had resolved the *Trent* Affair. Earlier they had negotiated the Lyons-Seward Treaty that bound Britain and the United States together in putting an end to the Atlantic slave trade. Seward was strongly antislavery and an American expansionist, although his aim was to do this by purchase and persuasion, not by Yankee intervention or force of arms.

Lyons was a British diplomat in the classic mold. A man of real ability, he was highly regarded by the Foreign Office in London, which had the greatest confidence in his judgment of affairs in Washington. Later, in the Paris Embassy, he was thought of as the most able diplomat in the Foreign Service.[9]

Seward's correspondence with Lyons, and later with his chargé d'affaires, William Stuart, shows that the State Department was conscious of the questionable legality of the U.S. marshal's actions in keeping Carlin in detention after the rest of the crew and passengers of the *Memphis* had been released.

The diplomatic exchanges also reveal how British power and influence in relation to that of the United States was strikingly different in the 1860s. The British envoys in Washington knew that they could exert power by merely threatening referral to London. Sometimes the British diplomats felt underused by the Liberal government in Westminster. Both Lyons and Stuart found that they had to remind Earl Russell, their Liberal foreign minister, that, in the words of historians James and Patience Barnes, "Some Americans were spoiling for a fight with the United Kingdom. Anti-British feeling went back many years."[10]

However, this should also be viewed in the context of sentiment in England. Hostility towards the North was stronger among the British upper classes than in the rest of the country. Despite the distress in the cotton towns of Lancashire, much working-class sympathy was said to lie with the North and with the antislavery argument. Liberal opinion in Britain also favored the North and sympathized with the distress of the laid-off cotton mill workers. This was reflected in similar circles in Europe. An instance of this is seen in the case of James Venning, an Englishman who was a lecturer in English at the University of Utrecht. He gave at least two lectures on the poetry of Shakespeare in aid of the distressed operatives of Lancashire.[11] The political balance in England between the interests of the various classes ensured Britain's formal neutrality, a position that was reinforced by U.S. Ambassador Charles Francis Adams's "superb diplomacy."[12]

William Stuart in Washington handled the initial correspondence in the absence of Lyons, who had returned to England on sick leave in mid-1862. Stuart was an Eton- and Cambridge-educated career diplomat who had served in Paris and Athens. After two spells as *chargé d'affaires* in Washington during Lyons's absence, he served in the British Embassy in Constantinople.

On 12 October, Stuart wrote to Secretary of State Seward sending him a copy of Turner's letter. He instructed Consul Archibald to visit Carlin in prison to determine whether he had taken an oath of allegiance to the United States and whether Carlin had tried to disguise his identity on the *Memphis* by using the name Carlingford.

Archibald reported that Mr. Edwards, his vice consul, had taken a sworn statement from Carlin answering Marshal Murray's allegations. Carlin had "positively and with apparent truthfulness, denied the whole of them with the single exception of that which represents him as having been formally in the Coast Survey Service." Carlin said also that he had not used the name Carlingford to hide his real identity. Stuart then advised Seward that it was "his duty, as instructed by Earl Russell to request that you will have the kindness to issue the necessary orders for Carlin's release."[13]

Seward responded on the fifteenth, confirming that he had requested the secretary of the navy to order Carlin's release as soon as it was evident that James Carlin had been born in England. Clearly, the Americans could not prove any change in his nationality. Both parties assumed that his discharge would take place immediately, and there the matter rested. On 6 November, Earl Russell directed that Mr. Turner in Liverpool should be advised that orders had been issued for the discharge of James Carlin.[14]

# Chapter 15

# Still a Captive, Late 1862

. . .

However, Carlin was not free. In early November he smuggled a note to the British consul in Baltimore, who wrote to the embassy in Washington telling them of his situation. Lord Lyons had to write again to Consul Archibald on 19 November asking him to "ascertain when Carlin had actually been discharged." On 26 November Archibald confirmed that Carlin was still held in Fort Lafayette. Carlin later stated that Lord Lyons had been astonished to hear of his continued captivity.[1]

Lord Lyons quickly passed this information to Seward, who contacted the secretary of the navy. Gideon Welles replied in detail on 6 December. He held that "the mere fact that Carlin is, or was, a British subject, even were it indisputable, would not entitle him to his release—As a British subject may be made a Prisoner under circumstances which would divest him of his neutral character and to the right of protection of his government."[2]

Welles emphasized that Carlin had "enjoyed the protection and patronage" of the U.S. government "to a degree which it is not usual to extend to those who are neither native or adopted citizens." He noted that "were he inclined to be ingrate, [Carlin] had the power of most deeply injuring the government." He also accused him of deserting the service although Carlin left the Coast Survey in good order well before the outbreak of the war.

Welles, presenting the Navy Department's view, comments that "the facts of the case are such as, according to the principles of International Law would throw upon him the onus of proving that he had not forfeited his right of protection of a government disposed to be sincerely neutral."

On December 9 Seward wrote again to Bache to inquire whether Carlin had taken the oath of allegiance, as required under the fourth section of the Act of Congress, 1 June 1789.[3] Bache replied that Carlin was not engaged in the office in Washington but that such details of service as the taking of an oath would be the responsibility of the commander of the vessel on which they first served. He added, "He did not know that, before the breaking out of the rebellion, they [oaths of allegiance] were required of the Sub officers and crew of vessels generally, by the naval officer in charge of Hydrography." Nor could he find out the facts as Carlin's commanding officers had left the U.S. Navy for "service with the rebels."[4]

Gideon Welles, secretary of the United States Navy, 1861–1869.
Courtesy of Library of Congress.

The officer in question was probably John Newland Maffitt, then in command of the schooner *Gallatin*, which Carlin had joined on 1 April 1856. On 29 September 1862, soon after his confinement in Fort Lafayette, Carlin wrote to Edwin McMasters Stanton, the U.S. secretary of war. He asked for a short parole in order to visit Washington and sort out the question of his nationality. He was confident that he would be released once the government had the correct information. He also mentioned that he had written to Bache. He suggested to Stanton that he contact Bache, who was a "person who knows him, worthy of such trust."[5] Stanton, Seward, and the district attorney of the Southern District of New York then conducted an extensive correspondence, trying to lay blame on Bache for the failure of his department to naturalize Carlin on entry to the Survey.

Quite why Carlin thought he could obtain his release by visiting Washington personally remains unclear. He may have known of documents that could clear him, or indeed that would prove the Americans' case. He may have felt that some discreet money would ease matters in his favor. Perhaps he just wanted the chance to escape and planned to take the same careless attitude to the new parole that he had taken to the parole that secured his release after the *Alert* affair. However, Carlin preferred to present himself as a honorable gentleman worthy of a parole when he responded with indignation to Bache's refusal to help.

While most of the official letters would have been written by clerks, acting on behalf of their masters, Bache's exchange with Carlin is revealing, as Bache was himself doing the writing. Carlin's respectful letter to Bache was met with a curt inquiry from Bache asking when he would take an oath of allegiance to the United States. Bache said that he was under the impression that Carlin was a secessionist.

Carlin replied in terms that show a degree of hurt and disappointment. He "cannot but regret that a simple request, which no one Gentleman ought to refuse another—of whose honor he had at least some slight proof, should have met so uncourteous a reply."[6] Bache's disparagement no longer fitted Carlin's view of himself as a man of property and some wealth, a long way from a master's mate being paid thirty-seven dollars a month.

Bache replied immediately to to Seward's letter of 9 December. He was clearly irritated by Carlin's request for his reference for parole. His response is typical of Bache's approach. His delight in subtle but pointed remarks shows why he earned a formidable reputation as a political operator in Washington. Bache finished his letter to Seward by pointing him to the War Office and asking "by what means he [Carlin] had first obtained his discharge, if indeed he has been discharged since his capture in the *Memphis*."[7] Bache was keen to deflect blame from his department and pass it on to the War Department, which had released Carlin previously, and to the U.S. Navy, whose seconded officers did not administer the oath in accordance with the Constitution.

Whatever the merits of Carlin's case, he had succeeded in creating a stir within the corridors of Washington and spreading discord and bad feeling between government departments. As we shall see, he was equally adept at doing the same with British colonial officials.

On 4 December, Dr. Bache sent a note to Gideon Welles admitting that he did not know whether James Carlin was, or claimed to be, an American citizen, or took any oath of allegiance. Bache also mentioned the statement from Lieutenant William Budd that Carlin was in command of the *Memphis* when he captured the vessel.[8]

At this point in mid-December 1862, things had come to an impasse. Seward and Welles, as we might expect, were adamant that Carlin was too valuable to the Confederate cause for them to release him. But it had become clear they could not prove that he had been naturalized.

# Chapter 16

# Diplomatic Power Play, Christmas 1862–January 1863

. . .

B ehind the scenes, James Carlin's father had taken the initiative. He made a sworn declaration of his son's Norfolk baptism before a justice of the peace in Belfast. He also asked that the "proper" authorities in Washington supply information about the charge under which his son was held and to state whether he continued to be a British subject or had become a naturalized citizen of the United States. This document found its way to British Consul Archibald in New York and then to Washington. On 12 December the consul reported that he had found Carlin still in Fort Lafayette.[1]

The diplomats then set to work. A pattern of move and countermove signals the sway of their arguments. On 14 December, Lyons wrote an "unofficial" letter to Seward informing him of the solemn declaration of nationality from Belfast. He did not send a copy as he did not want to delay matters with even more papers and the younger Carlin's nationality was "no longer disputed."

In Lyons's view, the case had turned on whether the prisoner had taken U.S. nationality at some point or in any way forfeited his claim to British protection. Lyons then emphasized that Carlin had solemnly denied taking American citizenship. Lyons continued by saying that, as Carlin had been in prison for some four months, there had been ample time for U.S. authorities to find evidence if any existed, and that he hoped there would be no further delay.

At this point, politics in Washington were affected by events on the battlefield, where the advantage was swinging towards the Confederacy. On 13 December Confederate forces defeated a larger Union army at the Battle of Fredericksburg, Virginia, some fifty miles south of the White House. While the Confederates suffered nearly five thousand casualties, the Union army lost thirteen thousand. The Confederate guns fired down from Marye's Heights on the Union troops of General Burnside as they crossed the Rappahannock River to enter the old town of Fredericksburg and scale the rise behind the town. The Confederates, however, failed to press their advantage, losing their best opportunity to end the war in their favor.

By 14 December thousands of wounded were arriving in Washington by hospital ships and being carried from the quays under the eyes of a shocked populace. Recriminations flew, and President Lincoln removed General Ambrose Burnside as commander of the Army of the Potomac. Lincoln himself came under intense political pressure from those in his own party who had never really accepted this outsider president from the West.

Seward, too, had to look to his political position. Lord Lyons would later describe him as inclined to speak very loudly and become a "braggadocio" when discussions warmed up. Like Lincoln, Seward had had no previous exposure to foreign affairs before his appointment as secretary of state. He was an able man with a love of the classics but regarded by the British as dangerous and inclined to view relations with Britain as "good material to make political capital of . . . and that they may be safely played with without the risk of bringing a war."[2] Gideon Welles in particular had formed an aversion to Seward, and he and Secretary of the Treasury Salmon Chase hated his attempts to assert undue influence on Lincoln by "back-stairs means" and attempted a Senate-led move to have him removed.[3] A *Charleston Courier* report later called him that "lying faithless trickster in the State Department."[4]

Seward replied to Lyons on 16 December using forceful tones: "I refer to the Case of James Carlin. It is a peculiar, perhaps exceptional one. He was employed as a pilot in the naval service of the US government." After listing Carlin's ships and commanders, he noted that Carlin's service ended on "April 30 1860 after the present insurrection broke out into Civil War."[5]

This was a curious mistake. Seward was still trying to imply that Carlin was a "deserter" from U.S. naval service. However, Lieutenant Fauntleroy's letter of 30 May suggests that he left the service in good order on 30 April 1860. South Carolina did not declare for secession until 20 December 1860. Hostilities broke out only when Confederate forces shelled Fort Sumter across Charleston Harbor on 12–13 April 1861.

After describing Carlin's blockade-running activities, Seward made his play by stating, "It is deemed incompatible with the public safely to release him from confinement at the hazard of his returning to the same hostile pursuits. He will therefore be detained in custody but the District Attorney at New York will be instructed to prosecute him for aiding and abetting the internal enemies of the United States."[6] The previous weekend had been crucial to Seward's survival as secretary of state. Lincoln and his cabinet supporters faced down Seward's detractors, who capitulated, leaving Lord Lyons relieved that Seward had survived what had amounted to a coup attempt against the unpopular secretary of state.

At this point Lord Lyons and Seward seem to have met and discussed the case in private at a Christmas event. On Friday, 26 December 1862, Lord Lyons wrote a lengthy confidential note to Consul Archibald in New York, going over Carlin's case:

It is announced to me that he will be detained in custody, but that the
District Attorney at New York will be directed to prosecute him for aiding
and abetting the internal enemies of the United States. It is apparent that this
is a last device of someone who is determined to find a pretext for retaining
the Prisoner. It may however be difficult to counteract it, as at first sight the
bringing a man to trial seems all that can be demanded . . . a material point in
the present case would be the manner in which Carlin was brought into the
hands of the United States authorities he having been captured on a British
Vessel seized on a charge of breach of blockade. In fact my present impression
is that the whole proceeding is entirely unwarrantable . . . and that sooner or
later Carlin must be released on the demand of Her Majesty's Government.

Lyons then admitted that he might be mistaken on this point but, "taking all
things into consideration," he felt that it would be wrong not to let Carlin know
that he would probably be released if he guaranteed that he would not return to
either the Northern or Southern states during the war. He believed that the "prejudice" against Carlin stemmed from his service in the Survey and his use of this
valuable knowledge against the interests of the United States. "If the Authorities
could be assured that he would keep at a distance from both sections of the country their principal motive for detaining him would be done away with."[7]

Lyons wished "that Archibald would let some confidential person see Carlin,
and ascertain from him whether, if the United States authorities offered to release
him on his giving a solemn assurance that he would not return, he should wish to
obtain his liberty on these terms."

Lyons emphasized to Consul Archibald that he, Lyons, "does not advise him
to follow this route but that it is only from a sense of compassion for his long
imprisonment that he reluctantly concludes that it would not be right for me" to
withhold the chance of obtaining his freedom. He also emphasized that Carlin
must "not give assurances unless he means religiously to observe them"; he could
not then expect the British government to come to his aid again.[8]

On 26 December, Lyons wrote to Earl Russell reporting that Seward's position
had weakened so much that he was "plainly not in a position to make any conces-
sions at all to neutrals." Seward could not be seen to be helping Britain to obtain
cotton or in any other way. Seward, while still vulnerable to attack by his enemies,
appeared to risk his political standing by making moves to save Carlin by offering
him his parole on condition he leave both the Northern and Southern States. He
must have seen this relatively trivial affair as a threat to his relationship with Lord
Lyons and the outcome of many other matters they were attempting to resolve
without serious escalation.

Lord Lyons next wrote to Earl Russell on 10 January, confirming that he had received "intelligence that Carlin was still in prison." This was a long letter rehearsing

all the previous correspondence and included nineteen enclosures with copies of all the previous correspondence.[9]

Lyons had already commented on the way the Americans suspended *habeas corpus* when dealing with military and civilian arrests during this period. Lyons continued: "I have since that time been unremitting in my endeavours to induce the Government of the United States to release him—the authorities seem determined to keep him in prison." Having failed to prove that he took an oath of allegiance, they now said that he was a danger to public safety because of his knowledge of the blockaded coast. Lyons stated that it had been announced that Carlin would be "prosecuted, in due form of the law, for aiding and abetting the internal enemies of the United States."

Lyons was obviously concerned by this turn of events and his letter laid out his frustration, giving an analysis of the British view. He said he had not failed to point out to Secretary Seward "the many inconveniences and embarrassing questions to which this proceeding may give rise." This must have been a reference to the awkward fact that James Carlin had made many runs though the blockade, showing that it was ineffective and undermining its legality. He may also have been referring to the fact that Carlin had been held under a mistaken belief in his nationality and was thus unlawfully detained for months without being formally charged. Lyons commented, "Even if we admit that the prosecution is not a mere device, resorted to at the last moment, in order to serve as a pretext for holding Carlin—can it be held to be any justification of his being held for five months without legal process—or offer of a trial?"

He posed the rhetorical question: "Is Carlin a British subject, liable to be prosecuted for acts hostile to the United States committed within the [Confederacy]?" He also raised other technical points of law relating to the British recognition of the secession states as belligerents and posed another fundamental question that still has resonance today: "Does the manner in which his person came into the possession of the United States, that is to say his having been seized on board a British vessel captured for breach of the blockade, affect the right of the United States to bring him to trial?"[10]

Lyons requested instructions from Her Majesty's government, adding that he had sent a note to Seward relating the present position and announcing that he would inform London that Carlin was still in prison with little prospect of early release. This was a veiled threat. London would have understood Lord Lyons's escalation of the heat of the exchanges and the threat implied by his reference to London.

Lyons instructed Archibald to keep a close watch on Carlin and inform him if any legal proceedings were imminent.[11] He may have feared that there would be a quick treason trial without the opportunity to make these points in open court. There were also unstated concerns about what might follow a quick conviction.

If Murray had his way and Carlin appeared on a hangman's scaffold, the result would have stirred up British public opinion, causing grave difficulty to Palmerston's Whig administration.

Lyons's greater interest in Carlin's case on his return from sick leave in London suggests that he may have had some private instructions on the matter while visiting Earl Russell in London before his return to post. Russell seems to have asked to see the file although the clerks in the Washington Legation were handling scores of similar cases.

Lyons informed Archibald that Seward "has shown a wish to devise a means of effecting a satisfactory arrangement—he has in fact, I think, been himself anxious to grant release and begged me to ascertain from Carlin whether he would engage to leave the country and not return to the Northern or Southern States during [the war] and if satisfactory assurances of this could be given, the release might be obtained." Lyons hesitated to tell Carlin about this proposal but felt that it was "hardly fair" to keep it from him as his liberty was at stake. He instructed Archibald in New York to find out Carlin's reaction but not to advise him either way.[12]

Archibald replied on 6 January in a confidential letter to Washington that "Carlin unhesitatingly rejected it." Isolated in Casement Six of Fort Lafayette, James Carlin turned down the offer. He was prepared to take the risk of conviction for high treason, convinced of his innocence of the charge of changing nationality. He also mentioned to Archibald that he "had a little property in the Carolina's that he was anxious to get out of the country." Carlin then asked Archibald to thank Lord Lyons for his interest in his case.

Replying to Archibald on 10 January, Lyons begged him to keep himself constantly informed of "Mr." Carlin's condition and to report forthwith any change in his condition. He particularly wanted "immediate Intelligence" with full details of any legal proceeding against Carlin. Suddenly Carlin had become *Mr.* Carlin. Perhaps he had earned Lord Lyons's respect by refusing an underhanded deal to secure his release?

We can only speculate as to this sudden rise in his status. The change to *Mr.* Carlin was more significant then than it would be now. Similarly the pace of events had quickened. Letters were dashed back and forth, with everyone showing great concern for Carlin's wellbeing. Perhaps Lyons suddenly saw in Carlin's case an opportunity to make a point in Washington or on a wider stage to show that Britain did not let down its subjects when they were in need.

Suddenly, following Lyons's trip to Europe, Lyons was anxious to secure Carlin's release. Perhaps he had heard something about the revengeful attitude in New York during a visit he made to the city that deepened his concern. Or perhaps Ella Rosa had been able to use her reputed family connections to get a word said on her husband's behalf in places where it counted.

Seward's response to Carlin's rejection of the offer to release him against assurances, was that there was "nothing left" but to begin the prosecution. His language implied that he knew that Carlin faced a death sentence if the court's findings went against him. Both Seward and Lyons seemed to have feared that, with Robert Murray running the game in New York, this could be the likely outcome.

This was the point at which Lord Lyons played his top card. On 10 January he advised Seward that he had referred the matter to Earl Russell and that the matter was now in the hands of Her Majesty's government. This letter has the tone of a formal diplomatic *démarche*. It had become clear to Seward that neither the U.S. Navy nor the Coast Survey had evidence of any change of nationality by Carlin, while on his side he had produced sworn testimony of his British birth. Seward was highly conscious of the strain in Anglo-American relations over matters concerning British subjects, and instructions were issued to release Carlin:

Department of State, Washington, Jan 12 1863.
My Lord, [Lyons]
With reference to the case of James Carlin which has been the subject
of correspondence between this Department and your Legation, I have
the honour to acquaint you that the Attorney of the United States for
the southern district of New York has reported that in his opinion, and
from testimony in his possession and now obtainable there could not be a
successful prosecution against that person in that district for high treason.
The Navy Department having been apprised of this fact, was at the same
time recommended to direct the release of Carlin. A letter of the 10th inst.
From Mr Welles announcing that an order to that effect has consequently
been issued.
I have etc W. H. Seward.[13]

With commendable *sang froid* Lord Lyons avoided any sense of triumphalism but allows an air of quiet satisfaction:

Washington
January 13, 1863.
My Lord, [Russell]
With reference to my despatch No.27 of the 10th instant, I have the honour
to transmit to your Lordship a copy of a Note from Mr Seward stating that
as it appears that there could not be a successful prosecution for high treason
against James Carlin, an order has been issued for his release.
I have the honour to be with the highest respect My Lord, Your
Lordships most obedient, humble servant—Lyons.[14]

While Lyons thought that his *démarche* had won the day, the district attorney of the Southern District of New York had also been occupied with the case. The State Department had handed the case papers to E. Delafield Smith during a visit he made to Washington and had also received a more recent letter on the subject from Seward. Delafield Smith's letter of 7 January reveal the views of the New York officials. Writing to Seward, he said that while he

> had hoped to obtain testimony enabling to institute, and sustain, at least for
> a time, a prosecution against this culprit. After several interviews with Mr.
> Marshal Murray, I am satisfied that no such evidence is within our reach, at
> least for the present. It is probable, that with such an affidavit as the Marshall
> could make, I can't obtain from an United States commissioner, a warrant
> for the arrest of Carlin. But upon the examination allowed him by law, his
> discharge would be speedy and certain. The same want of witnesses places his
> indictment, at least for the present, out of the question.[15]

Even if Marshal Murray had committed perjury, as he seems to have been prepared to do, the case would not hold. Carlin had been unjustly detained and held for five months without substantive charges against him being made and tested in court. Carlin was the fortunate recipient of the conjunction of the eventual rule of law in New York and the tacit threat of imperial displeasure by the United Kingdom.

When safely back in Nassau, Carlin told the *Charleston Courier* correspondent about his experiences in Fort Lafayette, recalling that "life in the Bastille was not very agreeable." The *Courier* described Carlin "as a gentleman of character and intelligence," who was well known in Charleston. He told the *Courier* that the prisoners had not been allowed to go beyond the doorsill of their casement, but after two months of vigorous protest, they were given twenty minutes outside in a restricted space.[16]

According to Carlin, the guards played tricks on the prisoners to lure them into "crimes" that could then be harshly punished, and they generally mistreated their captives. Some were locked in small cells in solitary confinement for minor infringements. Morale was low, and in his words to the *Courier,* Carlin said the prisoners "wear an expression of unutterable sadness. Deferred hopes, separation from loved ones, mental and bodily inactivity all tell upon the spirits of the unfortunate victim." In the same interview, Carlin confirmed that just before he was about to leave the fort, he had been offered an oath of allegiance to the United States that he had refused indignantly to take. He also mentioned that in place of the oath he was offered a parole on condition that he did not return to the North or South during the conflict. This, too, he refused.

He said that he had left behind about thirty-five prisoners. These included Colonel Zarvona, or "The French Lady" as he became known, who in the *Courier's* view seemed to have been abandoned to the "devilish hate of his enemies." Zarvona, whose real name was Richard Henry Thomas, had fought with Garibaldi in the struggle for the unification of Italy and was something of a hero in his home state of Maryland. He became a strong secessionist and was determined to commandeer Northern ships for the Confederate cause. His party succeeded in boarding the steamer *St. Nicolas* and delivering it to the governor of Virginia. He had been captured attempting to take the steam vessel *Mary Washington* while posing as a French lady passenger—hence his popular nickname. Thomas was exchanged in mid-1863.[17]

James Carlin also spoke of John Robinson, described as a "colored man" in the terminology of the period, who was held with them in the fortress but was "quite old and was dying from the severity of the climate to which he was not accustomed." Robinson had been captured while attempting to run the blockade and was taken to Fort Lafayette in irons and held for eight months. On his release in February 1863, he had been encouraged to enter the service of the United States as a pilot on Northern gunboats operating in Savannah and Charleston for one hundred dollars a month. He feigned old age and infirmity. In fact, he was fifty, and fearing he would be press-ganged, he made his way to Nassau. There he must have contacted his fellow ex-prisoner James Carlin, who helped him return home. Interviewed in Savannah, the *Charleston Courier* described him as belonging to James's new command, the *Ella and Annie,* and praised him for his "fidelity and honesty." In apparent good faith, the paper commented that Robinson was "joyfully returning" to his old widowed mistress and his "bondage."[18]

The following is a list of prisoners held with James Carlin in Fort Lafayette, New York. It comes from the pocket Bible presented to Carlin while he was a prisoner in Fort Lafayette after his capture on 31 July 1862 on board the British steamship *Memphis.*

> Autograph of fellow prisoners in casement No. 6, 4 October 25, 1862.
> James Carlin, Hunstanton, England. Captured on the *Memphis.*
> Thomas Potts, St. John, New Brunswick. Captured in New York,
>     June 13, 1862.
> Edward S. Jones, Warrenton, North Carolina. Captured on Filey Island,
>     South Carolina, September 21, 1862.
> M. H. Galdding, Savannah, Georgia. Captured in Nassau, New Providence,
>     Bahamas, July 22 1862.
> J. B. Vincent, Charleston, South Carolina. Captured in Bull Bay,
>     South Carolina, July.
> Ernest W. Cecil. Captured on 22 November, St. Marys Co., Maryland
> Berry Worthington. Arrested Carroll County.
> John Nicol, M.D. Arrested 11 October 1862 in New Haven, Connecticut.
> J. A. Machado. Arrested 11 October 1862 in New York City.

John Hippins Jr. Arrested 17 August 1861 in Norfolk, Virginia.

David Shuan. Arrested 28 August 1862.

M. [?] Corbett, arrested April 1862 in Virginia.

Ellison B. Olds,. Arrested August 12 in Ohio.

William H. Child. Arrested 20 December in Gainboro, Alabama.

H. R. Marks. Captured at sea, Houston, Texas.

Richard Finn. Captured at sea, Pensacola, Florida.

J. W. G. Innerarity, Coast Florida 1863 Mobile, Alabama.

Captain A. C. Grensfell. Arrested Dec. 21.

Here are the prisoners listed by James Carlin in the account he gave to the *Charleston Courier* in Nassau on 17 February 1863.

Captains D. B. Vincent, S. Burrows, H. Lea, J. Murray, and H. Smith of Charleston; F. Hernandez, H. Cessar, and J. Neil of Savannah; A. C. Moore, J. Rollins, and J. Jameson of North Carolina; J. C. King, H. R. Marks, and J. Jamison of Texas; and John Hipkins [*sic*] Jr. of Norfolk, Virginia, who had been a prisoner since the beginning of the war.

Imprisonment in Fort Lafayette, rejection by Bache, and rough handling by the Southern District of New York Court and the guards at Fort Lafayette—indeed the whole *Memphis* embroilment—changed James Carlin. He had come face-to-face with the reality of anti-Southern and anti-British sentiment in the North. He had faced shells and gunfire before, but Budd's shell exploding between the masts of the *Memphis* had come too close for comfort, and Carlin emerged from Fort Lafayette a different man.

Bache's sharp and offhand rejection of Carlin's appeal to him must have stung and may well have worked away in the recesses of his mind and afflicted his later life. The gentlemanly game was over, and it was time to take the war seriously. When he emerged from the casements of the fortress, he seems to have been more determined and focused. His blockade-running activities increased in frequency and vigor, and he took drastic steps to take revenge for his mistreatment and rejection.

Prospects for the Confederacy had changed for the worse. General Robert E. Lee's thrust into Maryland had been halted at the Battle of Antietam. This battle is often seen as the moment the war turned decisively in the Union's favor. Confederate President Jefferson Davis's hopes of recognition by the European powers had faded. Lee's Northern invasion strategy had failed, and he had been forced to withdraw to Virginia. President Lincoln seized the moment. What was arguably a tactical draw was presented as a Union victory. Lincoln issued the Emancipation Proclamation that came into effect on 1 January 1863. This freed all slaves in the ten states still in the Confederacy. It did not compensate owners, nor did it free slaves in the four border states of Missouri, Kentucky, Delaware, and Maryland, or in the occupied secessionist state of Tennessee. But Lincoln had declared his intention.

# Chapter 17

# Carlin Stakes His Claim,
# January–July 1863

. . .

Writing to Consul Archibald from Fort Lafayette on 7 January 1863, a few days before his discharge, James Carlin made a defense against the charges he faced. His frustration is palpable. The threat of being tried for high treason must have been ever present in his mind during this period of great tension and may well have caused the shadow that came upon him in later life.

Fort Lafayette Jan 7. 1863
Sir, [Consul Archibald]
Permit me to mention a few facts concerning my case, and likewise to draw a comparison, which will shew [sic] the extreme inconsistencies that the U.S. government has practiced towards me.

I would have called your attention to this when you were here but did not want to detain you in your hurried visit.

I am accused of using to the detriment of the U.S. government, a knowledge of this Coast, which I am said to have obtained when in their service. I positively deny being guilty of the above charge, and although I admit knowledge of the coast, it is no more than is necessary to me in my profession as a mariner, and when I joined their service it was at the friendly invitation of an officer with whom I was on intimate terms, and with no particular view of obtaining the knowledge referred to.

Permit me to make the following comparison. The Officers in the Army and Navy of the so called Southern Confederacy, have obtained a thorough knowledge of their profession in the Service of the government and for the most part at its expense. Yet they have used this knowledge against this government for several months, and although Citizens of the country and when captured are found bearing arms in hostility to the US Government, they have invariably been released within a short time after their capture and of course without punishment.

Per contra, I the acknowledged subject of a Neutral Power, captured upon the High Seas, a peaceful passenger upon a British Steam ship am thrown into a military prison for five months, held upon a charge of which I am not guilty, with no immediate prospect of release.

In view of the forgoing facts and the other proofs now at your disposal, I trust it may be quite pardonable in me if I demand most respectfully of the proper authority, that some decisive course of action be adopted in this now sufficiently aggravated case of wrong and injustice.

I do not deem it necessary to quote any further proofs bearing on this case, but many others are at hand such for instance as Earl Russell's communication to the Secretary of State W. Seward, affording protection to all British subjects captured inside the present blockade as it at least secures them from imprisonment.

Hoping that you will excuse this long letter, I beg to remain, James Carlin[1]

Carlin was set at liberty unconditionally on 12 January 1863 after some five months as a prisoner of war. He called on Consul Archibald two days later. This was more than just a courtesy call. Carlin wanted to discuss the serious business of compensation. Lyons told Russell that under the circumstances of Carlin's detention, he "had no difficulty in causing Mr Carlin to be informed that I will submit to Her Majesty's Government, his request that compensation may be demanded for him."[2]

Carlin then overstepped the mark. Carlin "safely affirm[ed] that one thousand Dollars per day would not exceed his income in clear gain if he had not been placed in prison." Archibald commented that Carlin did not hesitate to claim this sum, which amounted to upwards of £200. "If allowance were made for the depreciation of paper currency his demand would be some £140 per day or £51,000 per annum."

Clearly, Carlin based his claim for loss of earnings on the rate he was usually paid for running the blockade. The extraordinary size of this claim can be seen from the relative value of $1,000 in 1863 that now equates to $18,800 per day if assessed on the adjusted U.S. Consumer Price Index. Over five months, this would have amounted to some $2.8 million at today's values.[3]

Although the blockade-runners would only have earned their high daily rate for time at sea, perhaps fourteen days in a lunar cycle, it is a measure of the appeal of blockade-running. His letter of claim gives us his view of the events he had just gone through.

New York Jan 16 1863
Dear Sir, [Consul Archibald]

In consideration of my long imprisonment, I am convinced the US government will not hesitate to make some adequate compensation for my heavy losses sustained during an imprisonment of five months, from August 1, 1862 to January 12, 1863. My imprisonment however in the fort commenced August 11.

It would be impossible to make a correct estimate of my exact losses, but I can safely affirm that One thousand dollar per day would not exceed my income in clear gain, if I had not been placed in prison. In view of this fact, and also the fact that I have had my feelings outraged, that my health has suffered during my stay in the damp uncomfortable Casement of the Fort, I do not hesitate to present the above claim for damages and respectfully beg that you will take the matter in hand calling in whatever legal ability you may think proper in this case, the payment of such however to depend on the success in the case.

Having been captured on the high seas, passenger on board the Memphis, on my way to Liverpool on private business, the charge of having given aid to the enemy of the U.S. government is made. To this I have only to say that having property in the so called southern confederacy, I adopted the plan of running it through the then ineffective blockade of that coast and with no intention of giving aid to enemies of this Government.

In reference to the exact amount claimed, I beg you to consider the fact of my false imprisonment. However, make such modifications as you may deem judicious and proper.

Permit me to remain,

James Carlin

My Post Office address is Nassau. N.P. West Indies.[4]

Lyons did not reject Carlin's extravagant request out of hand, but instructed Archibald to let Carlin know that he would submit his request for compensation to the British government.

Writing on 6 March, Lyons thought it right to let Earl Russell know that Carlin might have earned something like the sum he mentioned if, instead of being imprisoned, he had been employed as a pilot on board vessels trading with the Southern ports and had successfully run the blockade every day during the whole period.

This letter reflects Lyons's personal views on the whole episode. He noted that Carlin's contention that he was merely a passenger on the *Memphis* seemed improbable but that he was "not lawfully detained in prison." He also gave Earl Russell his views on Seward's confidential offer to release Carlin on a pledge to leave both the Northern and Southern states. Lyons commented that Carlin refused to make such a pledge because he intended to return to his former activities. Lyons added that he had made sure that Carlin was told that he could not look to British protection were he caught running the blockade again. Russell was apparently so concerned with the personal details of the case that there is a marginal note suggesting that the foreign secretary himself referred the letter to the law officer at the Foreign Office.

On 22 April the law officer wrote that "H.M. government is clearly of the opinion that Mr. James Carlin is entitled to pecuniary compensation for an imprisonment of five months." He added that "the reasonable inference is that there never was any serious intention of instituting a criminal prosecution against Mr. Carlin and that the suggestion of such intention was a mere pretext for his detention really desired upon other and legally inadmissible grounds."[5] This seems an admirable summary of the whole affair.

On the question of the amount of compensation, he stated that "Mr. Carlin's own estimate appears to be very extravagant and is not likely to be listened to by the government of the U.S." He suggested that Archibald write to Carlin, proposing that he moderate his demand for loss of profits and make a reasonable addition for personal annoyance and the loss of personal liberty and the plain injustice of the sentence under which Carlin suffered imprisonment. He recommended that, if Lord Lyons thought such a revised demand was reasonable, it should be presented to the U.S. government.[6]

Lyons wrote to Archibald in New York on 9 May, saying that he was instructed by Earl Russell to direct Archibald to enter into communications with James Carlin on the question of submitting a moderated claim on the basis suggested by the Foreign Office law officer. It is curious that Earl Russell, with Great Britain's foreign affairs to direct, should involve himself in such a detail. While all such letters written by Foreign Office clerks would have gone out in Russell's name, the tone of the letter implies that it was the earl himself who issued these instructions. Russell wished to make a point against the Americans.[7]

From the tenor of Lyons's next report of 25 May to Earl Russell, it is clear that he was not optimistic about the value of pursuing this claim. He noted that Carlin had returned to his old profession and had already made "five successful voyages between Nassau and Charleston and that he has recently sailed on a sixth voyage." Carlin was making up for lost time.[8]

Archibald's report to Lyons develops this. He stated that Carlin's first trip after his release was on Alexander Collie's steamer *Ruby* as pilot, and two further voyages on the *Ruby* as commander and had then taken charge of the large American-built steamer *Ella and Annie*, which had a capacity of thirteen hundred bales of cotton. Archibald believed that "parties in Havana" owned this vessel. He reported that Carlin had made two trips and "at last accounts was absent on a third voyage."[9]

Lyons pointed out that even if Carlin moderated his demand, it would still be for a "large sum, because the profits of piloting vessels through the Blockade are very large." Lyons then asked Russell an awkward question. When judging the reasonableness of Carlin's moderated demands, should he consider Carlin's occupation as a pilot a legitimate one and to forward an estimate of his losses on a calculation of the gains he would probably have made running the blockade with "average success"?

Lyons emphasized that he would have to explain to the government of the United States the basis of his calculations and why they were larger than the "gains Mr. Carlin would have made in ordinary employment." He commented with irony: "that government would naturally be extremely reluctant either to admit that Mr. Carlin would have been frequently successful in escaping from their cruisers or to compensate him on the basis of his average profits as a successful runner."

On 9 July the Foreign Office law officer consulted with the Crown law officers and suggested that "Mr. Carlin should estimate the amount to be claimed, so far as loss of his time is concerned, upon a calculation of the ordinary earnings of a pilot and without reference to the outstanding gains derived from running the blockade."[10]

Carlin apparently thought that the whole affair was not worth pursuing on this basis and the question of his claim faded away. The lengthy file closes with a report from Mr. Charles Edwards, acting British consul in New York to the principal secretary of state in London, confirming that the appeal in Circuit Court of the case of the steamer *Memphis* had failed, and that it was unlikely to go to the U.S. Supreme Court for reasons of cost and its unlikely success.

James Carlin made two later claims against the United States government. The first was for the steamer *Cecile* being fired at by Union forces, and the second related again to his imprisonment after capture on the *Memphis*.[11]

There is a curious postscript to this story. Earl Russell appears to have gone to some lengths to secure Carlin's release. The foreign secretary, or his clerks, also wrote numerous strong letters in support of other British sea captains captured by the U.S. Navy and most were promptly released. But none of these captains had Carlin's specialist knowledge of the Southern coast. Washington had been obliged to release Lieutenant Commander Budd's prize prisoner. This suggests that the British Foreign Office might have favored Carlin's case over those of other English captives. Earl Russell was an old cabinet colleague of George Villiers IV, Earl Clarendon, and influence may have been applied.

Chapter 18

# Resumption of Trade
## "The Intrepid Carlin," January–May 1863

• • •

On regaining his freedom, James Carlin returned to blockade-running with a vengeance. Clearly determined to recoup his losses from his enforced absence, he soon found his way back to Nassau. The gold rush atmosphere in this tropical outpost must have been a relief after the casements of Fort Lafayette and the cold of a New York winter. Nassau was full of opportunists from across the world—all those who could sense quick money. The wharves were piled with bales of cotton and the harbor crowded with long, rakish, lead-colored steamers.[1] The newly constructed Royal Victoria Hotel, with its two hundred rooms, was the scene of lively parties. The boarding houses were packed and seamen slept on every veranda. New warehouses were put up along the north side of Bay Street, and the colony's treasury found itself with the funds to increase the salaries of officials by 25 percent.[2] But Carlin knew where to go and who to see, and he was quickly back in the thick of his trade.

Augustus Hobart-Hampden recalled that everything in the little Bahamian port was *"couleur de rose."* In contrast with Wilmington, "Everyone seemed prosperous and happy. You met with calculating, far-seeing men who were steadily employed with feathering their nests, let the war in America end as it might; others who in the height of their enthusiasm, put their last farthing into Confederate securities anticipating enormous profit: some men, careless and thoughtless, living for the hour, were spending their dollars as fast as they made them, forgetting that they would never see the like again." There were rollicking captains and officers of blockade-runners and drunken, swaggering crews; sharpers, looking out for victims; and Yankee spies.[3]

Carlin must have been anxious to return to Ella Rosa and assure her that their lives were back to normal: comings and goings, drama and risk, but also profit and excitement. Their third son, Samuel Edward, was born in November 1863.

This is a confused period in Carlin's record as he moved from ship to ship and port to port. Accounts differ, and dates do not always match. One report suggests that on his release from Fort Lafayette around 11 January, Carlin left New York for Europe and went to the River Clyde in Scotland, where he took command of the *Ruby* for its first voyage out to Nassau. William Oswald Dundas recounted that he had sailed down the Clyde on the *Ruby* with Captain Carlin in command. Dundas named George W. Wigg as the owner of the *Ruby*, and said that he sailed with them from Glasgow to Dumbarton Castle, where Wigg left the ship after wishing them all "bon voyage." Dundas, a supercargo (a clerk responsible for the shipping documentation, customs clearance, and sale of the cargo), said that they were carrying forty thousand pairs of English-made army shoes "held together in the old way by stout twine through the heels of each pair."[4]

Dundas wrote that "Mrs Rose O'Neal Greenhough [*sic*]," the Confederate spy, inveigled Carlin into giving her a passage from Liverpool on the *Ruby*, and that he gave in to her out of a sense of gallantry. Rose Greenhow had been in Paris lobbying Napoleon III and his consort Eugenie for the Confederate cause.[5] He also linked Carlin to the loss of the *Ruby* and the death of Rose after the *Ruby* went aground. In his version, Rose leapt over the side into the surf with a bag of gold coins on her belt and went straight to the bottom. But Dundas was wrong about Carlin's captaincy during this voyage and other details. Rose Greenhow died when the British blockade-runner *Condor* ran aground while being pursued by the USS *Niphon*. The $2,000 in gold she had on her person dragged her to the bottom when a wave overturned the ship's boat as it was headed towards the shore.

The I&E Company records show that Captain William Walker brought the *Ruby* to Nassau. Carlin is reported as pilot of the *Ruby* in February and was soon busy as its captain, running the blockade into Charleston and making £1,000 per trip, plus all the extras that came a captain's way.

The *Ruby* was a "river class," iron-built, side-wheel steamer originally intended for the Irish Sea traffic out of the Clyde. Built by Henderson, Coulborn and Company in Renfrew, the vessel was rated for 400 tons and was 209 feet long, with a beam of 19 feet and a draft of some 8 feet.[6] It was owned by Alexander Collie & Company, which worked closely with Fraser, Trenholm and Company in Liverpool. A Union naval report credited the ship with "great speed" and described the *Ruby* as follows: "fore-and-aft schooner rig; no bowsprit; has two smoke pipes, one standing forward of the wheelhouses, the other in line with after part of paddles; has a house forward of mainmast; also one abaft foremast; has a light hurricane deck between the paddle boxes, steam drums on deck."[7] This gave the ship a distinctly different appearance from the sleek lines favored by the later runners.

By 15 March 1863 the *New York Times* correspondent in Nassau was reporting that Captain James Carlin, "recently released from Fort Lafayette as a British subject," had already made two successful trips and had just left on a third. The *Charleston Courier* listed his arrival with the *Ruby* on 11 March, which was probably his second trip through the blockade after his release from Fort Lafayette. The *Nassau Guardian* newspaper reported that Carlin had brought in the steamer *Ruby* on 11 April.[8] However, on 5 April a secret agent working in Nassau for H.S. Olcott, a special commissioner of the War Department, had reported that Carlin was now captain of the *Ella and Annie,* and was due to sail for Charleston on 7 April.[9] Stephen Wise reports the ship as clearing out of Charleston on 18 April.[10]

The Carlin family house on Church Street, Charleston, South Carolina.
Photograph by the author.

Carlin and Ella were back in the money. On 20 March 1863 they contracted to buy No. 43 Church Street in Charleston for $8,000. This is a fine "Single House" in the local style. With spacious first-floor rooms, it has deep covered piazzas, or verandas, making it shady and cool. The house still stands on the southwest corner of Church and Water Streets in central Charleston with the outbuildings that once housed the domestic slaves.

It had been the property of William E. Mikell and part of the estate of General Jacob Read, a Revolutionary War hero who served in the United States Senate from 1795 to 1801. James and Ella Rosa Carlin were cautious about this purchase as the title was transferred to the Reverend William Yates to hold in trust for James and Ella and their children. Had they lost confidence in the outcome of the war, sensing trouble ahead?

At the end of April, the Reverend Yates wrote to the editor of the *Charleston Courier* to acknowledge the receipt of $1,500 from Mrs. James Carlin. Yates passed $500 to the free market, $250 to his marine school, and held a further $500 to be disbursed by himself as chaplain of the Seaman's Bethel. At about this time James and Ella purchased another plot in Charleston at 8 Logan Street near the corner with Tradd Street. On 6 May the Reverend William Yates, acting as trustee for Carlin, his wife, and their children, bought a second slave woman named Dinah and her children, Betsy and Sam, for $2,500.[11]

Making havelocks for the volunteers. *Harper's Weekly,* 29 June 1861.
Courtesy Ernest F. Hollings Library, University of South Carolina.

This trust document does not reveal if this was a legal device to ensure that Ella and her family had independent means should Carlin be captured again or killed, or whether they anticipated uncertain political times ahead. Perhaps they sensed the wind and felt that it was time to secure their local assets against sequestration if and when the Confederacy collapsed.

While these arrangements were being made, Carlin took the *Ruby* to Mobile, Alabama, arriving from Havana on 16 May. He cleared outward bound on 22 May, heading for Havana again and on to Nassau. Havana was favored for the Gulf routes despite tedious customs and port officials as it had a deep-water harbor with docks and warehouses and bulk coal at cheaper rates. The blockade-runner and ex–U.S. Navy officer Lieutenant John Wilkinson regarded the city's sanitary arrangements as woeful.[12]

Captain Ferdinand Peck then took over the *Ruby* and left Nassau on 8 June with a cargo of merchandise for St. John, New Brunswick. This was the *Ruby*'s last trip. Carlin's luck had held again. Although the *Ruby* had make eight successful runs through the blockade, it was wrecked on a reef between Folly Island and Morris Island on 10 June 1863 while under the command of Captain Peck. He had been deceived by a false light into thinking he was safely in Folly Inlet. The crew set fire to their ship to prevent the cargo from falling into the hands of the Union forces and were fired on for their pains as they waded ashore through neck-deep surf, losing one crewman.[13]

By the end of June 1863, the U.S. Navy had captured 127 ships suspected of running the blockade. Fourteen of these were steamers, twelve of which were British. The rest were sailing vessels of various sizes, some twenty-four of these being British. The Federal blockade was becoming more effective, and runners' losses rose.

Chapter 19

# The "Commodore" of the I&E Company
## "Knights of the Sea," June–July 1863

. . .

In the early years of the war, the legislature of South Carolina had debated forming its own transatlantic line of steamers to develop direct trade with Europe, but did not take any executive action. It was not until William Cantel Bee proposed a joint enterprise between the state and his company that General Assembly approval for state participation was obtained. There were to be further tussles between the Confederate government in Richmond and the various state legislatures over government rights to a proportion of cargo space in ships running out of Southern ports. South Carolina eventually decided to purchase its own state-owned blockade-runners in January 1865, but by then it was all too late.

The Importing and Exporting Company of South Carolina was initially organized as an unincorporated stock company by some ninety-seven businessmen in Charleston in March or April 1862. Founding shareholders included Captains James Carlin and Ferdinand Peck. The John Fraser Company was the largest stockholder. By January 1863 the original shareholders had made a return of 158 percent before the loss of its two first ships, the *Cecile* and the schooner *Edwin,* forced the first company's liquidation.[1]

Capitalizing on their financial success, William Bee and his associates formed an incorporated company in December 1862, allowing the directors to offer shares to the general public to raise capital for more ships. The business was managed by Bee and Charles Tunis Mitchell, two local cotton factors and commission merchants, hence the commonly used name the "Bee Company."[2] The South Carolina legislature had chartered five companies in Charleston for blockade-running between 1862 and 1863, but the I&E Company was the first and largest of these five and was famed for the success of its captains and the profits it made for shareholders.[3]

The stock was in demand and the company raised its capital to $700,000 in January 1863. By 1 May 1863 the stock was selling at 700 percent above par.[4] At the end of the month the subscribed capital had reached $1 million. This was used to buy sterling at an exorbitant 100 percent premium. Confederate currency was not exchangeable overseas, and the Confederacy had to buy sterling bills to pay for its European purchases. W. C. Bee was to be president through to early 1865. The directors were D. Jervey, William P. Ravenal, C. T. Mitchell, and Benjamin Mordecai. All were experienced cotton merchants and exporters. James M. Calder was their Liverpool agent, with Henry Adderley acting for them in Nassau. Mordecai, one of the company's cotton purchasing agents, "ranged far afield" searching for supplies with up to $200,000 in Confederate currency in hand to make deals before sellers knew that they were agents for blockade-running firms, which would have pushed up prices.[5]

The shareholders came from among the wealthiest citizens of Charleston. Carlin is shown on the master share list of 1863–65 as owning thirty shares with a face value of $1,000 each. (One of his stock certificates is currently for sale with a specialist dealer at the same price.) The largest shareholders were John G. Milnor, with seventy-eight shares; Henry Adderley and Company of Nassau, with seventy-three; and Benjamin Mordecai, with forty-six. Theodore Jervey, James Carlin, and four others held thirty shares each; C. T. Mitchell held twenty-nine; John Fraser and Company had twenty-five shares; and Ravenal and the director of Fraser, Trenholm held only four shares. James Calder, the agent in Liverpool, had none.[6]

Carlin's large stockholding suggests that he took much of his passage fees in shares while investing heavily in the stock of the company for which he worked. Doubtless, there were few other opportunities to invest local currency as profitably. His holdings soon represented a very considerable fortune. Ella Rosa must have felt that her investment in the lowly master's mate had paid off.

By 19 May 1863 the par value of $1,000 I&E Company stock was $8,500. By 9 September 1864 this had grown to $25,500 per share, although a large element was consumed by the heavy depreciation of Confederate treasury notes and by high price inflation in the South. Carlin's holding of thirty shares was worth some $750,000. In today's values this equates to about $14 million, using the adjusted Consumer Price Index as a guide.[7] Lynda Worley Skelton states that "stock in other Charleston blockade-running firms with a par value of $1,000 sold for much less."[8]

There were some 245 other stockholders spread around South Carolina, Georgia, North Carolina, and Virginia. Others lived in Nassau and even New York, or had close connections in the city. Skelton calculates that 72 percent of the shareholders held onto their stock from initial incorporation until the defeat of the Confederacy put an end to blockade-running. Carlin was to keep his stock until 1876, when Peter J. Barbot, the company treasurer, paid the final dividend of forty cents per share.

While profiteering and fraud were widespread in some of the blockade-running companies, the I&E Company is credited by the *Charleston Courier* with operating in an honest, even generous way, with the government giving them a free hand to bring in whatever supplies they needed at rates comparable to those offered to other, more commercial importers.

For the first two years of its operations, most of its freight was confined to the needs of the government. This contributed to the inflation of prices for manufactured goods by restricting supply of imported domestic necessities. Those goods that got through were sold at public auction, returning large profits to the importing combines. The success of their first ventures prompted the I&E Company to raise more capital to purchase additional ships. Skelton makes the point that the fact that the prices were high did not mean that the suppliers were necessarily profiteering by fixing high prices. Instead, this was a reflection through the open auctions of the very high demand for such goods.[9]

*Ella and Annie* flying the Confederate flag.
Courtesy of Naval History and Heritage Command.

In August 1863 cotton could be bought for six cents a pound in Galveston and sold in France or London for fifty cents or more. But shipping costs were exceptionally high, and ship and cargo losses would have eaten into these returns. The most detailed financial example we have for a voyage is Stanley Lebergott's calculations for the successful runner *Banshee,* owned by the Anglo-Confederate Company on a run from the Gulf coast. These show gross earnings of $130,000 on the inward cargo and $120,000 for the outward trip. He calculates that the net return on a round trip was $221,400, or a profit of 132 percent.[10] This is without amortizing the cost of the vessel or taking into account insurance on the risk of losing the vessel and the cargo. Lloyds of London was quoting between 15 and 20 percent, indicating the anticipated capture rate for vessels running into the Confederacy. Cotton prices differed between the Gulf and East Coasts of the Confederacy, reducing margins for the I&E Company.

During 1863 and 1864 the company operated the *Ella and Annie, Alice, Fannie, Ella, Caroline,* and *Emily,* all of which they owned. Skelton gives details of the operations of the *Ella and Annie,* which started in April 1863, and describes the range and variety of the cargoes it carried.

The *Ella and Annie* was previously the *William G. Hawes,* a packet boat built in 1860 for Charles Morgan's Southern Steamship Company and designed for the New York–to–Galveston run, calling at New Orleans. It was luxuriously fitted out with generous passenger cabins and a large freight capacity.

Iron-hulled with a double deck, the *Ella and Annie* was a side-wheel steamer of some 747 tons, with two masts carrying schooner-rigged fore and aft sails. Some 239 feet long, it had a 33-foot beam and a depth of 10 feet in the hold, giving it a capacity for some 1,440 bales of cotton. It was powered by a 50-inch-diameter cylinder with a 12-foot stroke, transmitted by a walking beam. The Louisiana government had earlier seized it for use as a gunboat, but its high speed, large capacity, and maneuverability made it far better adapted to running the blockade. The *William G. Hawes* was used on the Havana run until New Orleans fell to Union admiral David Farragut in April 1861. It was moved to the Atlantic, running the blockade from Charleston and Wilmington for the I&E Company under its new name *Ella and Annie.*[11]

Carlin brought the steamer into Nassau from Havana on 3 April 1863, with a cargo consigned to Henry Adderley and Company. Within days, it was on its way to Charleston, where it arrived safely after an easy run with a mixed cargo of merchandise and Havana sugar. The acting British consul, H. Pinckney Walker, informed the British Foreign Office that no Union warship had challenged the vessel.

It took the *Ella and Annie* only a week to load 1,251 bales of cotton, most of which was taxed, showing it was for private owners. Only 58 bales were duty-free, suggesting that they belonged to the government. Carlin took the *Ella and Annie* out of Charleston on 18 or 19 April and ran through the blockade to Nassau. The *Charleston Courier* reported that Carlin had been sighted off the Hole-in-the-Wall lighthouse on the southern point of Great Abaco Island on 25 April. A Federal gunboat then chased him for several hours. Using the *Ella and Annie's* superior speed, he escaped to make the round trip in nine days. The *Charleston Mercury* of 1 May, 1863, noted that it was the "quickest that has ever been made" and praised Carlin as one of the the the most successful of runners. The *Charleston Courier* of 29 April, 1863, commented, "Captain Carlin certainly knows how to run the blockade." Making up for lost time and lost revenue, Carlin was prepared to risk Union gunfire to avoid being captured once again.

The *Ella and Annie*'s cargo was auctioned off by various parties. There were groceries, liquors, oils, drugs, hardware, gunpowder, dry goods, stationery, and shoes. The absence of any quantity of munitions shows that this was a company trip, and we can surmise that Carlin had his own consignments on board, his captain's perk.

He was out to sea again on 7 May carrying 1,277 bales of cotton, of which only 67 bales were duty-free for the government account. Arriving in Nassau on 9 May, he was back in Charleston on the twentieth, having been spotted by Union vessels that had fired on the *Ella and Annie* as it sped past.

The *Charleston Courier* interviewed Carlin again on 21 May. Speaking from the runner, he said that the *Ella and Annie* was "fitted up in a neat and handsome style, her staterooms and officers quarters affording most excellent accommodation and her beautiful model indicates her fast sailing qualities." Theodore D. Jervey describes the ship as painted a creamy-white at the suggestion of Captain Carlin, who insisted that this color was "the most invisible of shades."[12]

The *Courier* commented that the choice of color seemed justified as the *Ella and Annie,* under the command of James Carlin, was "one of the most remunerative vessels that enters our harbor." He compared Carlin and his crew to "Knights of the Sea, who scorn alike the Bastille and fleet of an impotent, implacable foe." This extravagant phrase gives today's reader a flavor of those times and the romantic notions that still inspired the Old South. But the steamer "made not less that ten successful runs into and out of" Wilmington and Charleston.[13] The reference to the Bastille must have resonated with Carlin after his unintended stay in New York. Skelton comments that this comparison was "far more complimentary than accurate," suggesting that the "Knights" did not live up to the chivalrous image the Charleston press tried to present.[14]

Letters in the I&E Company Records at the South Carolina Historical Society show that Carlin had joined the company as captain of the steamer *Ella and Annie.* He was the firm's senior captain and took responsibility for the other captains in the fleet and was asked to recommend their rates of pay. He was thus supervising captain for the company and effectively their "commodore" [15] in merchant marine usage.

Carlin's terms of agreement of 25 August 1863 with William C. Bee and Company, acting as agents for the I&E Company of South Carolina, show the rewards available to successful captains.[16] As master of the *Alice,* he was to be paid half of all passage money for the first outward trip to Nassau. This was a valuable concession as passengers paid handsomely, and sometimes in gold, for their safe voyage out of the Southern states. He was also to receive $4,000, payable in Nassau for the ship's outward trip. For the first inward trip, his pay was $15,000 in Confederate currency (about $900 in gold).[17] He was to be paid the same amounts for the second round trip, but the third trip was to be $3,000 in gold for the outward trip to Nassau and $13,000 in currency for the trip back.[18]

For the subsequent voyage, the rate would be negotiated on the basis of the demands of the government in Richmond, the available cargo space of the ships, and the profits of the company. Captain John Egan, while acting as captain of the *Alice* in Carlin's absence, was to be paid by Carlin himself.

In a separate letter, Carlin gave his opinion on the pay for Captain Frank Bonneau, who made one trip as master of the *Orion,* but was to be master of the *Ella and Annie.* Carlin suggested that he be paid $2,000 to take the *Ella and Annie* to Nassau, payable in Nassau. The currency of the amounts payable in Nassau were not specified and could be taken as being in U.S. dollars rather than the devalued Confederate dollars. Carlin advised that Bonneau be paid $10,000 Confederate dollars to take the *Ella and Annie* into Wilmington and $2,500, payable in Bermuda or Nassau, for running the ship safely into St. George's. His compensation for further trips would be subject to negotiation with the agents. These recommendations were to be a source of friction between Bonneau, Carlin, and the company. Carlin seemed to have preferred the smaller, shallower-draft *Alice* to the larger *Ella and Annie.* Doubtless he wished to reduce his chances of being captured yet again and appreciated the greater flexibility of the shallower vessel.

Carlin as senior captain became responsible for eight other captains: Thomas J. Moore, (*Fannie*), John Egan (*Alice*), Frank Bonneau (*Ella and Annie*), C. B. Grant, D. Dunning, P. F. Kennedy (also *Fannie*), C. J. Barkley (*Ella*), and L. M. Hudgins (*Caroline*). These were a challenging group of men of independent mind and, in one case, a vainglorious personality. As we shall see, Bonneau presented the greatest challenge.

The I&E Company owned or operated the *Ella and Annie, Alice, Fannie,* and later the *Ella, Caroline,* and the *Emily* during the period in which Carlin was overseeing their operations in Charleston. In the earlier stages of the war, the company had run the schooner *Edwin* and the highly successful steamer *Cecile.* The *Fearless* and the brig *Sarah Flagg* were also associated with the I&E Company. A synopsis of the William Bee Company papers in the South Carolina Historical Society archives states that there were twenty-three vessels in the fleet.

Having raised $1 million through their rights issue, the I&E Company set about buying new vessels to replace the *Cecile* and add more suitable runners to their fleet. Two English vessels were brought over the Atlantic from West Hartlepool. These fine vessels had been built on the Clyde for the Baltic trade between St. Petersburg and Lübeck.

The *Orion* arrived in Charleston on 8 May 1863. Lynda Skelton, working from the Bee company papers, states that it was commanded by Captain William Walker for the I&E Company, sailing under British colors.[19] Walker was the preferred captain for these transatlantic voyages. After a successful run under the command of Captain Frank Bonneau, who returned to Charleston on 23 May, the *Orion*'s name was changed to *Alice*. However, both Stephen Wise and Eric Graham state that the *Orion* was renamed the *Fannie* while its sister vessel, the *Sirius*, became the *Alice* after its arrival in Charleston. Whatever the confusion over the change of names, Wise notes that between them the *Ella and Annie*, *Alice*, and *Fannie* made fifty-two trips through the blockade.[20]

The *Orion* and *Sirius* were both side-wheel steamers 231 feet long with a beam of some 26 feet and a hold depth of 13 feet. The *Charleston Daily Courier* reported that the *Alice*'s "cabin and staterooms were unexcelled by any of the steamers then in port."[21] Carlin was obviously taken with the vessel as he moved his command to the *Alice* on 6 June. It was newly registered in Charleston, and he was credited with being the first to fly the Confederate ensign in Charleston Harbor.

Hubris struck, however, only days after Carlin assumed command of the *Alice*. He was taking the ship out of Charleston, loaded with at least 994 bales of government cotton, when it collided with the *Chicora*, a Confederate ironclad warship. The prow of the gunboat tore a hole in the forward port beam of the *Alice*, and salt water flooded in, nearly rising to the main deck on the stern. The *Alice* had to return to its wharf for repairs on a hole on the waterline some two feet long and two inches wide. The *Charleston Courier* congratulated the captain for the success of his efforts to push forward the repairs and published a "card of thanks from Captain Carlin to the generous friends who have rendered their assistance in getting his handsome steamer out of her late difficulty."[22]

During this five-day delay for repairs, Carlin had the captain's office improved and the staterooms enlarged to make more storage space. He was able to deliver 1,000 bales of cotton to H. Adderley and Company in Nassau on 22 June. After a quick turnaround, he cleared outward from Nassau on the twenty-fourth on the *Alice*, supposedly bound to St. Johns.

In truth, Carlin took the *Alice* back to Charleston, arriving on 27 June and breaking his own record with a quick three-day run, completing the round trip in eight days and six hours. The inward cargo included goods for General P. G. T. Beauregard, the local commander of Confederate troops. We can judge the general's Louisiana tastes from his consignment, which included claret, figs, and cheeses, but there were also twelve sheets of plate iron for the army.[23]

Meanwhile, the *Ella and Annie* arrived in Charleston on 21 June, so either its reported departure date or the naming of Carlin as captain for this trip are examples of the misinformation that is rife in these shipping documents. This may have been the result of deliberate obfuscation on the part of the local shipping agencies involved to prevent useful intelligence from being cabled to Washington or confusion among numerous disparate sources.

John Egan was captain of the *Alice* for its next trip to Nassau in July. After his return trip the *Charleston Courier* printed a letter of thanks from the passengers for his skill and coolness under fire. Egan continued as captain of the *Alice,* making five successful return runs. The *Alice* was to make twenty runs for the company before being returned to England for sale in the spring of 1864.[24]

The humiliations of capture, imprisonment, and the harsh physical conditions of Fort Lafayette had changed James Carlin. He adopted a more belligerent role and joined in the Confederate navy's efforts to rid the Charleston approaches of the Union navy by helping finance and deploy an innovative weapon.

Chapter 20

# Charleston Under Siege, 1863

. . .

While James Carlin had been a prisoner of war, the Union army had been fighting its way deep into the South. During the first two years of President Lincoln's blockade, the Union navy had been kept well offshore by Confederate batteries at the harbor entrances. The runners had been able to enter most Confederate harbors once they had they evaded the outer cordon. However, by the end of 1862, the North's massive mobilization effort started to pay off, and the Union army began to occupy strategic sites on the coastal islands near the mouths of the main Confederate ports and attack the protective batteries. Combined with a "closer in" policy by the blockading squadrons, this led to a marked rise in the number of captures. In South Carolina the Union was winning ground, and Charleston was under siege. Despite the initial success of the I&E Company ships, they faced an increasing risk from the Union fleet and had greater difficulty slipping safely into Southern ports.

The Richmond government was well aware that if it could break the blockade by driving off the Union's warships, it would not only relieve a vital port but also place an onerous burden on the North: the cordon could only be reimposed by legally establishing a new blockade. The Washington government would then have to engage in the formal process of informing all foreign nations of its reinstatement with all the consequent delays and legal arguments and embarrassments. Breaking the Union navy's hold would reopen Southern ports for weeks and make it difficult for the Northern courts to order the confiscation of captured prizes.

This multiple goal was attempted on the night of 30 January 1863. Commodore Duncan Nathaniel Ingraham responded to criticism from the city's inhabitants, who were frustrated by the sight of two Confederate gunboats idling in the harbor, and ordered his ships into action. With Commander John Randolph Tucker and Lieutenant Commander John Rutledge, he set out with the CSS *Chicora* and CSS *Palmetto*. Under the cover of a thick haze, the small ships made a surprise attack. After a brisk engagement, the Confederate gunboats drove the entire blockading squadron out of Charleston Harbor.

The foreign consuls were then taken on a tour of inspection to show them that the harbor had been cleared and the blockade lifted. HMS *Petrel* happened to be in Charleston, and Captain Watson of the Royal Navy took the British consul, Robert Bunch, on a trip five miles beyond the blockading fleet's normal positions. After scanning the horizon, they found no sign of the Union navy, which was then based down the coast at Port Royal.

In a meeting between the consuls and Captain Watson, it was agreed that the blockade had been raised, and a declaration was issued to that effect. The government in Richmond received this news with delight and sent a message to James M. Mason and John Slidell, who were now representing the Southern states in London and Paris, with instructions that they should inform Earl Russell and the French government immediately. However, Earl Russell refused to accept that the blockade had been broken, and indeed it was reestablished later the same day when the Union navy resumed its previous positions. The Confederates' success had been very limited.

Gideon Welles of the Navy Department in Washington was determined to capture Charleston and close the port. He ordered the USS *New Ironsides* to reinforce the attacking Union forces. It arrived off Morris Island with the returning blockading fleet.

This formidable vessel would prove to be one of the most successful ironclads of the conflict. It was modeled on the British navy's HMS *Warrior* and the French battleship *Gloire*. Both were the leading ships in their respective navies. Built as a conventional broadside ironclad, the ship was 232 feet long, with a width of 57 feet 6 inches and a draft of 15 feet 8 inches. Displacing 4,210 tons, it was powered by two horizontal direct-acting engines of 700 horsepower.[1]

The *New Ironsides* was armed with two 150-pounder Parrott rifled guns, two 50-pounder Dahlgren rifled guns, and fourteen 11-inch Dahlgren smoothbore guns with a range of just over a mile. The gun ports, protected by swinging steel shutters, were seven feet above the waterline but had a limited field of fire. The ship's sides and the gun deck were sheathed with plates of four-inch armor. Sandbags were used to barricade the fore and aft woodwork sections to a depth of up to nine feet.

Sandbags were also spread on the spar deck to reduce the concussion of shell strikes that had shattered deck bolts, which then hit the men below like bullets. The hull was of oak from the forests of Pennsylvania and some twelve inches thick at the waterline. The large crew of 460 men and officers illustrates its power. General Beauregard noted that "this ironclad steamer threw a great deal more metal, at each broadside, than all the monitors together of the fleet; its fire was delivered with more rapidity and accuracy, and she was the most effective vessel employed in the reduction of Battery Wagner."[2]

In response to this threat, the Confederate navy tested a series of novel ideas. Electrically detonated mines were tried but rejected in favor of mechanical ones.

These were attached to ropes and laid in lines at crucial points in the outer sections of the harbor and the channels between the islands that protect it from the open ocean. Small boats were also used to place mines where they could be exploded under the enemy's ships or where a ship maneuvering in the outer harbor would strike them. Radical new efforts were made to counterbalance the weight of the enemy's warships and firepower with the limited means available in the boatyards and engineering shops of Charleston.

Captain Francis D. Lee, a brilliant young army engineer, was in charge of these developments in Charleston under the command of Major Stephen Elliott, who had a special interest in torpedoes. Lee designed a torpedo boat, *Lee's Ram,* and started building the wooden hull, but he was unable to obtain a suitable steam engine and steel plates from the navy, and the project was set aside in favor of other schemes.

Lee's first spar torpedo was tested under extremely primitive conditions. An old twenty-foot-long canoe was rowed into the side of an abandoned vessel in Charleston harbor. The device succeeded on its second test. The resulting explosion stove in the side of the barge, which then sank. General Beauregard promptly ordered further efforts along the same lines.

The first attempt to use spar torpedoes against the enemy was on a dark night in March 1863, when Lieutenant William T. Glassell, in command of "Lee's canoe,"[3] pulled out of Charleston Harbor with a seven-man crew. Their task was to attack the bark-rigged USS *Powhatan,* a side-wheeler of 3,765 tons and fifteen guns. The boat was seen and the alarm raised. One of the crew panicked and backed his oar, and the small craft was swept past its target on the swift current. These experiments persuaded the Confederates that they would have to use steam-powered vessels to deliver the explosive charges. After the Civil War, these pioneering technical forays led directly to the development of high-speed torpedo boats armed with self-propelled torpedoes that could deliver the explosive to the point of impact and ensure detonation.

In this atmosphere of alarm, General Pierre Gustave Toutant Beauregard, commanding the defense of Charleston, instructed Captain Lee to proceed with the development of a steam-powered, spar-torpedo boat. The ram was to be armed with a twenty-two-foot spar projecting forward of the bows. These were to carry three sixty-pound explosive charges tipped with a percussion cap. While the spar torpedo was first invented by Robert Fulton in 1801, it was not until Captain Lee took up the challenge that any real success was achieved, and senior commanders came to appreciate the weapon's potential.

The spar torpedo was based on the concept that water cannot be compressed, only displaced. The pressure exerted by the explosive charge was forced through the weakest surface, that portion of the target's hull damaged by the explosion.

Provided the spar was at least ten feet below the waterline, the density of the water was sufficient to protect the torpedo boat from the main blast although it could be deluged from the water forced to the surface. The sharp forward point of the torpedo was to be rammed into the side of the vessel to penetrate sufficiently for the main force of the explosion to enter the vessel and expand upwards within the hull.

While *Lee's Ram* carried percussion caps that exploded the charge on contact, the British Royal Navy developed electrical firing mechanisms that allowed the launch to retire, leaving the warhead stuck in the side of the target vessel until the attacking craft was at safe distance for the charge to be activated. By the 1880s the British had fast steam launches that carried a long spar on a tipping mechanism armed with a percussion torpedo. A forward gun was mounted on the vessels, along with a quick-firing machine gun mounted on the stern, to protect the crews from their quarry's rifle fire.[4] These early torpedo boats became an important element in naval tactics. Once an attacking boat had maneuvered close in to a warship, below the lowest trajectory of the latter's guns, the warship crew could only respond with boomed nets and rifle fire from the deck as a last resort.

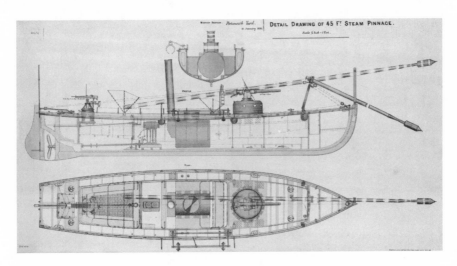

Royal Navy spar-torpedo forty-five-foot steam pinnace of 1880.
© National Maritime Museum, Greenwich, London.

To the increasing frustration of Charleston's traders and the blockade-runners, a ring of ironclads and formidable-looking monitors was closing in on Charleston's outer harbor and making incursions across the bar into the inner harbor. The Union navy, benefiting from the industrial might of the North, produced many more warships and converted more captured blockade-runners to naval use.

The big guns of the monitors were a grave danger to the city and its defenses. These strange vessels were a particular development of the American Civil War. The monitors had a very low freeboard and were flat decked, giving a minimal target for enemy fire. Compared with a conventional broadside warship like the *New Ironsides,* they provided a cost-efficient platform for one or two large guns housed in rotating turrets. Their low center of gravity aided their stability and thus the accuracy of their guns in moderate-to-calm water. Armor plated for protection, a monitor looked more like "a cheese box on a raft" than a warship. Their armament could throw heavy shells that were used to batter the land defenses General Beauregard had erected once he resumed command in Charleston in the fall of 1862.

Charleston and its environs. *Harper's Weekly,* 28 March 1863.
Courtesy of Peter Newark's Pictures.

On 6 April 1863 Beauregard sent a telegram to Brigadier General H. W. Mercer in Savannah, Georgia, reporting that nine ironclads had crossed the bar and were moving to engage his forces. He asked whether a diversionary Confederate naval force could be sent out of Savannah. On the same day he reported in a further telegram, this time to General Samuel Cooper, adjutant and inspector general, that twenty-four wooden vessels, including the USS *New Ironsides* and six monitors, were off the bar and that two monitors appeared to be on the Charleston side of the bar. Also, sixteen steamers and eight schooners were in the mouth of the Stono River and off Cole's and Goat Islands. He reported that the steamers were active all night and were landing troops on Goat Island in the morning.[5]

On the same day, in a telegram to James A. Seddon, the Confederate secretary of war, Beauregard reported that the threat had increased. The ironclads were moving in, and there were now thirty-three vessels in Stono River. Although some of these reports were later retracted, the growing danger was very real.[6]

There was widespread alarm in Charleston. General Beauregard appeared to have the "wind up," as on 6 April he ordered Captain Francis D. Lee to be ready to ensure, at a moment's warning, the complete destruction of the torpedo ram that he was developing. This small vessel was lying on the stocks in the navy yard in Charleston, waiting for armor plate and funds to complete its fitting out.[7]

Captain Tucker, "commanding afloat" in Charleston, instructed Lieutenant W. A. Webb to visit a Mr. Wagner of John Fraser and Company and demand steamships for the defense of the harbor. Webb was told that if he met resistance, he was to say that "he must and will have them" and to use force if necessary, citing the authority of the secretary of the navy. He was also instructed to arrange this with Wagner "quietly and pleasantly if possible."[8]

Attack by the Federal *Ironsides* on the Harbor of Charleston at 3:30 P.M. on 7 April 1863.
Courtesy of "The Civil War in America from the *Illustrated London News*": A Joint Project by
Sandra J. Still, Emily E. Katt, Collection Management, and the Beck Center of Emory University.

On the morning of 7 April, the Union fleet sailed "slowly and majestically up the main ship channel towards Charleston."[9] The monitor *Weehawken* led the procession, followed by three other monitors, then the *New Ironsides,* and finally four more monitors.

By the afternoon of 7 April the *New Ironsides* and the other warships were heavily engaged in trying to reduce Fort Sumter in the middle of Charleston's outer harbor, but their shells had little effect on the thick walls of the fortress. Well-directed counterfire was poured on the approaching ships from Fort Sumter and later from Fort Moultrie and the batteries on Sullivan's and James's

Islands. As the fleet crept closer to Charleston, the Confederate guns found their range on the buoys that were set in the channels as range markers, as ordered by General Beauregard.

The Charleston waterfront was crowded with spectators. We can imagine James Carlin and his wife, Ella Rosa, and her little household watching as the falling shells sent up great spouts of water next to the invading ships, and their hurrahs when a shot hit one of the monitors or the *New Ironsides*. Their splendid panorama of an apparently decisive action must have given them confidence that the South could still win the war.

At one point during the attack of 7 April, the *New Ironsides* was anchored exactly over a large electrical mine that a desperate Confederate engineering officer, Langdon Cheves, was planning to detonate. But because of the faulty insulation of the long wire that connected the mine to the electrical firing mechanism, he was unable to set it off. As Cheves reported: "The confounded thing would not go off when it was wanted."[10]

During this action the *New Ironsides* received over fifty hits from the shore guns but sustained little damage, as no shells penetrated its heavy armor. This demonstrates a striking element in naval warfare of that period. Iron-plated ships were able to take numerous shells and solid missile hits. Unless they caught a monitor at the base of a turret or an ironclad at some other critical point, damage was usually slight.

Nevertheless, the Confederate land batteries scored some 520 hits on the Union warships, which were sufficient to turn back the monitors, and the fleet retreated out of range. The Union admiral Samuel Du Pont, in command of the attack, later wrote, "Merciful Providence had permitted me to have a failure instead of a disaster."[11] The gunners of Charleston had won a considerable if short-lived victory, and General Beauregard was given full credit for the defeat of the "ironclad fleet."

The April offensive delayed work on the development of the spar-torpedo rams. However, trade had ceased, the wharves were empty of ships, and Charleston's merchants were near collapse. Drastic and ingenious measures were urgently needed to rid Charleston of the continuing menace of the *New Ironsides* that barred access to the open sea.

By early July the Union navy was still in Charleston's outer harbor, and there were reports of five thousand Union troops landing on the small islands at the mouth of the Stono River. The first assault was made on Fort Wagner on Morris Island on 11 July.

General Beauregard was desperate for further action against the Union warships in the harbor, but he met with delay and procrastination from Captain Tucker. On 12 July the general again wrote to Tucker urging action against the ironclads to protect Confederate earthworks on Morris Island and to prevent the threat, if they fell, to Fort Sumter. He suggested the use of the state gunboat and torpedo ram, which he had been assured could be speedily made ready to move with efficiency by steam, though unmailed. These and such of the steamers of light draught, like the Juno, if provided with the spar torpedo contrivance, together with the flotilla of iron boats already prepared for the service, could make nightly attempts to destroy one or more of the monitors; an event which . . . would be of incalculable importance to the defense intrusted [*sic*] to us.

To dislodge these monitors without endangering our own iron-clads, ought to be effected, if possible without loss of one hour that may be avoided.[12]

On 18 July, as the crisis continued and the Union land forces crept closer, General Beauregard wrote again to Captain Tucker. He repeated that it was of "the utmost importance to the defense of the works at the entrance to the harbor that some effort should be made to sink either the Ironsides or one of the monitors now attacking the works on Morris Island. . . . The stake is manifestly a great one and worthy of no small risk." He proposed that "one vessel such as the Juno, provided with the spar torpedo, 2 or 3 officers and a few men . . . would be as effective at night for the end in view as a flotilla of vessels of the same type." The matter was urgent and he wanted action as "the time [was] rapidly passing away when that assistance can be of any avail or value."[13]

By the end of July, the preparations for the ram had run into a further series of snags. Lee wrote to General Beauregard's aide-de-camp, Captain A. N. T. Beauregard (the general's brother), explaining the situation and urging continued support for the project. Lee had heard the vessel was to be surveyed to determine whether it was fit for its purpose. He pointed out that the hull of the vessel had been presented to him as suitable by John L. Porter, the chief naval constructor, and that a board of survey by naval engineers acting for the Navy Department had assessed that it would make six knots, nearly double that of other vessels in the harbor.[14] This turned out to be optimistic.

Captain Lee stressed in his letter that everyone had approved the vessel until the point when it was placed in the water, at which time its faults must have become clear, not least its leaks. Opposition was growing. Lee added that he did not know if the new condemnation was part of the "prejudice" against torpedoes that had been shown at every point during its construction.[15]

Lee respectfully requested that the commanding general "withhold his final judgment" until he had completed the "vessel proper" and had placed the armor where appropriate. He was at a loss as to how to pay for the work on the torpedo boat that would be completed within a week, but ready for use at night only, as it was still without armor plate. This positively identifies this vessel as Lee's unarmored ram named the *Torch*.[16]

Lee mentioned another small, cigar-shaped steamer based on the "Winans' model"[17] as nearly complete at Stony Landing on the Cooper River, about thirty miles from Charleston. It was financed and built by local merchants, including Theodore D. Wagner and Dr. St. Julien Ravenal. This vessel was later named the *David* and completed a successful spar-torpedo attack on the USS *Ironsides* in October. In the meantime Carlin was working with Lee to ready a vessel for offensive use.[18]

The *Torch,* as it was eventually known, had been built on the same basis as a conventional gunboat but was much smaller and "tub like."[19] This, the first steam-powered vessel to be used to deliver torpedo charges, was powered by an old, redundant steam engine from the Savannah tugboat *Barton* and, as Captain Lee noted, was said to have a top speed of six knots. In tests, however, it never exceeded four knots and was desperately lacking in power. A curved cutwater, or canvas-covered shield, had been built over the bow to protect the little vessel from being flooded by the backwash from the explosion of the torpedo charges as it was deep in the water, heavily ballasted with granite blocks. Only the pilothouse, smokestack, and cutwater showed above the waterline. The vessel was also painted Carlin's pale grey so as to be nearly invisible in the dark, and it was fired with an-thracite coal for a minimum of smoke and sparks. There appears to be no record of its dimensions, but for comparison the *David* was fifty-four feet long with a beam of just over five feet.[20]

The "prejudice" that Lee mentioned came from some professional naval and military officers who had reservations about using what they considered under-handed means of achieving their goals. Mines, torpedoes, and submarines, new-fangled gadgets, were viewed with great suspicion, regarded by many of that era as devious and dishonorable weapons. Lee, as an engineer, scientist, and officer, would have been all too aware of charges from his colleagues against his honor as an officer and gentleman. This sentiment was to affect others further down the ranks, too.

James Carlin had no such scruples and was growing increasingly frustrated with the lack of action against the Union navy inside Charleston Harbor. In his letter to A. N. T. Beauregard, Lee stated that Captain Carlin, who had already proposed to purchase, complete, and take charge of the ram, had called at his office and offered to command the new ironclad steamer *Charleston,* arming it with tor-pedoes and using them against the enemy's fleet. He had asked for Lee's assistance in fitting out the torpedoes for this new venture.[21]

The CSS *Charleston* had been laid down in December 1862 and constructed in the city's shipyards. It was nearing completion when Carlin made his proposal to use it offensively against the blockading squadron. Lee had assured Captain Carlin of his cooperation if his proposal met the approval of the general. The CSS *Charleston* would also prove to be underpowered with unreliable engines. As the strongest of the warships available to the Confederates, it later served as flagship for the Confederate squadron and aided the CSS *Palmetto State* and the CSS *Chicora* in defense of Charleston. Commander Isaac N. Brown, a regular naval officer, was appointed its captain.

Although Carlin's bid to become commander of the biggest Confederate States Navy steam warship in the harbor was not taken up, it showed the authorities that he was prepared to take a naval role to save the city from destruction by shellfire and reopen the harbor.[22] Theodore D. Wagner and his partners in John Fraser and Company were also keen to help and raised a $100,000 reward for the sinking of the *New Ironsides* and $50,000 for a monitor, in the hope of pushing the project forward.

Lee wanted his spar torpedoes to be tried out, stating in his letter that "Captain Carlin's full knowledge of the harbor, his cool courage and determination, all point to him as one peculiarly adapted to the proposed service, and I feel an abiding confidence that under his skillful management the torpedoes, so long unused, will yet accomplish something for the safety of this city."[23]

On 2 August 1863 General Beauregard wrote to Captain Tucker, giving his opinion on the best use of the private steam vessels seized from commercial interests in Charleston. Beauregard's view was that they would be of more use in the defense of Charleston Harbor than they would be if sent to other theaters of the war. Beauregard was "convinced the time for their effective employment for the defense of this harbor is now, in some effort to destroy at night the Ironsides and other ironclad vessels of the enemy, which are being formidably used for the destruction of our [defensive] works." He thought that if they could not be put to this use quickly, then there was little point in retaining them.[24] The ram was Beauregard's pet idea and he was determined to see it through.

On the same day, Lee wrote the following report to Brigadier General Thomas Jordan, Beauregard's chief of staff:

> I am in receipt of your communication of yesterday and would respectfully report that the additional cutwater is being prepared for the torpedo ram.
>
> In obedience to the commanding general's instructions, I submitted the plan of attaching spar torpedoes to the sides of the vessel to Captain Carlin's consideration, and at the same time informed him of the commanding general's determination to leave the details of the arrangements to his (Captain Carlin's) decision. Captain Carlin in reply expressed his preference for the use of the torpedo only in the bow of the vessel, with extra torpedoes on board, to be attached should the opportunity offer for immediate renewing of the attack. The reason Captain Carlin assigns is that, should he fail with his bow torpedo, in the time required to swing round with the tide in order to strike with those on the other side, would be amply sufficient to insure the destruction of his vessel by the enemy.

To provide against any possibility of failure in the torpedo and to multiply the chances of success, I have proposed the use of three torpedoes in the bow after the manner shown in the accompanying sketch. Captain Carlin highly approves of this arrangement, which is now being carried to execution.[25]

Lee was still finding Captain Tucker obstructive. On 3 August he again wrote to Jordan, complaining that he had received a communication from Tucker saying that he was not prepared to receive the torpedo boat until he could find officers and crew, and he asked his line commander for instructions.[26]

Lee was also having difficulty funding the work on the torpedo boat and paying the bills for its conversion. He wanted to know if he should discharge the crew as he had no means to pay them. He had written to Captain Carlin "at whose instigation the vessel was prepared for service, and who is cognizant of all the pecuniary arrangements, to take immediate steps towards a final settlement. From the evidence of everyone connected with the vessel she has exceeded, both in speed and seaworthiness, the expectations of all." In his language, his description of the finances, and his tone, he was distancing himself from the whole project. This view is confirmed by the next paragraph, in which he asks to be "relieved from his present duties immediately on the adjustments of the claims now existing against the ram, and assigned to active duty in the field."[27] Carlin had injected some urgency into the whole matter. Lee's letter shows that he financed the completion of Lee's unarmored ram from his own pocket.

Carlin was soon involved in the planning. He would have been well aware of the symbolic aspects of the arrival of the *New Ironsides* off Charleston and alarmed at the closer blockade that the Union Fleet was now able to effect. He also understood the international and legal aspects of the blockade. The new inner position of the blockading fleet demonstrated the greater effectiveness of the blockade and made it more dangerous. This action also changed the legal status of those trying to run through the Union fleet, making it impossible to argue against the legality of the blockade and putting them all in greater jeopardy if caught.

Between 17 and 23 August 1863, Union artillery on Morris Island directed heavy fire against Fort Sumter in Charleston Harbor. In the midst of all these dramas, Carlin took on a martial role and embarked on a carefully planned but risky expedition. With the runners' activities much reduced and the city in grave danger, action was needed.

What happened next gave James Carlin his small place in the history books. His "Kind Providence" ordained that he should appear in the right place and with the right qualifications to play a major role at the absolute point in time when naval warfare changed its form to that we now recognize as "modern."

Chapter 21

# The CSS *Torch* Incident
## Drama and Treachery, August 1863

• • •

Report of Ensign Porter, U.S. Navy
USS New Ironsides
Off Morris Island, South Carolina, August 28, 1863

SIR: In obedience to your order of the 26th instant, I hereby submit
to you an account of the visit of the enemy's vessels to this ship a few
nights since.

At 1 a.m. on the morning of the 21st instant, I saw a strange vessel,
sitting very low in the water and having the appearance of being a large
boat, coming up astern very fast. I hailed the stranger twice, receiving for
an answer to the first hail, "Aye, aye," and to the second, "I am the 'Live
Yankee,' from Port Royal." Beat to quarters immediately and threw up
rocket. In the meantime the stranger ran rapidly past our broadside and
fell athwart our bows, where we could bring no guns to bear upon her. She
remained there a few minutes and then started off rapidly in the direction
of Fort Moultrie. Meanwhile our chain had been slipped, and backing astern,
the bow guns were fired at her, but with what effect I can not say. From the
time she was first seen until she left us not more that five minutes elapsed.

Benj. H. Porter, Ensign.[1]

This small incident was a pivotal incident in naval history. It was the first de-
ployment of a small steam-powered vessel in an attempt to sink a large warship
by maneuvering explosive charges next to the hull. It led directly to widespread use
of fast torpedo boats in naval fleets around the world.

The experiment with the CSS *Torch* is mentioned in many histories of the naval
aspects of the American Civil War, but historian Raimondo Luraghi has highlighted
its significance in a naval context. He calls the idea itself "excellent," even if it was
to take further work before it became "fruitful." More usefully, as Luraghi points
out, was the alarm and fright it caused in the Union blockading squadron, which

kept its distance thereafter, staying farther out to sea and relieving the city of the immediate threat of bombardment from the sea approaches.[2] While the *Torch* incident may have given the Union navy cause for concern and eased the bombardment of Charleston, it made the task of the runners no simpler. Marcus Price's figure for entrances and clearances from Charleston shows a total of ninety-four vessels making successful trips in the first quarter of 1863. This shrinks to twenty-five for the second half of 1863, with eighteen in July before the *Torch* attempt.[3]

The events of the night of 20 August 1863, as retold in official reports and by James Carlin, appear straightforward enough. Research has revealed that, beneath the surface, there was another untold story. Both sides were playing an intelligence war with spies and contrabands crossing to either side. The individuals involved also had their own consciences to appease. Some participants were civilians who could not face the brutalities of war or found themselves on the wrong side of the conflict and did what little they could to aid "their" side. Charleston was a small city, and the cast of characters tends to reappear in other guises in other parts of the story of Carlin's life. Even the Reverend William Yates had his role to play. The finale leaves us contemplating the futility of it all.

The most detailed version of that night is given by W. P. Poulnot, who claimed to have been executive officer on board the *Torch*. His tale is told in the *Charleston News and Courier* of December 27, 1895, some thirty-two years after the event. Doubtless, the Sunday newspaper's journalist went to work on his reminiscences, putting Poulnot in the center of the action. As with many such memoirs, the facts surrounding the event are often either vague or inaccurate, but the story doubtless gained from the retelling. Others have used these sources, and the tale has been much retold.[4]

Poulnot seems to have retained a clear enough memory of the events and of his shipmates on what must have been the most memorable day of his life. Other, perhaps more reliable facts come from the official reports of both the officers on board the *New Ironsides* and General Beauregard. Carlin's cool and laconic account appears in full in appendix 1. Poulnot gives a detailed record of the preparations for the daring expedition, and he creates the sense that everyone involved realized that it could have resulted in death for all concerned.

The disastrous effect on the supply logistics of the Confederacy and the loss of earnings for the runners themselves gave ample reason to mount this risky adventure. There was also the $100,000 in prize money offered by Theodore D. Wagner and his partners from the John Fraser Company for the sinking of the *New Ironsides* and the extra $50,000 for sinking a monitor. Poulnot said that English supporters, the Confederate government, and local millionaires all combined to offer prize money amounting to millions in Confederate dollars. Whatever his motivation, Carlin was so keen to see the destruction of the *New Ironsides* that he offered to buy the *Torch* with his own funds, although this was not taken up by Lee and the navy. He had become the "ingrate" that the Union secretary of the navy, Gideon Welles, wrote of, but he would have taken delight in taking revenge for the indignities of the Tombs and Fort Lafayette prisons.

Poulnot was employed by the Arsenal, the government agency preparing the *Torch*. He said that it had just been completed at Baird's shipyard as the "smallest gunboat." Built like a conventional wooden vessel, its sides were originally pierced for four 300-pounder Columbiad guns. It was intended for use as a floating battery. This gives an indication of its size and explains its capacity to hold twelve soldiers, plus the four crew members of the gig and the rest of the officers. It was painted light grey in the style of the blockade-runners and floated "part submerged."

The gunboat's "much worn" machinery was only able to achieve about four knots. Poulnot said that its shield was boarded over and canvassed to obscure the light from the furnaces.[5] The little vessel was taken to March's dry dock, where Poulnot measured it up for the necessary ironwork. Duncan Cameron, the foreman of the blacksmith's yard at the Arsenal, undertook the work. Poulnot obtained a twenty-four-hour leave from Major J. T. Trezevant, who was commanding the Arsenal, and persuaded Carlin to take him on as volunteer executive officer.

The 1 August launch was delayed by a day when the propeller became entangled with a hawser on leaving the dry dock and the vessel had to be hauled out again. On relaunch it was taken on a short test trip around the harbor and pronounced fit for service. Meanwhile, the crew members were living well on their own stores, but without the benefit of alcohol, which Carlin had banned.

The *Torch* was then moved to the head of the North Atlantic Wharf, but was found to be leaking badly. Twenty laborers and some hand pumps were rushed over from Adam, Damon and Company, and the problem was overcome for the moment. There were further reports that the *Torch* leaked badly and that it could only be kept afloat by continual bailing.

Informers, too, had their part to play in this many-layered event. Admiral John Dahlgren, commanding the Union blockaders, informed his fleet that "it was rumored that the enemy have a ram near Fort Johnson."[6] Reports of a ram under construction in Charleston had actually circulated among Union naval officers a year earlier. J. B. Marchand, commanding the USS *James Adger*, had reported to Du Pont on 2 August 1862 that "four contrabands, one a female, came off from Charleston to the USS *Vandalia* in a boat procured from the navy yard." These informants reported on the military strength of the Confederate forces defending Charleston but also stated that two vessels were being built in the city, one of which was a ram that was "very sharp forward with 2 feet thickness of wood, and the sides [were] roof shaped."[7]

Poulnot said that he went to Major Caspar Chisolm, the officer in charge of the Torpedo Bureau, and collected the six 75-pound torpedoes to arm the vessel. These were loaded onto the *Torch* and placed under guard. Poulnot was ordered to the Orphan House steeple to observe the position of the blockading fleet and to keep a special watch out for the USS *New Ironsides* with the intention of setting out at eleven o'clock that night. At dusk, he returned to the *Torch* to find that all was ready except that they lacked a fireman to stoke the furnace of the boiler. A desperate hunt for a fireman then took place, but all refused the dangerous task. Their departure time was approaching; something had to be done. At seven o'clock, someone remembered a man named Habenicht, who was in jail under a sentence of death for desertion from Fort Sumter. Poulnot hastened to General Beauregard to request an order for his release if Habenicht would agree to act as fireman. This they both agreed to. He was released to Poulnot's care on the understanding that Poulnot would be responsible for Habenicht's safe return to custody.

With the clock ticking, Poulnot then took a chance. Habenicht pleaded to be allowed an hour with his family. Poulnot agreed and arranged to meet up with the stand-in fireman at the post office at 10:30. Given that most steam boilers need some hours of careful firing up before they achieved sufficient steam pressure, we can assume that the boiler had already been lit.

True to his word, Habenicht reappeared at the *Torch* on the stroke of 10:30 P.M., cool enough to offer his new commander a cigar. It later emerged that Habenicht had not deserted from Fort Sumter but had returned late from a forty-eight-hour leave in the city. He had been prevented from returning on time by a gale. He had tried to get back and eventually made it to the fort when the gale subsided. However, the fort's commander, Alfred Rhett, had ordered a court-martial that found him guilty and sentenced him to be shot at the racecourse. Habenicht's view appears to have been phlegmatic. He was going to die either way, so he reasoned that it was better to die with glory than ignominy.

On the strike of the clock, as 11:00 P.M. rang out, the warps were slipped, and the *Torch* made its way out through the harbor, avoiding the defensive obstructions and mooring briefly at Fort Sumter to borrow ten or twelve men from the First South Carolina Artillery. Their task was to act as marine guards and protect the *Torch* from the crews of the Federal picket launches that swarmed the lower harbor.[8] The volunteers, excited with the prospect of high adventure, were soon on board under the command of Lieutenant Eldred S. Ficking.

Visibility was limited in the darkness. Carlin, the pilot, and Poulnot were only able to see objects silhouetted against the dark loom of the land. The *Torch* made its way down the ship channel, past the protective booms, and out into the wider harbor between the Union blockaders and the Morris Island batteries. There was no moon and only a light swell from the prevailing southwesterly wind. Carlin said that at midnight he "sighted the [*New*] *Ironsides* lying at anchor in the Channel of Morris Island, with five monitors moored immediately in a S.S.W. direction from her, and about 300 yards distant. One monitor was anchored in the direction bearing upon Battery Gregg and about half a mile distant."[9]

Poulnot commented that "at slack water the great broadside of the monster *New Ironsides* was open to our view, showing black against the leaden sky."

When they were within a quarter mile of their target, Carlin was feeling so confident that he would strike the unarmored bow section that he ordered Poulnot to lower the torpedo boom some twelve feet below the surface and make fast the supporting guy ropes.

At this time the *New Ironsides* was lying across the channel with its bow pointing towards Morris Island. As the *Torch* ran parallel to the side of the warship, Carlin realized that they would miss striking the side of the *New Ironsides* square on with their torpedoes as the warship started to swing to the now-ebbing tide.

When they were one hundred yards from the *New Ironsides,* they could see the sentry on the forecastle. Poulnot said that the sentry had his "musket on his shoulder as he 'bout faced from the port rail to march his beat," implying that the *Torch* was approaching the *New Ironsides* from the bow as it lay to its anchors pointing upstream into the flow of the ebb tide.

Running on a parallel line, Carlin "steered up," keeping the swinging warship on their port bow. When they were within forty yards of the huge ship, Carlin stopped his engine and ordered the quartermaster to put the helm "hard astarboard," an order that would turn the *Torch* to port on an attack line at a right angle to his previous course.

In his report to General Beauregard, Carlin was clear that the failure of this order led to the failure of his expedition. In Carlin's words:

I noticed the slow obedience of the ship to her helm, and again gave
the order, repeating it three times. It was a moment of great anxiety and
expectation, and not doubting but I would strike her, I was obliged to
attend to the proper command of the officers and men and restrain any
undue excitement. In this I was ably assisted by the cool, courageous
bearing of Lieutenant Fickling, who commanded the force stationed for
defense. I discovered as we ranged up alongside that in consequence of the
*Ironsides* being in the act of swinging to the ebb we must miss with our
torpedoes, but feared that her chain cable would either ignite them or detain
us alongside. In either case we must have been captured. A kind Providence,
however, intervened and saved our little band from such disaster.[10]

This was the critical point of the attack. While the *Torch* was steaming on a close but parallel course to the direction in which the *New Ironsides* was lying at anchor, it presented little obvious threat to the much larger vessel and could pass for a U.S. Navy launch going about fleet business. The moment the *Torch* turned onto a line that would take it on a collision course with the side of the ship, the officers and crew were clearly stating their business and could expect prompt and powerful response from the great guns of the warship. At this crucial moment, the *Torch* turned into the potent weapon Lee had planned.

As the *Torch* steamed towards the larger vessel, its speed was increased by the quickening power of the ebbing tide (and also perhaps some component of the speed of the river current). Carlin had to calculate the precise moment to turn to ensure that the *Torch* hit the *New Ironsides* square-on amidships, even though the warship was also moving with the tide. He had to compute the upstream component of his new course in order to compensate for the effect of the tidal flow on the hull of the *Torch* as it ran almost broadside to the stream for those last forty yards. He had to judge whether the *Torch* had sufficient speed, at the moment of turning, to carry his vessel the forty yards to the ship and arrive at the impact point with sufficient velocity to activate the percussion caps of his torpedoes. This would have to be calculated giving due allowance to the extent to which the tight right-angle turn would take speed off his vessel. He also had to consider the drag effect of the lowered torpedo on both the vessel's speed and on the dynamics of the turn across the ebbing tide.

USS *Ironsides* in fight trim.
Courtesy of Library of Congress.

Many of these intuitive calculations and judgments would have been second nature to a man of Carlin's sea experience, but he had had no practice runs or training sessions—just a quick trip around the harbor. No wonder he attributed the failure of his mission to the failure of the helmsman to make the turn as ordered. We must assume that this was the fault of the wheelman James Patney. It is of course possible that he was unable to hear Carlin's order or that he misunderstood it, although this seems unlikely given the size of the *Torch* and Carlin's repeated orders.

We can also give Patney the benefit of being unsighted behind the curved foredeck shield, but it also questions the role of the pilot Thomas Paine, who should surely have been helping with these maneuvers. Certainly no blame seems to have been attached to either man.

Was this yet another case of Northern sympathizers infiltrating Southern ranks with disastrous results, or was it incompetence, poor discipline, lack of training, or pure fright by an ordinary merchant seaman untrained in naval combat? Patney probably turned the helm as directed, but the *Torch* was in the grip of the tidal stream and had little extra forward way. It could have been making a good speed over the ground, but its actual speed through the water could have been less than either the wheelman or Carlin calculated. The *Torch* would have far less steerage than its apparent speed would indicate was likely. The rudder would have little effect on the mass of water that was moving at nearly the same speed as the *Torch,* and the turn would be slow and delayed. With the benefit of hindsight this seems a likely explanation for the failure of the turn. Carlin and his fellow blockade-runners preferred more maneuverable side-wheelers to screw-powered vessels for exactly these reasons. They could make sharp turns at low speeds.

Meanwhile the crew was preparing to face death or glory. Poulnot was seated on one of the spare torpedoes with a tophaul line in his hand, preparing to fire by hand if the torpedoes on the spar failed to ignite.

As Carlin realized that the initial attack would fail, he faced two further severe alarms. His torpedoes were down and armed. His vessel was ranging against the side of the warship and rapidly being driven towards the anchor chains by the strengthening tide. Carlin feared that these would either detonate the torpedo or catch and detain the *Torch,* leaving it exposed to rifle fire or boarding from the crew of the *New Ironsides* and the likelihood of the low-sided vessel being swamped by the rushing current.

Poulnot reported that at this point the *Torch* struck the *New Ironsides* amidships on the portside "stem on." Carlin and his crew were prepared for a huge explosion, followed by a great backwash and upswelling of water. If they survived the initial blast, they half expected to be swamped and flung into the foaming water close under the side of a mortally wounded leviathan that might roll over them if it capsized and sank.

But, there was no explosion. Nothing happened except that the crew of the *New Ironsides* were alerted by the sound of the torpedo barrels scraping the side of their vessel. Then the officer of the watch, Ensign Benjamin H. Porter, standing directly above them at the port gangway, leaned over the rail and hailed them twice and sent up a rocket to illuminate the area and warn the rest of the fleet.

The huge bulk of one the greatest warships afloat was looming over their tiny vessel. The ebb tide was strengthening all the time. The *Torch* was alongside, hampered by the torpedo poles and in danger of becoming entangled with the *New Ironsides*'s gangway. The tide was threatening to force the little steamer onto the battleship's anchor chains. If the *Torch* had become caught under the chains, it could have capsized or flooded in minutes.

"Hello!" replied Carlin in what must have been a pretty calm tone. In Poulnot's version, events very nearly got completely out of hand at this point. Lieutenant Fickling raised his rifle and, cocking it, took aim at the head of the *Ironsides* officer of the watch as he peered over the bulwarks.

"Hold on! Let me make that fellow stop talking," said Fickling as his men also raised their rifles. Carlin pulled Fickling's gun down and ordered the soldiers and crew to remain silent.

"What steamer is that?" hailed the officer above them.

Carlin's reply remains a classic for cool thinking under pressure and was repeated throughout Dixie in the days that followed.

"The steamer *Live Yankee* with dispatches from the admiral," he replied to the head silhouetted against the night sky above the dark hull.[11]

"Where are you from?" demanded the United States naval officer.

"Port Royal bound to Wilmington, N.C. put in here short of coal," replied James.

"Lower a boat and send her on board," ordered the *New Ironsides*'s officer.

"Aye, aye, sir,"[12] answered Carlin without the least intention of complying with either request. All this occurred in the space of about three minutes, while the two vessels ranged against each other as the flood tide swung the *New Ironsides* at its anchor.

Carlin, Poulnot, Fickling, and Paine the pilot pushed the vessels apart at the bow of the torpedo boat as far as the oars and poles would allow. The tide forced them farther apart. The *Torch* was so close to the side of the larger vessel that it could not bring its guns to bear. Carlin gave the engineer the order to "go ahead," but the engine had stopped. Poulnot leapt below and with Habenicht labored with the starting bar to restart the engine caught at dead center. After several attempts, they succeeded in pointing the vessel away from the *New Ironsides* and made off one hundred yards or so.

Now they were alarmed that the *New Ironsides* would blow them out of the water or launch boats loaded with boarding parties. To cover their withdrawal, they opened barrels of pine rosin they had brought with them and fed lumps of the stuff into the boiler furnace. This burned furiously, giving off such dense smoke that "no one could see or scarce stand it, away from our vessel."

As Poulnot returned to the deck, he distinctly heard the order given for the *New Ironsides* to clear the decks for action and the boatswains' pipes and drums. There was a further order: "Load! Ready! Fire." The warship had slipped its chains and backed astern to allow its bow guns to fire at a lower trajectory. Poulnot was amazed to see and hear two shells from one gun. One shell exploded on the starboard quarter close aboard, depositing a considerable amount of water on the afterdeck. The other shell flew overhead and exploded over the starboard bow. Carlin seems to have maintained a course that took him on a line directly ahead of the warship, thus ensuring that the retaliatory shots passed to either side of the little vessel. Poulnot stated that nine double-shotted guns were fired at the *Torch* without much effect, except that the small vessels of the Union fleet scattered in alarm at the shooting.

Doubtless, with the $50,000 prize in mind, Carlin then contemplated attacking one of the five monitors moored nearby. With a faulty engine and the *Torch* taking on water, he had second thoughts, considering it "almost madness to attempt it" and turned for Charleston.[13] As the *Torch* passed close to some of the small launches from the U.S. fleet, they took the *Torch* for some "death-dealing man trap or a phantom Flying Dutchman" and kept their distance.

Captain Stephen C. Rowan, the officer commanding the *New Ironsides*, seems to have tried to make light of the incident. His report is succinct: "August 21, 1863— At 1 a.m. wind S.S.W., force 1, weather b.c., saw a strange looking vessel coming up astern very fast, and upon being hailed he answered, 'Live Yankee, from Port Royal.' Beat to quarters, fired a rocket, slipped the chain and fired several guns at the stranger, but as he passed he grazed our bows, and then kept directly ahead, so that we could not get our battery to bear on him. At 1:20 he disappeared under the land."[14]

In the dark the *Torch* was no longer visible in the starlight and made good its escape, lost against the dark mass of the coast. On the way back to Charleston, Carlin returned the volunteer marine corps crew to Fort Sumter. It is clear that the soldiers had little appreciation of the danger they had been in as they agreed that they had had a "splendid trip and enjoyed the fun." As they steamed back against the tide, the crew of the *Torch* enjoyed the confusion of the blockading squadron that had been much alarmed by the excitements of the night.

Poulnot moored the *Torch* to the North Atlantic Wharf but had to move it to West Point Mill the next morning, when most of the crew returned to their homes full of their exploits. Tales of the "Live Yankee" soon spread throughout the South. As Milton Perry notes, J. B. Jones, a clerk in the War Department, "wrote of it in his diary, exulting over the statement, confidently expecting greater things." Perry also comments that there really was a Union steamer named *Yankee*—"a 328-ton paddle-wheel gunboat mounting three cannon."[15]

Early the next morning, the *Torch* was moved to avoid the shelling of the city from the Union warships that started at sunrise. And what of the redoubtable Mr. Habenicht? Poulnot reported that he returned him to General Beauregard's office and told the general of his "constancy and bravery," whereupon the general gave him a lecture and released him from the army.

Poulnot's account rounds off the tale. After their return to Charleston, the crew discovered that the man who had manufactured the torpedoes had made a deathbed confession as he lay dying at the Pavilion Hotel. Ruck was a Northerner from Boston who had been a trusted employee and official of the Confederate government and a coppersmith by trade. Appalled at the thought of such a "death dealing instrument" being used against his own people, Ruck had filled the torpedoes with sand and sawdust.[16]

Thus, it was little wonder they did not explode alongside the *New Ironsides*. Poulnot commented that this was probably the best thing that had happened "for, as certain as day, if they had gone off none would have been left of the *Live Yankee*'s crew and some think the crew of the *Ironsides* would have been in other quarters about this time." Was Ruck's action treason, treachery, or a tender nature? Ruck certainly took a serious risk sending the torpedoes out unarmed. Perhaps he knew that he did not have long to live and chose to take the risk for the sake of his Northern origins.

Carlin was in the anomalous position of being a British merchant marine captain on the books of the Confederate navy as a pilot, yet in command of a vessel under the authority of the Confederate army, reporting directly to an army general. Beauregard persuaded Carlin to retain command of the *Torch,* but no further actions were undertaken. His executive officer, W. P. Poulnot, had sought his appointment directly from Carlin and thus reported to him, having obtained a twenty-four-hour pass from Major Trezevant, commander of the Arsenal.

The pilot, Thomas Paine, an associate of Carlin's in other ventures, became famous as a blockade-running pilot and was lost at sea as captain of a new steamer built to run between Tampa and Havana. The wheelman James Patney later died of injuries sustained on the *Starlight* on the St. John's River. Charles Boughton was taken on as the deckhand. He later "became a wreck "and "followed the seas." One engineer was Thad Sims, who later carried out foundry and iron work in Charleston. The others in the engine room were Mr. Veronee and Charles Fitzsimmons, both Charleston engineers. The armorers were John D. Clancy and Archibald Whitney, volunteers.

These two gentlemen did not expect to share any prize money but went on the trip for "the excitement and to display their bravery." The name of the cook/steward is unknown, but he "served on the ram *Arkansas* and volunteered to go in any capacity. He proved to be a good and handy fellow, without a shirt or a friend. The officers raised a purse of $1,000 Confederate money, for this man."[17]

The Whitehall gig that the *Torch* carried as a lifeboat was the property of the Reverend William B. Yates, pastor of the seaman's mission and friend and mentor of James and Ella Carlin. He must have felt that it was the most practical help he could offer on what was clearly a risky venture. Four schoolboys formed the gig's crew. These may have been from the seaman's school run by Yates. They, too, performed good service and received a purse of Confederate money as their reward. Sadly, the good pastor's gesture was to cost him his gig as it was swept overboard and lost, perhaps following the shell explosion that swept water over the starboard quarter.

While the immediate aims of the expedition were not achieved, the overall results proved more satisfactory. The close-in blockade eased slightly as the Union navy moved farther down the estuary towards the open sea. Within two days of the exploit, Captain J. F. Green of the USS *Canandaigna* reported that a steamer had run the blockade outwards with an "almost uninterrupted passage out in the vicinity of six [U.S. Navy] vessels."[18] While Stephen Wise records that the *Fannie* left Charleston on the twenty-second, there was little further activity by the runners of Charleston until June and July 1864.[19]

The next attack against the USS *Ironsides* was by the famous semi-submersible CSS *David* on the night of 5 October 1863. The ironclad was damaged but did not leave Charleston waters until May 1864 when it went north for repairs. During this period Confederate engineers in Mobile, Alabama, had been developing a submarine named after its inventor Horace L. Huntley. The *Huntley* was delivered by rail to Charleston in August 1863 and entered the race to sink the USS *New Ironsides* and win the $100,000 reward being offered by the John Fraser Company. Like the *Torch,* the *Huntley* was armed with spar torpedoes. It could stay submerged for some two hours, although the crews suffered greatly from lack of fresh air. In any event, it failed to sink the *Ironsides,* but its actions led the Union warships in the Charleston approaches to take extensive protective measures. The *Huntley* was the first "submarine" to sink a warship. On 17 February 1864 the USS *Housatonic* was struck by the Huntley's spar torpedo, and the resulting explosion forced the warship on its side and filled the hull with fumes.

The submarine sank on at least four occasions.[20] The forty crewmembers who drowned during its development and later patrols are commemorated on a memorial in White Point Gardens in Charleston. Below them, on a separate plaque are listed the crew of the torpedo launch *Torch.*

When Charleston fell and Admiral Dahlgren entered Charleston, he reported that he found nine torpedo boats and that he had raised two that had been sunk in the harbor prior to the evacuation. Why these were not used in further attempts against the invaders is unclear, but precautions were taken to guard against further spar-torpedo boat attacks. Calcium lights were set up to illuminate the area around the large ships and booms, nets were deployed, and two tugs patrolled around the USS *Ironsides* at night.[21]

Carlin was still enjoying his fame from the incident on 24 September 1863, when he dined with the diarist Edmund Ruffin at the house of S. Stoney. Ruffin was a significant figure in the Old South. A gentleman planter, writer, and political commentator, he made his greatest contribution as an agricultural reformer. The "Lively Yankee" repartee tickled the ironic senses of at least one acute observer of Charleston life under siege.[22]

# Chapter 22

# Trouble in Bermuda
## Or How Not to Run the Blockade,
## September–November 1863

. . .

I n the months leading up to the August attempt against the USS *Ironsides*, the
Bee Company's senior captain had been busy running the blockade with the *Ella
and Annie* and the new vessel the *Alice*. In the midst of his involvement with the
*Torch*, James Carlin had to deal with the affairs of the company and with a particularly feisty Southern captain. This would prove to be his trickiest executive task.

Frank N. Bonneau, first mate and later captain of the *Ella and Annie*.
Courtesy of the Naval History and Heritage Command.

Carlin had caused more excitement in Charleston on 6 June 1863 when he
appointed Frank N. Bonneau as captain of the *Ella and Annie*. Bonneau had been
the ship's first officer and was well known locally. All Charleston flocked to visit
him on board his new command, offering "tenders of congratulation."[1]

Charleston newspapers described Bonneau as "young and gallant" and "our fellow townsman," and contemporaries called him "a splendid, handsome courtly gentleman."[2] He had served in the U.S. Navy before the war and joined the Confederate cause as captain of an army artillery company. He took up blockade-running at the instigation of his uncle and patron, Commodore Duncan Nathaniel Ingraham, who was dissatisfied with the commercial caution of the civilian English captains and wanted to introduce a more military spirit into the vital military supply line. Bonneau certainly showed the dash and élan in command of the *Ella and Annie* that went some way to justify his remarks, in the *New York Times* in 1892, about the timidity of the English captains under Federal gunfire. Despite his subsequent boasts and the excitement of the local press, his "career with the Company was short and controversial and ended in failure."[3]

Bonneau's buccaneering did not appeal to William Bee, who preferred a more cautious, business-like handling of his property. Bonneau's lackadaisical approach to getting urgent supplies to the Confederate forces contrasts with the quick turnarounds managed by his senior officer. His handling of the *Ella and Annie* highlights the difference in approach between naval officers and more commercially minded captains drawn from the Merchant Marine.

The presence of the Union navy in the outer harbor did not prevent Bonneau from taking his new command out of Charleston. The *Ella and Annie* was reported unloading 1,122 bales of cotton locally valued at $239,567 in Nassau on 25 June. The close-in tactics of the U.S. Navy increased the risks of the run into Charleston, and the main Confederate effort was being switched to Wilmington, North Carolina.

Bonneau took the *Ella and Annie* into Wilmington in the second week of July with a cargo from Nassau. As Carlin tackled the *Ironsides,* he may have given little thought to Bonneau engaged in the Wilmington–Bermuda run. However, problems were approaching. By 13 August the *Ella and Annie,* with Captain Bonneau as master, was at Mrs. Todd's Wharf in the town of St. George's at the northern tip of Bermuda after a run of some seventy-one hours. After unloading its cotton, the *Ella and Annie* was controversially moved to an anchorage in the outer harbor.

In her thesis, Lynda Worley Skelton says that it was at this point that Captain Bonneau ran into the trouble that caused the I&E Company difficulties with the Confederate government, with whom the company was already in various disputes over the proportion of government and military cargo it carried. Bonneau's actions or the lack of them also gave Carlin a taste of the responsibilities that came with his post as senior captain. The following events owed much to Bonneau's exuberant nature and his Southern "devil may care" character. His subsequent correspondence with his employees shows the resentment Southern pilots and captains held against their foreign, usually English, rivals.[4]

Major Smith Stansbury, the Confederate ordnance agent in Bermuda, faced delays getting the *Ella and Annie* loaded with its return cargo, but the greatest difficulty was with Bonneau. What should have been a turnaround of a few days dragged on and on. Everyone except Bonneau grew more frustrated. Stansbury knew that Bonneau was drawn to Hamilton by a woman he had brought over from Nassau; he could hardly be wrested from her arms.[5]

Captain Bonneau then refused to bring his command back to the wharf in St. George's for reloading. Instead, the *Ella and Annie* was to take on its cargo from a schooner in the outer harbor, using lighters for the transshipment. This was time consuming and laborious. When the lighters were alongside, Bonneau then insisted that the *Ella and Annie* steam around to the southwest of the island and dock in Hamilton and load there instead. The lighters were to follow him to Hamilton, the capital city of Bermuda, some twelve miles away.

He later stated that this move was because water and rations were considerably cheaper in Hamilton than in St. George's, and he blamed delays on being allotted a berth in St. George's. His actions meant that Stansbury had to take the last consignment of arms across to Hamilton for loading. Initially Major Stansbury refused to do this, but Major Norman S. Walker, the Confederate government's military and financial agent, eventually overrode Stansbury and John Tory Bourne, the Confederate commercial agent who had supported him. Walker ordered Stansbury to load the arms in Hamilton.

On 13 October, Bonneau wrote a long letter to Bee full of excuses. He blamed exhaustion after a long trip, his own fever, chills among his crew, delays by the customs house, and the rivalry between the towns of St. George's and Hamilton. He also accused the Bermudan government of being hostile to him because he did not make "a bar room" of his ship while he was in port.[6] Skelton remarks that the officialdom of Bermuda seemed thoroughly disgusted with him, blaming his private pursuits for the loss of valuable military supplies.

In fact, Bonneau was being fêted and generally enjoying himself in Hamilton, a point he did not mention in his letters. Skelton notes that the *Ella and Annie* was the first Confederate runner to dock at Hamilton, and the merchants and dignitaries were anxious to celebrate Bonneau and his officers with a public dinner. Buoyed by his reception in Hamilton, Bonneau flaunted the Confederate flag.

The commander of the USS *Fort Jackson* complained that the *Ella and Annie* had "come out of the harbor for sea, and was then passing and repassing us, flaunting that symbol of the rebellion and occasionally dipping it to us in derision." He also complained of insults to his officers while on their way to visit the governor.[7]

It was not until 9 September that the *Ella and Annie,* disastrously delayed, cleared Hamilton for Kingston, Jamaica. Its real destination was Texas. Bonneau's dalliances had cost his cause a vital three weeks, but it was soon to create even more trouble. The ship carried an urgently needed load of munitions, including 500 cases of Austrian arms containing 12,000 weapons, nearly half a million rounds of ammunition, and 400,000 vital percussion caps, all that Stansbury had available in

Bermuda. Also included were 12 carboys of nitric acid, 10 carboys of sulfuric acid, 10 carboys of muriatic acid, a case of gum shellac, 5 cases of surgical instruments, saddles, emery abrasive, 10 kegs of horseshoes, and other military items.[8]

Following the terms of the Bee Company charter agreement with the government, Bonneau requested $10,400 for expenses for the trip to Texas via Havana from Major Norman S. Walker, the Confederate agent, who had his headquarters in the Globe Hotel. These funds were to cover 230 tons of coal at both Kingston, Jamaica, and Havana, Cuba, as well as port fees, which he regarded as being particularly high in Cuba.

He allocated $1,000 for a pilot to take them through the Sabine Pass, where Lake Sabine, a large salt-water estuary on the Texas-Louisiana border, empties into the Gulf of Mexico. This reference shows that the munitions were intended for Port Arthur to relieve the Confederate troops of the Trans-Mississippi Department. They were soon to be engaged in what became known as the Battle of Sabine Pass, the most significant battle in Texas during the entire Civil War.

The *Ella and Annie* was sighted by a Union warship soon after leaving Hamilton and chased back into St. George's Harbor, Bermuda. Bonneau set out again on 11 September but was hit by a heavy gale and had to return because the side boxes protecting its vulnerable paddle wheels had been carried away by large waves. The *Ella and Annie* had sustained other damage, and much of the cargo was ruined. The carboys of nitric acid had been thrown overboard by order of the captain, who was concerned that the chemical, stored in large glass jars, might explode as heavy seas tossed the ship about.

Bonneau estimated that it would take as long as two months to repair the damage to his ship. He appears to have been anticipating more time with his friend in Hamilton. On 4 September, Stansbury wrote to Colonel Josiah C. Gorgas, head of the Confederate Ordnance Bureau, reporting that he had transferred the most damaged part of the cargo of arms to the *Cornubia* to be run into Wilmington as soon as possible. There they could be repaired and preserved, as he had no faculties in Bermuda to handle them.

Confederate government officials were used to losses and delays, but believed they had a valid claim for damages against Bonneau. They wrote to President Bee of the I&E Company, charging that Bonneau had unnecessarily delayed the *Ella and Annie* in Hamilton. Their concern was amplified by the losses the blockade-running fleets were suffering as the Union navy grew larger and refined their tactics. As Steven Wise comments, "In mid-August, just as the South was beginning to replace the supplies lost at Vicksburg and Gettysburg, their luck began to run out."[9]

The lack of these armaments at a critical moment to the Confederate cause was a blow to the government. The Bee Company president felt the political repercussions and instructed his senior captain to go to St. George's and look into what had happened and to inform Captain Bonneau of the complaints against him. Carlin made the run to Hamilton on the *Alice,* captained by Egan, arriving in the second week of October. William Bee was critical of Carlin for appointing Bonneau as captain of the *Ella and Annie* and suggested that he was swayed by his previous friendship with the dashing Southerner. Carlin was anxious to avoid blame and returned with a letter from Major Walker expressing confidence in Bonneau as a captain, although Walker was bitter about Bonneau's culpability for causing the unnecessary delay in Hamilton.

Walker wrote to William Bee and Company in Wilmington from St. George's on 16 October:

> At the request of Capt. Carlin it gives me pleasure to inform you that any confidence in Captain Bonneau as an efficient officer is not influenced by the recent mishap to the Steamer "Ella and Annie."
>
> At the same time I must explain the conviction that there was a most unnecessary delay of the steamer at this port on a most useless expedition to Hamilton, and that the damage sustained in the recent storm was not of such a serious character as to render an abandonment of the voyage to Kingston necessary. The "Ella and Annie" will be loaded with government stores and sent to the coast with as much dispatch as possible. Your Obt. Servant - N. S. Walker.[10]

John Bourne was also critical of Bonneau, but complained that Carlin (calling him Capt. Corbin) had not come to see him (Bourne) during his visit to Bermuda "as he should have." He stated that "the principal detention and finally the unfortunate disaster came from Bonneau's order to move both the *Ella and Annie* and the lighters to Hamilton." He feared that this fact was "never communicated" to Captain Carlin nor was he made aware that this unnecessary transfer delayed the ship's departure by a week.[11]

While the *Ella and Annie* was being repaired in Bermuda, it was released from the government charter to Texas and commissioned to carry Confederate stores to Wilmington. It made its last run on 5 November, clearing St. George's for Wilmington together with the blockade-runner *R. E. Lee,* commanded by Lieutenant J. Wilkinson. There were two passes through the long Cape Fear peninsula; the runners would try to select the least defended.

After separating from Wilkinson off the coast of the Carolinas, the *Ella and Annie* met heavy seas and reduced speed. At 5:30 A.M. on 9 November, as the sun rose, the vessel was steaming south close in along the Cape Fear shoreline towards New Inlet, when it touched bottom on the shoaling outer beach. Bonneau said that they did not stop, but hauled away from the shore. At this point they sighted the Union gunboat *Niphon* dead ahead across their bow, steering north. The *Niphon* immediately steered to cut the *Ella and Annie* off from the beach.

USS *Niphon*, 1863.
Courtesy of the Naval History and Heritage Command.

Captain Bonneau was still living in Charleston in the 1890s when he was interviewed by the *New York Times* and gave a vivid account of these events:

> We being in three fathoms of water, I was much surprised to find a boat
> running so boldly for us. To pass outside him would be to lose my ship
> for he would then cut me off from the support I expected from our own
> batteries in a few miles more. To run my ship ashore at this point would have
> been madness for the beach here is an outer one, the sound extending inside
> of it for miles, and consequently I could expect no protection, and my whole
> ship's company would either be destroyed on this bold beach or taken by the
> enemy as prisoners. To turn back to sea was to give the ship to the enemy
> without an effort to save her.

Bonneau then showed his naval élan. Blocked from a seaward escape and too far
from the protection of covering fire from Fort Fisher on the Cape Fear River, the
*Ella and Annie* upped its helm and turned towards the *Niphon*. Desperate to escape, Bonneau maneuvered his ship to ram the *Niphon*, hoping to cut it and run
it over. He said that he tried to hail a warning to the *Niphon*, but was met with a
blast of grapeshot and musket balls.

The Union gunboat, reacting very quickly to its helm, managed to turn
away so that the *Ella and Annie* hit it at an angle, carrying away the bowsprit

and damaging the starboard stem and starboard boat rail. Both ships, tangled and locked together, raced side to side at great speed with their paddle wheels churning and grinding against each other.

Acting Master J. B. Breck, the commander of the *Niphon,* sent a boarding party over the clashing rails. Armed with cutlasses and pistols, they quickly secured their prize. Bonneau later claimed that one hundred bluejackets swarmed aboard his ship, firing to left and right.[12] Bonneau and his crew were made captive. The Union boarders then ransacked the vessel, quarreling over their booty until the flagship the USS *Shenandoah* came up and its officers stopped the looting. Breck later described how he found wood shavings and a keg of powder with a slow match attached, "ready to blow her up."[13]

The *Ella and Annie* was captured off Masonboro Inlet, on the northern shore of Cape Fear in four fathoms, eighteen miles from Fort Fisher, and sent to Boston with a prize crew for repair. Bought in by the navy, it became the USS *Malvern* and eventually became Admiral David Dixon Porter's flagship. It was wrecked off Cuba in 1895.

Bonneau and his crew were also taken to Boston, where Bonneau was at first given a local parole. He was tried and found guilty of trying to sink the *Niphon,* a conviction that carried the death penalty. Fortunately for Frank Bonneau, the presiding admiral admired his spirit, saying that he would have done the same thing. Bonneau was reprieved and sent to jail in Boston and then to Fort Warren before being exchanged for a Union prisoner. He returned to Charleston and continued blockade-running, making further successful runs in the *Hattie.*

Bonneau's troubles rumbled on until the end of 1864, with lengthy letters between Bonneau and Bee. On his release from prison and return to Charleston, he wrote to Bee claiming money he believed he was due for his earlier command of the *Alice* and trying to justify his actions. He made the spurious point that if the *Ella and Annie* had not been lost but had made another successful run, he and the company would not now be the subject of government blame for his delay in Bermuda. He also tried to deflect blame for the loss of the *Ella and Annie,* noting with some justification that other captains had lost ships and not been subject to such criticism. The commander of the *Shenandoah,* when reporting *Niphon's* success on 10 November, had the "gratification" of reporting the capture of the *R. E. Lee, Cornubia,* and Captain Robert Lockwood with the *Margaret and Jessie* during the same dark period of the moon.

On 12 December 1864 William Bee wrote to Bonneau, stating that when the latter had been placed in command of the *Alice,* Bee "had requested Capt. Carlin, through whose instrumentality you were placed in command of the *Alice,* and as your personal friend, and disposed to do you justice, to name those terms. He did so and at my request reduced them to writing." Bee's sentence continues at some length in the same vein: "You now claim . . . $10,000 in currency for the inward cargo of the Orion and five percent upon the gross value of each subsequent outward and inward cargo."[14]

Bee accused Bonneau of having been on the coast too late at night. Bonneau responded by listing captains who had left Bermuda at the same time and held the same opinions on the best tactics to use on that night off Cape Fear; he pointed out that numerous other runners also came to grief trying to run into Wilmington.

Bee appears to have withheld Bonneau's pay, queried his qualifications, and complained about his private cargoes, including cotton. In a bitter reply, Bonneau objected to his treatment, as he was the "oldest officer of the line." He clearly fell out with William Bee, although his relationship with Carlin survived the events in Bermuda, his capture, imprisonment, and his ill health while in Boston. He told Bee that he was "sure Captain Carlin will do me the justice not to undervalue my service."[15]

We do not know what Carlin told Bee about the events in Bermuda, but Bonneau's appointment, although popular in Charleston, cannot be regarded as a triumph. Bonneau made some successful runs and probably earned his keep. At the critical moment, however, his temperament cost the Confederacy sorely needed munitions and lost the company its best ship. The steady characters of the experienced, "foreign" sea captains proved a better commercial bet for their investors and for the South. Carlin had to deflect criticism for the selection of his friend and justify his actions, but William Bee retained his trust in his "Commodore" and was to give him another command.

# Chapter 23

# Preparing for Change, December 1863

. . .

A fter the capture of the *Ella and Annie* in November 1863, William Bee instructed James Carlin to go to England to purchase or commission vessels
for the company. Bee was in urgent need of more cargo capacity as he anticipated
a surge in business. He had been in negotiations with the Confederate treasury to
improve Confederate finances by centralizing control of cotton exports and ensuring the cooperation of the railroad companies with their capacity for obtaining
upcountry supplies.

The Confederate States Congress had passed regulations requiring all blockade-runners to reserve half their cargo space for government cargoes. There had
been many protests. The *Nassau Herald*[1] predicted that those who backed the
runners would withdraw from the trade, and commentators in Bermuda echoed
these concerns. William Bee had written to his friend Christopher G. Memminger,
the Confederate treasury secretary, supporting the move but urging "Memminger
to bring all shipping operations under one central control." To help Memminger
bring some efficiency to the export of cotton, Bee proposed that the "Secretary
take an interest for the [Confederate] Government in the Ships of our Company."
He wanted to operate for the Confederacy as a whole, not just South Carolina.

He told Memminger that he had sent Captain Carlin to England to build
"three more vessels of lighter draft, greater capacity and altogether superior to those
the English are building to sell to their Confederate cousins." He commented that
his vessels used Charleston and Wilmington as their home ports, as Captain Carlin
"thoroughly disapproved" of running ships between Florida and Havana as others
had tried. He continued: "The protection of the vessels and cargoes in those ports
is doubtful, and the tardiness and cost of transportation very great. Again as no
vessel is allowed to leave the Port of Havana after the light is shown at the Castle
at the entrance of the harbor, which is usually the case at sunset, vessels would be
compelled to leave while there was light enough to betray them and the chance of
capture greatly increased."[2]

Carlin had advised him that the runners should use Georgetown and the Santee River in South Carolina as alternatives if Charleston and Wilmington were inaccessible. "The Georgetown harbor could be kept open by a moderate force and a few long range guns," Bee wrote. "Vessels with a light draft as were to be built in Scotland, could run up the Santee River to the north Carolina Railroad crossing, and to the Peedees crossing at Georgetown."[3]

Carlin knew both of these areas from his days with the Coast Survey, and Bee was passing on his senior captain's expert views. Changes also had to be made to the way the railroads were used to bring cotton from the interior. The railroad companies also participated in the blockade-running trade, demanding rights to small percentages of cargo space as the price for transporting cotton to the ports against the conflicting interests of the military and the government.

The problem was not the availability of cotton but the allocation of the limited means to deliver it to the coast. Lynda Worley Skelton notes that a conflict existed between the need for the Richmond government to have the Confederacy's cotton delivered to the coastal ports and the operational needs of the armies in the field. Government departments, including the army and the navy, made direct contracts with the railroad companies, offering them a small percentage of the government space on the blockade-runners if the railroads would assign entire trains to ship cotton for the department.[4]

Railroad officials could buy cotton cheaply in the interior and sell it dearly in Wilmington. They often found it more profitable to speculate on selling their cotton in this manner instead of accepting the small amount of cargo space on the blockade-runners. Corruption was commonplace, and private cotton found a way to gain priority. Government cotton remained in the interior, while imported military supplies remained in the depots.

To counter these difficulties, the Bee Company secured the participation of the Charlotte and South Carolina Railroad Company, which had cotton waiting for transport to the coast. William Bee needed the means to turn this bounty into foreign currency.

Bonneau was safely out of the way as a prisoner in Boston, and the other Bee Company captains knew their business well enough. Carlin was to go to England to prepare the way for the anticipated increase in trade resulting from the efficiency measures implemented by the Confederate government and William Bee.

## Chapter 24

# Appointment in Scotland, December 1863–1864

• • •

C arlin made the run through the blockade and headed for Havana, where he caught the *Infanta Isabelle* en route via Cádiz, Spain, to London. Carlin called it one of the "finest ships afloat" and made the point that it was built by Denny and Company. From Cádiz there would have been any number of Mediterranean mail ships heading north to London, where they arrived on 10 January. After a busy month, Carlin reported back to his employers in Charleston from his father's home in Port Muck, Isle Magee, on the northern coast of Ireland.

This letter (see appendix 1) reveals Carlin's frenetic activity on his arrival in England as he rushed around the country by steam train, accompanied by John W. Sly who appears to have been a marine engineer. Carlin demonstrated a grasp of the technicalities of his trade, as well as an energetic and decisive manner. During his years commanding steamships on the eastern seaboard of America, he had gained enough knowledge of steam propulsion to specify exactly the vessels and engines he needed. The ships he ordered on the Clydeside were recognized as among the finest built for their peculiar trade.

The letter also confirms that William Bee had appointed Carlin as superintendent of the company's fleet. This post may have been intended to authenticate his status as a representative of the company when dealing with English shipbuilders and as supervisor of the shipbuilding process. It also regularized his position as senior captain and thus the commodore of family legend. He stated that he intended to "bring out" the ships he had ordered built, suggesting that he had no plans to give up seafaring.[1]

On arriving in London, he first called on James M. Calder, the Confederate agent in Liverpool. Carlin then made a comprehensive tour around the shipyards of Britain. He found that the shipbuilders of the northeast were busy with work and that costs had risen. There was no time to lose, and he had to press on to Scotland. He had consulted with his fellow captains and then made decisions based on costs and timing. He had been impressed by the fine steamers built by Peter Denny and his Clydebank firm Denny and Company. His judgment was to be vindicated by the exceptional performance of these vessels.

Peter Denny built the *Ella* and *Caroline* and the larger vessel the *Emily* for the Bee Company. He also built the *Imogene* under a later contract. Carlin allowed himself a self-indulgence by naming the first vessel after his wife, Ella Rosa. Carlin was to continue his relationship with Peter Denny for some years after the end of the war and joined him in several business ventures. Carlin family legend has James Carlin living for a while in a large house in Dumbarton, and it seems likely that he stayed with Denny at Helenslee, the mansion Denny had named after his wife, the daughter of James Leslie.

Peter Denny in 1868 by Sir Daniel Macnee.
© National Maritime Museum, Greenwich, London.

Peter Denny (1821–1895) and his elder brother William had been building ships on the River Leven from 1844. Their shipyards were under the shadow of the castle that sat high above on Dumbarton Rock on the north bank of the Clyde estuary. Denny's ship-designing skills were renowned, and the company's speedy ships were much in demand for cross-channel ferries. The Denny family was connected to the

Napiers of Robert Napier and Company engine works at Govan and maintained a close working relationship. The Denny yards went on to complete the famous clipper ship the *Cutty Sark,* and they built liners and cargo vessels for Britain's leading shipping lines until 1963. In all they built some twenty-two thousand ships, the highest number of any Clyde shipbuilder.[2]

While long, narrow ships were favored for blockade running, British shipbuilders found that there were limits to the speed advantage of a very narrow beam. The hulls became structurally weaker, the carrying capacity diminished, and engine space was restricted. The final blockade-runners combined both the admired sleekness of line with the sturdy construction of the Clyde river-class steamers.

Helenslee, Peter Denny's house in Dumbarton, in the 1870s.
Joseph Irving, *Book of Dumbartonshire,* vol. 3.

The Bee Company vessels were built at Denny's North Yard on the Leven. The twin ships *Ella* and *Caroline* were 225 feet in length with a 28-foot beam and 13 feet of depth in the hold; they drew 9 feet of water. The cargo capacity was 30,082 cubic feet or space for 600 to 800 bales of cotton. Accommodation was limited. The twelve to fifteen passengers were a valuable source of additional revenue during the absence of regular packet boats. With an iron hull, each ship carried two smoke stacks, iron masts, and iron paddlewheel boxes. The Napier-built oscillating steam engines were rated at 200 horsepower. These engines operated without complex valves, as the piston cylinders rocked or oscillated so that the head of the cylinder was alternately aligned with the steam inlet and outlet ports. Although they were inefficient, they were relatively cheap, small, and simple and thus ideal for these steamships.

On 18 January, Peter Denny offered to build two more side-wheel paddle steamers for James Galbreith, a partner of the shipbrokers Patrick Henderson and Company, agents for the Confederacy in Glasgow. Galbreith was acting for Carlin on behalf of the I&E Company. The price was £22,000 each on the basis that they were to be "adapted in every way for blockade running." Delivery dates were to be 15 July and 1 September 1864. Robert Napier and Sons at the Lichfield foundry was contracted to supply the engines for £10,000 each.[3]

Carlin ordered the slightly larger *Emily* at the same time. It was registered at 1,100 tons new measurement, compared to the *Ella*'s 634 tons. The *Emily*'s length was 155 feet, but it was wider in the beam at 34 feet, had 16½ feet of depth in the hold, and drew 10 feet of water. Its engines were rated at 300 nominal horsepower. The *Emily* was fitted out for twenty-five to thirty passengers. On 8 feet of water, its capacity would be 1,600 to 1,800 bales. It was destined to be the last of the Bee Company vessels.

The swift, clean lines and smart appearance of the runners *Ella, Caroline,* and later the *Imogene* drew admiring comments from the shipping correspondent of the *Dumbarton Herald*. Each launch was written up in the newspaper, and it was made very obvious that they were intended to run the blockade.

On 4 March 1864 Carlin signed an agreement with Peter's brother Archibald Denny at the Woodyard site for two more vessels similar to the *Ella* and *Caroline*. They were given the yard numbers 34 and 35 and the preliminary names *Charlotte* and *Maud Campbell*. The records are unclear about these vessels, and they were later sold to other parties.[4]

Carlin also ordered a fifth vessel very similar to the *Ella* that was to be a joint venture between Carlin himself, who owned twenty-three shares, and Peter Denny and the shipbroker James Galbreith, who held forty-three shares each. His partners allowed Carlin a further indulgence as this ship was named the *Imogene,* a name used by Ella Rosa within her family circle. The contract for this vessel was signed on 4 August 1864 with completion due by November. With construction underway, Carlin moved to Liverpool, the center of Confederate support in Britain.

The *Ella* was launched on 26 May 1864 by Miss M. Robson, the daughter of the manager of the Commercial Bank, which must have been involved in the financial arrangements. Carlin had wanted to appoint Egan as captain, but Egan was in Ireland on private business, so Carlin appointed Captain C. J. Barkley to take the *Ella* out on its maiden voyage. At about this point Peter Denny or Carlin must have commissioned the maritime artist William Frederick Mitchell to paint the *Ella* in the harbor at St. George's, Bermuda. This lively oil painting is now in the National Maritime Museum at Greenwich in London, although museum officials have no record of how it ended up in their collection.

Meanwhile, the *Alice* and the *Fannie* of the I&E Company of South Carolina "turned in a tremendous performance," according to Stephen Wise, who records that they made some forty-four runs (twenty-two return trips) through the blockade in the spring and summer of 1864.[5] The *Ella, Caroline,* and *Emily* were intended to replace these two busy vessels if they were captured or when they wore out. Captain John Egan had taken over command of the *Alice* on Carlin's departure for England and made five successful round trips. He joined Carlin in Liverpool in the spring of 1864. The *Fannie* needed repairs before the new ships were ready, and it had to return to Britain for refitting in May 1864. Skelton records that on 8 June, Captain Dunning took the *Fannie* to Bermuda and back to Greenock on the Clyde, where they arrived in early July 1864. Passengers included Captain Carlin, returning from yet another transatlantic trip, and Henry Adderley, traveling to England with his family.[6]

After the war, the *Fannie* ran between Stranraer and Belfast before being sold to the London and South West Railway in 1869. It ended its days on the French run and the Channel Islands service.[7]

# Chapter 25

# Liverpool and the Last Days of the Confederacy, March 1864–June 1865

. . .

James Carlin chose to settle his family in Liverpool, then the greatest port in Britain by both volume and value of goods handled and also the tonnage of ships registered. Liverpool merchants and the cotton mills of Lancashire and Yorkshire had extensive business relations with the Southern states in the years prior to the Civil War. Following on from these connections, the city became the center of the Confederacy's efforts to finance and deliver munitions and other essentials. The port also had the advantage of experienced shipping and confirming houses with the capacity to underwrite Confederate arms purchasing and shipbuilding on the basis of anticipated cotton deliveries to the port.

Liverpool was also the most important United States consular post, where U.S. Consul Thomas Haines Dudley faced strong pro-Confederate feelings among the locals. He received anonymous letters threatening him with death if he was found in the wrong place, or if he succeeded in stopping schemes that supported the rebels or promised them profits. He took special precautions over his mail and when he traveled to London to consult Ambassador Charles Francis Adams. He even used disguises when going about in the city.[1]

The Merseyside shipyards contracted to produce the armed raiders CSS *Alabama* and the CSS *Florida/Oreto,* the Laird Rams, and the other raiders that were to cause such havoc among Union merchant shipping. The United States government was particularly affronted that the British had tacitly permitted the construction of these vessels and had not made greater efforts to stop them from leaving British ports.

James Dunwoody Bulloch, a Confederate naval officer, had been sent to England in May 1861 to organize the Southern war effort in Europe and commission six commerce raiders. He set up his offices in Liverpool in the warehouse of Fraser, Trenholm and Company, well-established Charleston cotton brokers, who were to act as the overseas bankers and paymasters for the Confederate government.

His offices had a secret rear entrance for confidential visitors.[2] Bulloch hired expert legal advisors and set about testing the legitimacy of the Union blockade. The point at issue was the British Foreign Enlistment Act. Under this wide-reaching legislation, Bulloch, as a citizen of a foreign country, could purchase vessels, but he could not fit them out as warships. Confederate agents in Liverpool and Glasgow went to great lengths to send out armaments on separate vessels that rendezvoused well offshore with the new fast raiders the Liverpool yards had built for the Confederacy.

Engraving by Alexander Hay Ritchie depicting Sherman's March.
Courtesy of Library of Congress.

Dudley soon had detective agents at work tracking the activities of Bulloch's visitors and identifying Confederate ships with the potential to be warships that were being constructed in the local yards They went to great lengths to obtain photographs or accurate descriptions of these vessels and also those being bought to run the blockade. Records were obtained of ships leaving for the West Indies, and their names and cargoes were reported to Washington. Obvious blockade-runners were photographed, and copies were sent to the Union navy for distribution to their squadrons operating the Atlantic blockade and to U.S. consulates in ports around the world. Carlin would have been an obvious person of interest to this motley assortment of private detectives, investigators, and informers, and we can picture him going about his business in Liverpool and Dumbarton with half an eye cast astern.

Ella Rosa would have found a supportive and lively group of Southern women in Liverpool. There were grand balls and other fundraising events. In October 1864 a flag-decked Grand Southern Bazaar in St. George's Hall in October 1864 raised £20,000 for the Southern cause. While this would have eased her into the social life of the expatriate Confederates, it would have been little compensation for her separation from her fine house in Charleston and her domestic slaves. Events during the months that followed show that it was a good time to leave the Confederacy.

The "total war" that General William T. Sherman and the Union army inflicted on the South started with the destruction of Atlanta in September 1864 and continued through November and beyond when his troops marched to Savannah, pillaging and destroying everything on the way. Under siege and battered by gunfire, Charleston held out to the last months of the Confederacy but was evacuated on 10 February 1865.

The Waterloo Hotel, Ranelagh Street, to the left of the Lyceum Library.
Courtesy of Liverpool Record Office, Liverpool Libraries.

We have no certain date for when Carlin brought Ella Rosa and his three sons out of Charleston. We know that Carlin was in England from January 1864 until about May. So it is probable that he took his family with him on the run through the blockade from the Confederacy to Havana and then crossed the Atlantic on the luxurious Spanish mail steamer S.S. *Infanta Isabelle,* taking passage to Cádiz. Here

Ella Rosa would have her first glimpse of peninsular Spain. From family accounts, it was a memorable exit from Charleston under gunfire. There was no female accommodation on the stripped-down runners, and legend tells of a dangerous breakout from the Confederacy, with Ella Rosa and her three small children, James, William, and Samuel, hidden among the bales of cotton piled on the deck during their escape from Charleston. On another such run, a safe room was constructed of cotton bales for the wife of the former secretary of war, General George W. Randolph, who was leaving Confederate service for health reasons. We can imagine James Carlin going to ingenious lengths to ensure the safety of Ella and their small brood. Whether the family story is apocryphal or not we shall never know.

The Carlins' first daughter, Ella Imogene, was born in the Waterloo Hotel, Liverpool, on 28 November 1864. This establishment ranked with the Queen's Hotel as the joint second-best hotel in the city and was renowned for its turtle soup. The *Liverpool Guide* states that it was fashionable and frequented by Americans. The hotel became the temporary home of some of James Carlin's postwar ex-Confederate colleagues.[3] With the "Commodore" still making frequent trips to the Confederate states, Ella may have been content to stay there for her first months in England. They soon moved up the coast of the Irish Sea from Liverpool to the village of Waterloo, just north of Bootle.[4]

Carlin left no explanation for his return to England, bringing his family to a cold and unfamiliar land. Charleston was besieged and its citizens in danger. Those who could left. Was he merely obeying instructions to go to Europe to aid the Confederacy by using his skills to source and oversee the construction of specialist blockade-runners? Was he leaving America because the Union forces, especially the United States Navy, were out for revenge for his audacious attack on the *New Ironsides*? Did he sense that it was time to go, that the Confederacy was a doomed cause that had run its course? Charleston was closely besieged and subjected to frequent shelling; that was reason enough.

Doubtless there would be commercial opportunities in England, too. As soon as he settled his business in Dumbarton, Carlin headed for Port Muck in County Antrim where his father, the elderly Coast Guard, was living. He must have been anxious to show off his wife and small sons to family and friends. He would also have wanted to thank his father for his prompt and effective action to secure his release from Fort Lafayette.

His subsequent activities, especially his share in the *Imogene*, suggest that he had decided that the real money was being made by the owners of the ships that ran the blockade rather than the captains who faced the existential hazards. The time had come to risk his funds rather than his life.

Carlin was actively managing the movements of the I&E Company "fleet" from Liverpool and during his trips to Nassau and the Confederacy. On 30 July 1864 he wrote to Bee from the Queens Hotel, Liverpool:

My Dear Sir,

I trust ere this reaching you the S.S. Ella will have arrived in safety on your side of the Atlantic. I wish you would examine the ship and give your attention to the general outfit & condition of the ship and workmanship as if there is any serious wrong I would like please to know it at once.—cargo may not weight them down enough to be in the best running trim which should never be less leaving port than 6ft 10 better to be always about 7ft 2 if possible & on an even keel.

The large ship I hope will yet get ahead of time, this vessel will carry several tons of freight from here and I hope you will receive this in time to order whatever you want brought over. If you have any orders please send it in duplicate by Bermuda & Nassau. Am I right in understanding the name of the ship to be Fannie? I will mention on this that it is what I read in yours.

With many prayers for a peace at an early day,

I remain yours very Truly J. Carlin.[5]

This letter reveals for the first time something of James Carlin's attitude towards the war. His apparently heartfelt prayers "for peace at an early day" are the only suggestion that he saw that the cause was lost and that it was time to call a halt to hostilities. His recent visit to the Confederacy may well have shocked him, and the Atlantic voyage would have given him time to reflect on the tales of defeat, misery, and human loss coming from the recent participants in the great battles.

On 25 August 1864 he wrote to William Bee and C. T. Mitchell from Liverpool:

Gentlemen,

I have the honour to acknowledge your letter of July 4th expressing your disapproval of the appointment of Captain Barckley to the command of our Co's ships. I regret to inform you that the letter alluded to did not reach me in time to act according to the wishes there in expressed.

The first ship (Ella) has therefore been dispatched under the command of Capt. C Barckley. Even if your note had reached me in time to displace Capt Barckley I would have been obliged to give command to some one more a stranger to you & the work to be done than Barckley is, hoping the ship may arrive safe and that you may have the opportunity of disposing [unreadable] you soon after the completion of my duties here when all further explanations will be made forthwith.

I am Gentlemen yours very respectfully James Carlin

P.S the Caroline will take out 20 to 30 tonnes freight at £30 sterling per ton in advance which I hope may be to your satisfaction. It is proper to state that the ship (C) will be due at Bermuda on the 1st October or thereabouts. J. C.[6]

In common with other Liverpool Confederate captains, Carlin kept a list of the "good men on pay here for our ships. Many of our people here have ships and are offering any money for good <u>Engineers</u> and <u>Officers (Southerners)</u> men that understand this business and are trusty."[7]

At this point Carlin avoided running the inshore blockade himself and concentrated on the organization of his small fleet and the selection of efficient captains. The autumn of 1864 was to be a testing time as a yellow fever epidemic caused many deaths in Nassau and Bermuda, leading to a shortage of crewmen and a twenty-one-day quarantine was imposed on vessels entering Wilmington and Charleston. On two occasions the ship's agent Thomas E. Taylor was held in quarantine in Wilmington for fifty days, and his ship lost seven crew members to yellow fever. Numerous runners suffered the same frustrating delays.[8]

The I&E Company's accounts with James M. Calder for 19 November 1864 show Carlin receiving payment for wages in pounds sterling. The actual amount is not shown. Ships named include the *Caroline, Emily, Alice, Fannie,* and *Ella.* In the same month Egan took the *Emily* on its maiden voyage across the Atlantic to Nassau.[9]

SS *Ella* in St. George's Harbor, Bermuda.
©National Maritime Museum, Greenwich, London.

By 24 November the *Ella* had successfully run the blockade four times, and the *Caroline* had run through twice.[10] On 3 December the U.S. gunboat *Pequot* sighted the *Ella* off the coast of North Carolina while trying to make its fifth run into Wilmington. The *Pequot* gave chase, following the *Ella* for some sixty miles before losing it off Cape Fear.

Augustus Hobart-Hampden recalled that the Union blockaders formed a protective new moon-shaped semicircle off the entrance to Cape Fear River that the runners tried to "turn" by creeping past the "horns" at the ends. But the Union navy soon grew wise to this and stationed an anchored vessel close inshore at each extremity to fire signal rockets if a runner attempted to get by inshore. Illuminated and thus exposed to the fleet, the runner would be doomed to gunfire or the shallows. Numerous vessels ended up burnt out on the sands.

Just before sunrise the *Ella* was spotted by the USS *Emma,* which changed course to intersect it and opened fire. The *Ella* put its helm hard over for a dash inshore along the surf line but went hard aground off Bald Head Island at the foot of Cape Fear. The *Ella* had nearly made it around the corner into the safety of the mouth of the Cape Fear River and the protection of the big guns of the Confederate batteries at Fort Fisher. It was stranded in the shallows and battered by Union shells. Boarding parties from the Union warships tried to reach it but were forced away by Confederate counterfire, while those on shore rushed to salvage some of the cargo. Finally, a small boarding party from the USS *Emma* managed to get aboard the *Ella* and finish its destruction by placing a 24-pound howitzer shell next to its engine.[11]

The ship had been en route from Nassau with a cargo of gin, coffee, military goods, arms, and ammunition. E. Lee Spence notes that part of its cargo was a large quantity of 5½-inch rifled shells.[12] One hundred years later the remains were explored by a team of divers and archeologists, including the irrepressible Charles Peery of Charleston, South Carolina. One of the salvaged gin bottles now rests on the bookshelf above this author's desk. Sadly, it is empty. The *Ella* had paid for itself in its four runs as the cotton on two trips had already earned the Bee Company £54,000, and four cargoes must have covered its construction cost of £22,000 plus its operating overheads.

Carlin dispatched the *Caroline,* under the command of Captain Thomas B. Skinner on 17 September 1864. It was headed for St. George's, Bermuda, via Halifax, Nova Scotia. Its October manifest shows that it changed masters in Bermuda, and Captain L. M. Hudgins took the ship to Nassau, arriving on about 8 November with a mixed cargo of merchandise: brandy and whiskey, hardware, and bundles of sheet iron, casks of copper bolts, tin ingots, pig lead, spelter (zinc alloy), zinc sheet, lead, and one hundred bundles of iron ties (brackets).[13]

This cargo illustrates the sort of shortages that occurred in an essentially rural economy. Some items were transshipped at Nassau. George A. Trenholm, then Confederate secretary of the navy, recorded that a somewhat different cargo actually arrived in Wilmington. The alcohol stayed in Nassau, while the metal items eventually reached Wilmington on 2 December for government consignees, including direct supply orders for the army and navy.

The *Caroline* was back in Nassau by the end of December with 415 bales of upland cotton for the South Carolina Railroad Company worth $437,434 and barrels of rosin. Hudgins set out for Charleston again at the beginning of February 1865 but was unable to find a way through the Union fleet and was back in Nassau by the seventh. The agent Henry Adderley charged the I&E Company some £5,000 for disbursements for this failed run. Huggins took the vessel to Havana in ballast in February 1865, expecting to find a cargo for the Confederacy. He failed to reach Galveston and returned to England in March.[14]

In early July the *Fannie* arrived in Greenock on the Clyde for refitting. It returned to Nassau on 20 February 1865 in the dying days of the Confederacy. Charleston and Wilmington had been closed by occupying Union troops, so the *Fannie,* still commanded by Captain Dunning, left for Liverpool on 5 April. Skelton reports that Calder sold the *Fannie* and the *Alice* in August 1865 for £26,662 and one shilling.

The *Emily* left the Clyde in late November 1864 under the command of Captain Egan. It carried a mixed freight including two small marine engines for the Navy Department. It stopped at Cardiff, presumably to recoal, and made a quick twenty-three-day passage to St. Thomas before continuing to Nassau. Because of its deep draft, there was no question of the *Emily* trying to get into Galveston, and it was back in Liverpool by 25 April 1865.[15]

The Bee Company's investment in Carlin's new ships had just about paid off. Some valuable cargoes were delivered safely, but they were just a month or so too late to make really big financial returns.

Chapter 26

# The Last of the Cotton, April–May 1865

· · ·

As the war was winding down, Carlin worked the fleet of the I&E Company until the last moment. He even ran the blockade into Galveston, Texas, a couple of times from Havana, but the end was clear. His final run was to Galveston, in the *Imogene,* in the company of his old associate and trusted captain Charles Barkley.

A seaman named A. J. Forrest wrote a letter that offers a vivid glimpse of the voyage of the *Imogene* at the moment the Confederacy reached its end:

The Steamship Imogene arrived at Nassau about the middle of March 1865 after the capture of Wilmington by the yanks. She was a new boat and came direct from her builders in Glasgow. I was then first engineer in the Susan Beirne Mr S. [James Sprunt] being purser and about 19 yrs old. I joined the Imogene, Captain James Carlin (who is half owner) in April 1865 in the same capacity as in the B. We sailed from N[assau] on the 10th with a cargo of machinery for the Confederacy at Galveston. I had a very fine voyage, seeing none of the enemy ships and arrived at G[alveston] in good shape on the 16th. Where we took on a load of cotton and several ladies as passengers. On May 3 we sailed from G on a very dark night passing through the blockading fleet (one of which was the USS Fort Jackson that captured me on the *Wando*) in safety and made a fine run to Matanzas, Cuba where we arrived on the 7th took on some stores and ice and sailed for Nassau on the 8th with the last cargo of cotton from the Confederate States of America and discharged our deck load and sailed for Bermuda on the 14th making a fine run and arrived there on the 18th. Took on coal and supplies and sailed on the 23rd for the Azores where we arrived at Terceira, on the 1st of June. We found it to be a delightful and beautiful place. I took a ride over the island with the Chf. Engs. and his wife and was sorry when we had to leave it. After taking on coal and stores we sailed for Liverpool on the 3 [June] arriving there on the 10 June after a very smooth passage all the way across the Atlantic and left the ship in the Canada Dock on the 14 to take board ashore all being sorry at losing a good job. Write soon Love to you all Father.[1]

This expedition was to be the subject of a court action in London that illustrates the financial disintegration of the Confederacy in its last few weeks as the besieged capital of Richmond was overrun in the beginning of April 1865. Everyone was scrambling to save what they could from the wreckage.

When the Union forces occupied the Atlantic ports, blockade-running moved to Mobile, Alabama. In August 1864, when the sea approaches to that city were captured by Union forces, Confederate efforts moved on to Galveston and Corpus Christi near the Mexican border. Galveston was an important Gulf port and was the largest city in Texas in 1861, but when the *Imogene* arrived, the port was closely blockaded and fast running out of basic supplies. The city and its citizens were in turmoil. On 7 February the Union navy had captured two schooners, the *Annie Sophia* and the *Pet*, which had run into the harbor with 476 bales of cotton. However, they had failed to reach the steamer *Wren*, sheltering under the protection of the guns of Fort Point Battery. The *Will-o-the-Wisp* was shelled and then set afire while stranded off Galveston three days later.[2]

While the *Imogene* was not the last vessel to leave the Confederacy, it was the last blockade-runner to arrive in Nassau with a cargo of cotton.[3] Stephen Wise confirms that the *Imogene* was the third-last vessel to make the run into Galveston from Havana, arriving in Texas on 16 April.[4] The *Imogene* reported that nine vessels were loading cotton when it was there and that entering and leaving the port was easy.[5]

If the *Imogene* left Texas on 3 May, as Forrest stated, then only the *Wren* and the *Lark*, departing on 13 and 24 May, cleared Havana customs after the *Imogene*. The *Lark* had been rushed and looted by desperate local townsfolk on its arrival on 24 May and was lucky to get away the same day with only the crew of the crippled *Denbigh* on board. This steam runner had been boarded and burned by the U.S. Navy on that same fearsome day. Lairds in Liverpool had built the *Lark* and *Wren* for Fraser, Trenholm and Company, which had sold them to the Confederate government; both survived the war, as did the *Imogene*.

These events and the subsequent court action back in England should be seen against the background of the ongoing collapse of the Confederacy and its final days in the Western States. As the *Daily News* of London reported on 25 April 1865:

> The treasury is broken up, and, in fact had abandoned its functions before the fall of Richmond. It had no funds, no credits, and no means of collecting taxes. A forced loan had been made just before the evacuation by which two or three millions of dollars in specie were extracted from the Richmond banks, but this was not more than enough to ensure a safe retreat for the revolutionary leaders in foreign countries.

Confederate bonds were now left in Richmond in great bundles, and are now sold, I may mention for the comfort of English creditors of the concern, in the street, by the boys, at 5c the dozen, with a very feeble demand.

And it is to this more than aught else that Davis owes his downfall, for it is this which has left his storehouse empty. He himself and his colleagues, the Benjamins, Trenholms, Brekenridges, are probably at this moment occupied rather with the task of providing for their own safety than with public affairs.

Confederate president Jefferson Davis left Richmond late on 2 April and officially dissolved his government at a cabinet meeting in Washington, Georgia, on 5 May. Confederate forces on the Mississippi had surrendered on the fourth, which brought to an end plans to renew the fight from the Confederate controlled Trans-Mississippi. General Maury surrendered the Gulf forces the next day. There had been plans to form a government in exile in Havana or escape to Europe, but these came to nothing. Union troops captured Davis on 10 May.

By the time the *Imogene* left Galveston, the Confederacy was finished. The deals and contracts Carlin made in Galveston on 20 April would have been conducted in the knowledge that times were desperate, the Confederate government was no more, and Confederate financial documents and notes were probably worthless. U.S. Consul Dudley in Liverpool commented that the Southern merchants and their European supporters and financiers retained a naive and unrealistic expectation that the Union government would honor Southern bonds and cotton loans if the Confederacy were defeated.

Carlin was on board the *Imogene* as both captain and supercargo. Charles J. Barkley was to act as master for the passage to Havana as he was probably more familiar with the Galveston run than Carlin.

On 20 April 1865 Henry Samson, acting as Confederate States treasury agent for foreign supply, agreed with Carlin that 250 bales of cotton that Carlin had just "delivered" or sold to Samson in Galveston should be loaded onto the *Imogene* for delivery to the Confederate agent Charles Helm in Havana. He was to transship the cotton to Fraser, Trenholm and Company in Liverpool. The five bills of lading were signed by Charles Barkley and handed to Samson by Carlin as supercargo on 28 April 1865. Carlin, with his associate Peter Denny of Dumbarton, had a personal interest in the rest of the cargo. The function of a supercargo was to act for the cargo owners and protect their interests.

Carlin waited for a dark night to take the *Imogene* out, so he left Galveston on 2 May. The ship was sighted and recognized by a Union warship off Havana. Later, newspapers reported that a steamer, thought to be the *Imogene,* was sighted off Castillo de Morro, Havana, on 7 May. When the Union ship signaled the *Imogene,* it took off to the north under all steam with the English ensign at its peak and the rebel flag at its fore. The *Imogene* avoided capture and diverted to Matanzas, Cuba, arriving on 9 May. Here it dropped off twelve passengers, including Zack Davies, the Galveston pilot. Having picked up a Nassau pilot, the ship left on 11 May bound for Nassau. It then called in at St. George's, Bermuda, before crossing the Atlantic, arriving in Liverpool on 12 June. The blockade was lifted by proclamation on 13 June 1865 by President Andrew Johnson, Lincoln's successor.[6]

At £40 a bale, the consignment was worth some £10,000, or about £800,000, using today's UK commodity price comparison figures. It comes as no surprise that an involved lawsuit soon followed concerning the failure to deliver the cotton to Helm in Havana as contracted in Galveston. The actual ownership of this consignment was also disputed. After the failure to deliver in Havana, Trenholm claimed that the cargo should have been handed over to them on arrival in Liverpool.

When the *Imogene* arrived in Liverpool with 1,000 cotton bales, Fraser, Trenholm and Company demanded delivery of 250 bales on 13 May. Carlin and his associates refused to part with a quarter of the precious cotton. Trenholm immediately brought a bill of complaint seeking an injunction against the *Imogene's* owners to prevent them from disposing of the cargo and declaring that no one other than the claimants had an interest in the cargo.

The action was brought by the plaintiffs Charles Kuhn Prioleau, William Lee Trenholm, Theodore Dehon Wagner, and James Thomas Welsman, trading as Fraser, Trenholm and Company in Liverpool, Charles J. Helm in Havana, and Henry Samson in Galveston, all by then United States citizens again. Vice Chancellor Woods heard the application in the Chancery Court in London on 14 June 1865. The defendants were James Carlin, Charles J. Barkley, Charles Galbreith, and Peter Denny.[7]

The plaintiffs requested an injunction stopping the 250 bales of cotton from being disposed of other than to Fraser, Trenholm and Company or their assignees and that it had to be delivered as agreed and must not leave the Port of Liverpool.

The court responded with an order for the defendants to enter an appearance in the High Court of Chancery in Westminster, London, within eight days. As there appears to have been no further legal outcome, we must conclude that Carlin and the others complied with the court order and delivered the cotton as agreed or compensated Trenholm and Company, or that the order was withdrawn before the hearing in London after a settlement between the parties. Trenholm and Company were involved in at least four other cases in chancery in 1865.

The case remains unclear. If the delivery of the cotton to Samson in Galveston was a ruse to circumvent Confederate government rules preventing private cotton exports and the final ownership of the cotton remained the property of Carlin and his associates, they were within their rights to withhold delivery to Trenholm in Liverpool. If they had received a Confederate bill of exchange in return for the cotton in Galveston, then the cotton belonged to the defunct Confederate government that Samson represented and should probably have been delivered to Trenholm as consigned. It is unlikely that Carlin would have accepted valueless Confederate paper in Galveston in payment for a highly valuable consignment.

It may well be that Trenholm was trying to take advantage of the "ghost" ownership evidenced by the shipping documents produced by Samson. It appears as a "try on" motivated by Trenholm's perilous financial position. Carlin and the others appear to have owned the cotton Carlin delivered to Samson in Galveston and were merely retaining their own property once they arrived in Britain. By the end of the war, these dealings had become so involved that it seems impossible to unravel them today. Somehow they were all trying to salvage what they could in desperate times.

# Chapter 27

# Financial Matters, 1864–1866

. . .

Trenholm and Company was declared bankrupt in England on 16 November 1867.[1] Trenholm's partnership with Welsman and Wagner was dissolved on 13 March 1868.[2] In contrast, the I&E Company, run by William Bee, paid a substantial dividend in January 1865 of £50 per share plus $2,000 in Confederate currency. In December a further dividend of £70 was paid, amounting to £110 sterling per $1,000 share, plus $2,000 in Confederate currency. Skelton calculates that the eventual return on the original capital exceeded 200 percent.[3] Paper currency depreciation and rampant inflation in the South between 1862 and 1865 substantially reduced the real value of the investment.

James Carlin's dealing with William Bee and I&E Company were to be more profitable than his final dealings with Trenholm. Lynda Skelton estimates that the I&E Company carried a maximum of twenty-five thousand bales of cotton through the blockade during the course of the war at gross profits on cotton (excluding transport and other costs) of up to 400 percent.[4] However, costs were high, and only a portion of the cotton transported was on the company's own account, much of the rest being on the government's books.

Skelton records that the shareholders received four dividends between December 1863 and December 1865, each larger than the initial purchase price of $1,000 per share. The first dividend was in Confederates States of America dollars at $5,000 per share. The second in August 1864 was $2,000, half of which was paid in Confederate 8 percent bonds and the other half in "4 percent Confederates Certificate at par." In January 1865 the shareholders received $3,000 plus £50 sterling. In December 1865 they received £70 sterling. These seem like high dollar values, but currency exchange charges and high inflation in turbulent times reduced the actual return. Acting for the I&E Company, James Calder issued drafts drawn on Liverpool for interest due to shareholders to 31 December 1866. Ella Carlin received £50, as did James Waddell.[5]

Carlin held on to his shares in the I&E Company and to his property in Charleston, implying that he did not foresee how the endgame would play out until it was too late to sell at acceptable prices. His risky trip to Galveston may have been his last chance to convert his Confederate dollars and bonds into tangible assets and run them out to England as baled cotton. Confederate currency could only be exchanged in Europe at extortionate rates, and the Southern treasury was always hard pressed for foreign exchange.

A Carlin family tradition says that James and Ella lost everything with the collapse of Confederate bonds, and they certainly lost a substantial portion of their funds. The Richmond government's Currency Reduction Act of 17 February 1864 had forced President Bee of the I&E Company to buy nearly $500,000 worth of government 4 percent securities. With other government stock, the company then owned over $1 million of Confederate bonds. Skelton records that at the end of operations, its debt with Carlin was partially paid by 10,000 8 percent and 11,5000 4 percent Confederate bonds, plus another 50,000 4 percent bonds in the Charleston Importing Company and 2,500 stock in Kalmia Mills in Aiken County SC.[6] Carlin signed William Bee's receipt on 2 December 1865, showing that he quickly returned to Charleston after the end of the war. The bonds became worthless, and the shares in the Charleston Importing Company fared little better as the dividends were paid in Confederate currency.

While in January 1863 three Confederate dollars would have bought one dollar in gold, by January 1865 it took sixty Confederate dollars. Carlin's Confederate bond holding had amounted to at least $75,000 in bonds or 1,250 gold dollars. The Bee Company suffered severe losses from looting following the Union occupation of Wilmington and Charleston. The U.S. Treasury Department took quick action against the Charleston blockade-running companies, which were subject to Federal confiscations. Their chairman, Theodore D. Jervey, was jailed for two months.

I&E Company lawyers then filed an audacious claim against the United States for the property that been confiscated or taken without payment. These actions should be seen against the background of a series of refusals on the part of company directors and some Southern banks to cooperate with the Federal treasury agents. Their stand eventually paid off. Bee Company records for 1866 show that they retrieved two bags of gold containing $2 and $20 coins totaling $9,000 from the local Peoples Bank. In 1868 the United States dropped its claim against the company and Jervey. All the shipping operations had ceased, and the *Emily* and *Caroline* were sold for £15,000. Funds still in Liverpool amounting to £21,928 were used to pay two more dividends in 1874 and 1876—the final payouts from what had been in the exceptional circumstances a successful financial performance, although their activities had sustained the Confederacy for four long years.[7]

In an affidavit to Union government officials of 17 January 1866, William Bee stated that "it was a popular error that large profits were realized by the stockholders from the operations of the Company. When in fact, had the original subscription been retained in England it would, with accumulated interest upon investment, have yielded a larger return than has been derived from its employment in this enterprise." But Benjamin Mordecai, the company's cotton buyer, declared that the Bee Company was believed to have been the most successful company organized during the war.[8] Bee appeared to be dissembling in the face of postwar sentiment.

Marcus Price comments that three of the seven blockade-running enterprises incorporated by the South Carolina government—the Bee, the Chicora, and the Charleston Companies—managed to pay their stockholders dividends amounting to more than the par value held by them in shares. He emphasizes that, when estimating the profits realized by the stockholders, the real value of their original purchase, if paid for in treasury notes, had continued to devalue. Thus the stockholder had to receive a substantially greater return to make a real profit on their original investment.[9]

The I&E Company made money for its original investors, but at the end of the day, the captains of the blockade-runners, starting from modest merchant marine salaries, seem to have come out with the greatest relative gains.

# Chapter 28

# Life in England, June 1865–1871

. . .

Carlin arrived back in England in June 1865 knowing that General Robert E. Lee had surrendered at Appomattox Court House on 9 April. The South had lost, and the Southern economy had collapsed. Many Southern plantations were burned to the ground, and the fields lay uncultivated. Liberated ex-slaves scratched an existence alongside their previous masters in a ruined land or shuffled along country roads to the cities to form forlorn groups begging on the sidewalks. The fall of Galveston on 2 June put an end to any further blockade-running, and President Johnson formally ended the blockade of the Southern coast on 23 June 1865. Charleston had been looted by the occupying Union soldiers and their officers, and sections of the city were reduced to rubble.

In 1865 numerous ex-runners and Confederate naval officers washed up in Liverpool, where they found themselves exiles in a foreign and unsympathetic country. Back home carpetbaggers were busy taking revenge on the Old South, stripping it of privilege and wealth. Reconstruction was under way, and Northerners were determined to reward themselves for what they saw as their travails in the war they had just won.

Carlin still had money to spare and assets in the South. He was determined to get back to business. While there were those who proved keen to part him from his money, he seems to have met no opposition upon his return to New York, Charleston, or Louisiana.

His first task was to sell off his little fleet comprising the *Ella, Caroline,* and *Imogene,* as well as other vessels for which he was a titular owner on behalf of the Bee Company. This required the unraveling of cross-party shareholding arrangements. The shipping market was swamped with ex-blockaders, and shipbuilders still had unfinished vessels in their yards. It was almost impossible to sell all of the shallow-draft vessels that thronged the harbors of the Caribbean and Cuba. To add to their troubles, the Federal navy was disposing of the ex-blockade runners it had captured and pressed into service as makeshift warships.

To keep their property safe from expropriation by the United States government, Southern owners sent their steamers to Rio de Janeiro or back to Britain hoping to find a coastal market for their specialist craft. Prices halved and the ships in Carlin's charge were eventually sold for £15,000 each to a consortium comprising Peter Denny, James Galbreith, J. N. Beach, and Thomas S. Begbie, who had hoped to find a market in Brazil. Some of these ships eventually played a part in rebellions against Spanish colonial rule in Chile.[1]

By the end of the war, Ella Rosa and sons James, William, and Samuel and baby daughter Ella were safe in Waterloo, Liverpool, before moving to a house in St. Domingo Vale nearer the center of Liverpool. Between April 1868 and June 1874, the Carlins rented a series of houses in Everton, then a newly built suburb of Liverpool, where four more children were born.

It is a curiosity that from about 1871, Carlin or someone in his household added "RN" to his name in listings in commercial directories and other records. The normal use of "RN" is to indicate service in the British Royal Navy. There is no record of Carlin ever having served in the navy. The "RN" may have been added by someone in his household to show that the Carlin was not a mere merchant captain but had served on the books of the Confederate States Navy.

It is doubtful that Ella Rosa found Liverpool meeting the expectations of England she would have acquired in prewar Charleston and Southern plantation society, which had held a romantic view of Britain. In his book on wartime Charleston, Theodore Jervey described the city and its environs as "English to the core. Not only Charleston, but that great suburb which stretched from above Georgetown to the Savannah River along the rice plantations of the coast, a hundred miles and more, was English in sentiment, pronunciation, and prejudice. For three decades prior to the war the crowning aspiration of the region had been for direct trade with Europe."[2]

Although Liverpool was then a large bustling city, it was a far cry from the England of country estates and fine houses that the Southern gentry had tried to replicate in Virginia, the Carolinas, and Georgia. Ella Rose would never return to America. It was to be ten years before she would enjoy something of the lifestyle of which she may have dreamed.

Chapter 29

# Charleston and Florida
# Ventures, 1865–1869

. . .

Columbia's sewing machine. Mrs. Britannia: "Ah my dear Columbia, it's all
very well, but I am afraid you'll find it difficult to join that neatly."
*Punch*, 1 October 1864. Courtesy of Bristol Record Office.

With the exception of one more act of audacious gun running, the rest of
James Carlin's life is only glimpsed infrequently in passenger lists and local
newspapers. He had business to attend to in Charleston and his brother to visit in
Florida. He is found traveling up and down the Atlantic Coast in the company of
figures from his blockade-running days and renewing old acquaintanceships along

the coast. We can infer from these connections that he set about joining in the Reconstruction efforts then taking place throughout the South. He was soon in the company of carpetbaggers, expansionist politicians, and filibusters in Northern Florida. These soldiers of fortune had participated in prewar attempts to expand American interests in the Caribbean and Central America by invading and trying to take over whole nations.

His life became highly mobile with frequent shifts of scene and numerous transatlantic crossings.[1] His pattern was to return to his wife and family in Britain for a few months each year—just long enough to sign the birth certificate of the latest infant. On these documents, Carlin would be described variously as commission agent, merchant, master mariner, ship owner, gentleman, and even cotton planter. This was to be his life through to his mysterious disappearance from his family in London in 1881. Old Carlin aunts said he left Ella Rosa in London for another woman in the United States. If so, she has not emerged.

In Liverpool he associated with the ex-Confederate naval officers who had commanded the commerce raiders that had done so much damage to United States shipping. James I. Waddell, the captain of the raider CSS *Shenandoah*, had steamed into Liverpool to surrender his vessel to the British authorities. Waddell, John Newland Maffitt, and others had to make new careers to carry them through until attitudes eased at home and they were able to benefit from the various amnesties and pardons Washington eventually put through Congress. While the merchant captains who ran through the blockade soon found employment, this was more difficult for the naval officers who lacked formal British Board of Trade master's or mate's certificates of competency. James Bulloch, the head of the Confederate Secret Service in Europe, stayed in England and took to commerce. Maffitt qualified as a British ship's master, and gained command of the British steamer *Widgeon* on the South America run. The Brazilian government then charted the *Widgeon* as a transport on the Parana River in support of the triple alliance of Brazil, Argentina, and Uruguay in a vicious war against Paraguay. Maffitt had an uncomfortable year on the fever- and smallpox-ridden river. James Carlin turned to business.

Carlin looked across the Atlantic and saw a host of opportunities. It was time to start using the money he had accumulated, and he was soon in Charleston. The house on Church Street had to be secured, and there were accounts to clear up with William Bee and his associates. On 7 November 1865 he registered a copartnership in Charleston with Henry T. Thompson and his brother John M. Thompson, who under the name of Thompson Brothers traded in the wholesale grocery and general commission business. Carlin was to be the special partner and contributed $10,000 in gold to the common stock. This partnership was dissolved in November 1867, although the enterprise continued under Henry Thompson.[2]

Carlin joined his ex-colleagues John W. Sly, John Eagan, Charles Barkley, and John Ferguson in applying to the General Assembly of South Carolina for an act to form the Charleston Dredging and Wharf Building Company with an authorized stock capital of $25,000. This act was passed by both the state senate and house of representatives on 21 December 1865.[3] There appears to have been a falling out between the company and its founders, as by 25 November 1867 Carlin and others, as creditors, sued the company in the Admiralty Court in Charleston, receiving $900 in compensation plus costs. The company was again sued in 1868, suggesting that it was still operating until at least that time.[4] Carlin was also a signatory of a petition from Pickens County, South Carolina, for an additional magistrate.[5]

In addition to these ventures, Carlin had the twenty-five thousand shares in Kalmia Mills he had received from the Bee Company in 1864. The mill was one of thirty in Aiken County, South Carolina, on the border with Georgia. During the war the company purchased more land for expansion and ordered machinery from England for large-scale production of paper, cotton yarn, and cloth. The machinery had been brought over from England by one of the Bee Company vessels but had been held up in Nassau because of the "events of the war."[6]

By 1867, when Kalmia Mills was put up for auction, it was an ambitious project on some 4,000 acres with 78 workers' cottages, a dam, and a saw mill, and it had nearly completed the installation of 320 looms, 10,000 spindles, and other equipment of the latest English design, a paper mill, and 2 "wheel turbines." But the shareholders had overreached their finances, and their mortgage was called in. The land and machinery were auctioned on 23 April 1867.[7]

Carlin had not forgotten his adventures delivering the *Gladiator*'s cargo to the St. Johns and Indian River systems south of Jacksonville. Nor had he missed its obvious potential for development. East Florida is bordered with elongated lagoons running parallel to the coast and protected from the open sea by barrier islands of sand dunes fringed with palm trees. These lagoons allow marine traffic to avoid the uncertainties of the open Atlantic. They now form an important part of the Intracoastal Waterway running up the Atlantic seaboard of the United States from Key West to Norfolk, Virginia.

However, it was a desolate, insect-plagued wilderness in the decades after the end of the Civil War. The remains of Indian gardens could be seen amid the huge oyster-shell middens that lined part of their banks, and there were traces of the old plantations abandoned during the Seminole Indian wars. According to one description, "Wild orange trees grew on the hummocks. The river teemed with marine life while deer, bear and other game abounded."[8] The area grew oranges to equal the best from Havana and already had regular steamer connections to Jacksonville and the North. But the mosquitoes were ferocious.

Carlin soon established new contacts on the Indian and St. Johns Rivers. Later events show that Carlin had sought out his brother Charles, who had been bought out of the British Royal Navy in 1864 and had returned to America. The family of Charles's wife-to-be, Mary Moorer Joyner, had sold their plantation in Goose

Green Creek near Charleston and moved south to new lands in Florida in the company of other South Carolinians who had found it impossible to work their ruined plantations without slave labor.

John W. Joyner, Charles's brother-in-law, had settled in Sand Point, a tiny mosquito-ridden settlement at the head of navigation on the Indian River, which came to be known as Joynerville. Charles later opened a boat-building yard, and his wife bought property in what became the center of the town. This pioneer community centered on a saloon and trading store operated in 1867 by Joyner and Colonel Henry T. Titus, a huge, swaggering man who combined something of "Colonel Blimp" with the size and character of Falstaff.

Titus presented himself as a soldier of fortune and spun many tales of his "filibustering"—daring, private attempts to expand the United State's influence in Central America and the Caribbean But he had played an inglorious role in Narciso López's 1850 expedition to Cuba that was brutally crushed by the Spanish. Titus and other filibusters had to flee the US Coast Guard on board a vessel loaded with munitions en-route to Cuba.[9] These raids were organized from Jacksonville, where the main hotel acted as the filibuster headquarters. There was a strong Masonic connection that underlay much of the Cuban liberation movement. These attempts caused great excitement in the South, and battalions were also raised in New Orleans and Savannah. Their model was the successful Texas Republic that had expelled the Mexicans from huge swaths of the old Spanish Southwest.[10]

Prewar supporters had believed that an American takeover of Cuba would strengthen the South in its growing arguments with the Northern states over slavery and trade matters.[11] The flamboyant colonel later participated on the proslavery side in the disastrous affrays in the "Bloody Kansas" border wars of the late 1850s. Titus then commanded troops in Nicaragua for the arch-filibuster General William Walker, who had to sack him for incompetence. Titus had also been a blockade-runner on the Indian River until captured by Federal troops.[12] The settlement of Joynerville eventually became Titusville, the county seat of Brevard County, in 1873. Titus was a controversial figure, but he can be credited with laying out a spacious and attractive township in this stretch of wilderness.

Colonel Titus's wife, Mary, was the oldest daughter of General Edward Hopkins. The general had been a Confederate brigade commander during the Civil War and owned a plantation on the St. Johns River in 1867. He was a well-known figure in Jacksonville and had been mayor twice and had run for governor.[13] In 1851 his aide-de-camp in the Jacksonville militia had been a member of the committee formed to support the establishment of a Cuban republic. Edward Hopkins was president of the St. Johns and Indian River Railroad in 1878. This linked the Jacksonville–Tampa line from Lake Monroe to Titusville. It was completed in December 1885 to the joy of the local residents, who had raised $30,000 by subscription for the project. Hopkins was collector of customs for St. Johns upon his death in 1887.

William Henry Gleason.
Courtesy of State Archives of Florida.

The late Captain Carlin White of Jupiter said that his grandfather Charles Carlin and his great-uncle James Carlin did survey work for these local railway projects. He said that they also had dealings with the politician William H. Gleason and his wife, Sarah G. Gleason. Both were prominent figures in the region.

Gleason was an engineer and surveyor from New York, who had established himself in Wisconsin and later Washington. At the end of the Civil War, he moved to Florida and was appointed by the Freedmen's Bureau to make a topographical and agricultural survey of the Florida peninsula to assess its suitability for "Negro colonization." Although he recommended against these settlements, he was so impressed with the business potential that he brought his family to settle in Fort Dallas, now Miami, in Dade country. Using contacts made during his trip, he engaged in state politics and was elected lieutenant governor on the Republican ticket. Carlin would also have encountered William Hunt, the Gleasons' business partner in land deals. Hunt was by then superintendent of Charles Carlin's employer, the Life Boat Service.

Gleason was a keen expansionist, pressing for America to take control of not only Cuba but the British Bahamas as well. He was a close personal friend of the filibuster General Walker prior to the general's death by firing squad in Nicaragua. He believed that if Walker had succeeded in taking over Nicaragua, the country would have been annexed by the United States, and prosperity would have followed. Gleason tried to push through a series of canals and cuts to link the St. John and Indian Rivers with Biscayne Bay south of Miami, in effect creating the Intracoastal Waterway between Fernandina and Key West. But he overstepped himself in trying to oust Governor Harrison Reed of Florida by occupying his office while Reed was away. Reed's aide expelled him at gunpoint. Gleason would also try his hand at canning and exporting Indian River produce, but his scheme soon failed.

After his first postwar visit, Carlin was keen to be involved in business in this remote area. He returned to England on the SS *City of Baltimore,* arriving in Liverpool via Queenstown, Ireland, on 1 February 1866. By October he had formed a group of investors to promote a concession trading firm as the Florida Provision Company. The main partner was Captain Edward Tattnall Paine, then in Waterloo, Liverpool, but previously an antebellum cotton factor and rice planter of Charleston. The other shareholders were William Hasseltine and Colin Mackenzie, also of Waterloo, and Ann Sellman Iglehart Waddell, the wife of Captain James Waddell, both of whom were then in Liverpool.[14]

The Carlin house in Jupiter, Florida, in the 1900s.
Courtesy of the Loxahatchee River Historical Society.

The authorized capital was £5,000. Carlin and Paine held the majority of the shares and Paine was to be their agent in Florida. The company was to process and can fish, oysters, meats, fruits, and vegetables. The plan was for Paine to go to Florida and set about purchasing locations, machinery, boats, and nets and set up the operation.

By 31 May 1867 the shareholders were dissatisfied with the way Paine was handling their affairs and revoked his appointment, authorizing Francis C. Sollee in his place and giving him full powers to act on their behalf. Sollee's wife, Rebecca Louise, was another daughter of General Hopkins and thus the sister of Mary Evalina Titus.

Sollee had served as a quartermaster in the Georgia military during the Civil War, earning some fame for mounting an 8-inch cannon on a railway flatbed wagon in the defense of Jacksonville.[15] Acting on behalf of the Florida Provision Company, he sold two hundred acres of land in the center of Sand Point to Mary Titus in June 1868. This supports another report that the company owned much of the land on Sand Point, which became Titusville.[16] Charles Carlin and his wife also came to own a substantial plot in the center of the settlement at about this time. Sollee was a clerk in the post office in Jacksonville, Florida, in 1885.[17] By 1896 Captain Sollee was an inspector of customs in the Port of Jacksonville and gave testimony in yet another Cuban filibustering incident.[18]

A series of speculative Florida investment companies were registered in England in the immediate postwar period. Some proved to be out-and-out frauds on a credulous British public. The Florida Provision Company, with its local knowledge and contacts, had some appearance of substance in contrast with some of these Florida swindles.

Charles Carlin and his wife, Mary, then moved farther south and became leading members of Jupiter Township, where Charles was initially the lighthouse keeper and then the well-known captain of the Jupiter Life Boat. For many years they ran the Carlin House as a winter retreat for wealthy northerners.

James Carlin was now keeping company with significant local figures. They were a colorful bunch, some with dubious histories, but they probably suited his temperament and sympathies. They seemed to go down well enough in northern Florida, as they had political ambitions and some success in running for office. Colonel Titus, his brother-in-law Sollee, and Gleason, Walker, and Hopkins were connected by family ties and the dream of American hegemony across the Western Hemisphere. Their visions of taking over Cuba may well have led James Carlin into his next escapade.

# Chapter 30

# The Steamer *Salvador* and the Cuban Revolution, 1869

• • •

Then Cuba is the pride and joy of Spain. It is cherished as the only fraction left of the world which once owned Spain as a mistress. Cuba is the place whence revenue comes and whither every bankrupt Spaniard goes in order to rob ad libitu.

George Villiers, Minister, British Embassy, Madrid, 1836,
from *Life and Letter of the Fourth Earl of Clarendon*

On the afternoon of 7 May 1869, a small, two-masted paddle-wheeler steamed though the western entrance of Nassau Harbor and anchored opposite the market. In command was Captain James Carlin. The steamer was the *Salvador*, and it was well known around Nassau and Havana. It had left Havana in ballast on 22 February on a provisional register issued by the British consul. It was heading for Jacksonville but had been forced to stop at Key West for two months for repairs. On board were eighteen crew members, forty-two Cuban passengers, and a Mexican colonel named Medina. The events that followed became known as the "Salvadora Affair."[1] As the *New York Herald* commented at the time: "any one can see what she is made for." The paper's correspondent remarked that "the Cubans seem to be well satisfied with the Captain of the steamer and he is the proper man to carry passengers anywhere. . . . confidence can be placed in any vessel under his command."[2] Its intent was obvious to all. The evidence of the British officials and local West Indian boatmen gives a vivid and detailed picture of this episode in the island's history.

The sleepy colonial capital was fired up by the news that Carlin was back with a former blockade-runner and a crew that knew the business. The administration was roused. The era of the American Civil War had been high times in the Bahamas, and Nassau had thrived as never before and seldom since.[3] But as soon as the South was defeated, the town reverted to its lethargy, and the economy slumped and returned to its old occupation of wrecking, or the salvage of the numerous vessels that foundered on the dangerous reefs that surround the island group. The quiet life of the island was soon over. A widespread insurrection in Cuba put Nassau under the spotlight and carried its small affairs to the chancelleries of Europe.

Cuba had long been a target for freebooting American filibusters hoping to ride in on the discontent of the native-born Spanish population, expel the Spanish colonial government, and annex the island to the United States. Some may even have hoped to take it over on their own account. But this insurgency was to be a homegrown Cuban affair.

The Town and Port of Nassau, New Providence, Bahamas. Courtesy of "The Civil War in America from the *Illustrated London News*." A Joint Project by Sandra J. Still, Emily E. Katt, Collection Management, and the Beck Center of Emory University.

The Spanish Caribbean was in revolutionary turmoil in the years following the end of the American Civil War. Creoles (Criollo), or colonial-born Spaniards, in the remaining Spanish colonies allied with Republican and Liberal elements in Spain to rebel against rule from Madrid. Prominent Cubans formed a junta, or committee, in New York to support these efforts under the leadership of Carlos Manuel de Céspedes y López del Castillo, a Liberal Cuban lawyer. Mercedes Montejo de Sherman was the secretary of the Junta Patriótica de Cuba in New York, which had commissioned James Carlin and the *Salvador*.

The insurrection that was to become the First Ten Years' War of Independence started on 10 October 1868 when Céspedes and thirty-seven plantation owners in Oriente Province freed their slaves and proclaimed independence with the slogan "Grito de Yara" ("Cry of Yara"), with the initial aim of declaring independence from Spain and then joining the island to the United States. Open revolt broke out in the poorer Eastern Province and thousands of men were soon under arms. Céspedes, too, freed all his slaves and encouraged them to join the insurgent forces.[4]

The Rebel Manifesto protested the harsh rule of the Spanish governor, Captain General Francisco de Lersundi y Hormaechea, and the imposition of taxes with no political representation and/or civic rights or religious freedom. The Spanish officials reacted strongly and issued a decree in November 1868 closing all ports in the Central and Eastern Provinces of Cuba.

The Junta Central Republicana de Cuba y Costa Rica was in league with the big American banking dynasties of J. P. Morgan and the Seligmans, to whom Sarah Gleason was related. The junta operated from 71 Broadway in New York City and provided funds and organizational support to the insurrection. More radical members of the Cuban liberation circles were hostile to the New York junta, suspecting them of supporting annexation by the United States. While this was true of some junta members, it was strongly rejected by others alienated by U.S. restrictions on recruitment in the United States, arms purchases, and previous "Yankee" filibustering expeditions.

Carlos Manuel de Céspedes y López del Castillo.
Courtesy of monografias.com.

Elements in the U.S. government encouraged the Cuban revolutionaries or at least turned a blind eye to their activities, although they compromised U.S. relations with Spain and led to protests from López Roberts, the Spanish minister in Washington. While some Spanish governors were reform minded, the Spanish rule of Cuba was often brutal. Creole resentment was increased by the practice of restricting all government posts to Spanish-born *peninsulares*. There appeared to be an alarming lack of due legal process that shocked Americans and was frequently commented on in the U.S. press, which reported news from Havana in some detail.

Nassau was only some 250 miles from the northern coast of Cuba, and the southern cays of the Bahamas group were half that distance from the beaches and mangroves of Porto Principe Province. Cuban men were arriving in the town in some numbers, and they had been observed drilling and training in isolated houses. In April 1869 the British colonial secretary in Nassau reinforced the Spanish governor's decrees and issued a government notice stating that Governor General Francisco de Lersundi y Hormaechea had declared that all vessels found in Spanish waters with men, arms, and munitions on board would be treated as pirates and that the men would be shot immediately. This was followed by a similar forceful decree in March 1869 from Lersundi's successor, Captain General Domingo Dulce y Garay, First Marquis of Castell.

Nassau had become a way station for Cuban opposition. The 225 Cubans massing on the island were under the command of Colonel Rafael de Quesada, the brother of General Manuel de Quesada. Rafael had just returned from New York but had been resident at the Royal Victoria Hotel in Nassau for the winter of 1867–68.

The British governor also issued his own proclamation on 24 March 1869, reiterating the details of the Foreign Enlistment Act and delegating authority to customs and revenue officials to detain any vessel suspected of contravening the regulations and imprison the master and owners if they failed to pay the penalties imposed by the court. The proclamation made it clear that the act applied throughout Her Majesty's dominions, and details were published in the *Nassau Guardian*.

The *Salvador*'s arrival brought the promise of excitement to Nassau. While the heady days of the U.S. blockade may not have returned, Carlin certainly brought activity. His presence was soon known throughout the government, and the port authorities were instructed to search the vessel and keep a close eye on his activities. The consequences of his arrival eventually sounded around the corridors of Government House and stirred passions as far away as Lord Granville at the Colonial Office and Lord Clarendon at the Foreign Offices in Whitehall. The commander of the British West Indies Fleet in Jamaica and his Royal Navy superiors in Jamaica, Halifax, and Nova Scotia became involved, as did the lords of the Admiralty. Legal aspects also reached the legal chambers of the Judicial Committee of the Privy Council in Westminster.

The affair was to sour relations between the Royal Navy and the governor and his staff, and it made a number of senior individuals look to their pension rights while scratching around for scapegoats. The governor even felt forced, in all honor, to offer his resignation and that of his government. It also caused a stir in the corridors of Spanish ministries in both Cuba and Madrid.

# Chapter 31

# The Cuban Run, May 1869

· · ·

James Carlin was known in the Carlin family, in a romantic sort of way, as a "gunrunner" in the style of Joseph Conrad's unnamed protagonist in *Arrow of Gold*. But "blockade-runner" was the usual phrase for Civil War activities. Initially, such semantics seemed trivial. It was assumed that the use of the term "gunrunner" referred to blockade-running in the Civil War era.

This interpretation altered with the discovery that Carlin owned a ship named the *Salvador* in 1868. More records were found reporting its loss on the Cuban coast in 1870. *Salvador* seemed an odd name for a small, British-registered paddle steamer. Suspicions were heightened by the technical description of the *Salvador* in its British Board of Trade registry. It was a long, narrow steamship of the type used to slip though the U.S. fleet off the Southern coasts, and indeed, it turned out to be the former blockade-runner *Gem*.

The *Salvador/Gem* was an iron-hulled, side-paddle-wheeler built by James Henderson of Renfrew in Scotland in 1854. It carried two masts, the fore schooner rigged, and the after mast square rigged. The vessel was regarded as "very fast" and was said to be able to run at thirteen knots. There was a small deckhouse on the single deck. It was 161 feet long with a beam of 15.9 feet and draft of 7.5 feet, with a registered tonnage of 117. As the *Gem,* the ship had made a run through the blockade in August 1863 and March 1865 for the Charleston-based Cobia Company. After the war, the *Gem* was sold to Henry Rowland Saunders of Nassau.[1] By the time James Carlin came to own the ship, it was only good for carrying cattle or deck passengers. In the view of the mate, if a 10-pound gun had been discharged on board, it would have shaken the *Salvador* to pieces.

The colonial officials were immediately suspicious of the *Salvador* and its familiar master, and it was soon well known in the colony that Carlin was going to run a consignment to the rebels in Cuba. The receiver general, John D'Auvergne Dumaresq, was clamping down on what he viewed as illegal trade and ordered an immediate "rummage" of the vessel from "stem to stern." This was carried out with the help of the navigating lieutenant, a gunner, and a boatload of British blue jackets from the British ironclad HMS *Favourite*.[2]

Dumaresq asked for the naval party to include engineers and stokers as he admitted that he knew little about engines. The naval personnel were expressly to aid the search, not to assess whether the *Salvador* had been fitted out for warlike purposes. It was found to be in ballast with bulk coal in the hold and some suspicious packages that had been sent on board in Nassau, without the receiver's permission, by a Dr. Tinker, a Cuban national.

These were examined and contained coarse, brown woolen Holland shirts and trousers, military boots and gaiters, and hatbands and cockades. There was also a Winchester rifle, seven Spencer B.L. rifles, and empty flannel cartridge bags for light field guns. Two flags were found in another package, one an English ensign, and the other had blue and white stripes with a red triangle at the head and a star in the center. The hatbands contained the same device. These items were all detained but later released to the consignee, the local shipping firm of Tunnell and Loinaz, which had been contracted by the Cubans to handle the vessel. These findings confirmed the receiver's view that the ship was about to carry aid to the rebels.

Diejo Lionaz was a Cuban merchant with connections to Porto Principe in Camaguey Province. He had lived in Nassau for six years and had become a British citizen. He was away in New York during the events that followed but was later questioned as a witness. His partner, Wilbur Frisk Tunnell, a native of Georgetown, Delaware, handled the whole business of registration and obtaining clearances. Carlin had known Tunnell in the days of the U.S. blockade.

Tunnell provisioned the ship for forty-two passengers and eighteen crew for a voyage to St. Thomas as requested by Carlin. Tunnell was to testify later that he knew nothing of supplies for any extra passengers but had merely arranged for the bills to be paid. Dumaresq, who was also the registrar of shipping, granted the *Salvador* a permanent British register on 10 May after he had made a survey.[3]

Tunnell, acting on behalf of Martin Castello, also from Porto Principe, then made an application for customs clearance to ship some two hundred cases containing rifles, bullets and bullet molds, shells, swords, kegs of powder, and other items to St. Thomas in the Leeward Islands. This small island with a fine natural harbor was then a Danish possession that had been a favored ghost destination during the days of the Union blockade.

Much of this larger consignment had recently come in from New York and had been held in bond in the customs house at the port for some weeks. The swords had belonged to the Confederate government but had been sold a few days previously by the U.S. consul in Nassau, Thomas Kirkpatrick, on behalf of the U.S. government, which had been holding them in New York.

Receiver General Dumaresq was on the alert. The *Salvador* was going to continue its voyage with the passengers it had brought from Key West and was now to be loaded with more arms clearly destined for Cuba. Dumaresq sought the governors' approval for the clearance of this larger consignment, thus moving responsibility to the center of the islands' government.

The newly appointed governor, Sir James Walker, initially withheld permission. Acting on local legal advice, he reluctantly allowed the consignment when faced with a challenge by a lawyer acting for the Cubans. The governor had to accept that the consignment was declared to customs as a normal commercial transaction following the practice of the port authorities during the U.S. blockade, when ships were routinely loaded with munitions and cleared from Nassau with paperwork for St. John, New Brunswick, or similar neutral destinations. Blockaders sometimes carried a few passengers, but they did not take bodies of men intended for the Confederate ranks and were not viewed as "transports" in contravention of the British Foreign Enlistment Act.

Carlin would have seen the *Salvador*'s excursion as a repeat of his previous exploits. The rebels were well funded by New York bankers, and there appeared to be plenty of money to be made once again. His apparently careless attitude towards details of the British Foreign Enlistment Act suggests that he had not appreciated the extent to which the act had been under renewed focus following the United States' legal actions for Civil War reparations from Britain. The ground rules had changed in the past three years. While it was general knowledge on the island that the *Salvador* was to embark Quesada's eighty men, the Nassau authorities took no preemptive action to detain or stop them.[4]

By late afternoon on 10 May, the *Salvador* cleared Nassau customs for St. Thomas but was still in the western harbor with steam up and its funnels smoking. Carlin desperately needed to take on more fresh water both for his passengers and the boilers. While still moored opposite the market, he had dispatched Samson Stamp, a trusted boatman he had used since the blockade-running days of the *Cecile,* to get a message to Tunnell or, if possible, directly to the skipper of the water boat, Captain Lightbourn, asking him to come alongside as soon as possible. Boatman Stamp had run around town trying to fulfill his mission but could find neither Tunnell nor Lightbourn. Returning to the quay, Stamp was hired to take valises and a man named Carlos Verona out to the *Salvador.*

As Stamp and his party left the quay, the *Salvador* took off and headed for the narrow eastern exit with Stamp and his passengers rowing away in pursuit. Doubtless they were waving and shouting, but James Carlin was not waiting. With Nassau pilot James Storr on board, the *Salvador* hove its anchor and left the harbor under the eyes of the whole town and doubtless the governor and his staff watching from Government House.

Slipping through the familiar, shallow channel between Hog Island (now Paradise Island) and the mainland, the *Salvador* passed to the east of Fort Montague at 5:00 P.M. The island authorities and the commanders of the three naval vessels all thought the *Salvador* was well on its way to Cuba and that there was nothing they could do about it. James Carlin had left the Royal Navy stranded on the wrong side of the shallows and the set of the tide. Officialdom then packed up for the day.

The *Salvador* had not made off for Cuba. At dusk, it was anchored two hundred yards off Fort Beach, some three miles from its previous berth. It was about six hundred yards north-northeast of the fort and lying north and south, waiting for the tide with its bow pointing out to the open sea. This protected anchorage was used by captains who wanted to catch the tide out of the harbor but had to delay their departure for some reason, and Carlin had a reason to wait. He could not undertake a tricky voyage laden with passengers with no water on board.

Meanwhile, Stamp, still rowing strongly after the *Salvador,* had hailed Captain Lightbourn while passing his boat and gave him the message. Stamp and his crew pulled on until he reached the cemetery, where he set Mr. Verona ashore. By then it was long after dark, but he was able to see the *Salvador's* lights and rowed alongside. He unloaded the luggage and stowed it on top of the deck roundhouse as instructed by the mate Wells and went to sleep on the crowded deck. Wells later stated in his evidence that the *Salvador* would have left for Cuba the evening before if they had been able to fill the eleven-hundred-gallon tanks and extra water barrels in the harbor.

That evening three local boats, one of them a lighter, carried some men from the shore to the ship, but most of the men were sent back to the beach as the ship did not have sufficient provisions for them and was not ready. They were told to return in the morning between 3:00 and 4:00 A.M.

As dawn broke, the boats carried some eighty men out to the ship in small batches. Colonel Quesada supervised the embarkation in full uniform with his sword at his side. These men had been living nearby at Waterloo, a country house at the extreme end of Shirley Street, and at the Barn close to Fort Montague. The boatmen handling the transfer to the *Salvador* were well aware that two policemen were watching them from the nearby bushes.

And indeed all this had been closely watched by a small detachment of the island police force under Police Sergeant Hugh Fletcher McQuaird, supervised by Inspector Charles Sutton. McQuaird had observed the first group of some twenty-two Cubans being taken off to the ship at about 10:30 P.M. and had seen half of them return and move off to Waterloo. He then patrolled until 11:30 and returned to the town to report. Sutton and McQuaird then took a pony-trap and returned to the beach via Waterloo. Sutton left at about 3:30 A.M. to do his rounds of the town, leaving the sergeant and a constable on watch. At 4:20 A.M. they observed the return of the Cubans, and during the next hour they counted a party of some seventy-eight men being transferred to the *Salvador.*

At this point the police surveillance appears to have relaxed. Just before 6:00 A.M. Constable Dain relieved McQuaird, who went home to catch a few hours of sleep. Sutton, meanwhile, went to the office as usual in the morning. He later admitted that he did not ask for a report from the beach but worked in his office until 12:30 P.M. Then the island appears to have woken up to what had happened. At about midday the governor sent Sutton a message and then a note demanding to know if anything had occurred in reference to the Cubans during the night.

Sutton rushed around to McQuaird's quarters and met him en route to the police station. Only then did Sutton learn that seventy-eight more Cubans were now on the *Salvador*. The governor was astonished to learn from a verbal report from Inspector Sutton that the *Salvador* was still in the eastern harbor and that it had embarked a great number of Cubans. Sir James Walker was later to regard this delay as the "only blot in [his government's handling of] the whole transaction."[5] We can imagine the governor, the colonial secretary, the police inspector, the receiver general, and doubtless boatman Storm rushing about the little town like characters from a Gilbert and Sullivan operetta.

Sutton was sent to the attorney general with a request for a warrant, and Walker followed up by going into town and staying with the magistrate while he was taking the police depositions about the embarkation of the Cubans. Governor Walker then had second thoughts about the wisdom of being present during this process and left to avoid accusation of influence from James Carlin or the Cuban's sharp lawyer. He had instructed the colonial secretary to search for Captain Loftus Jones of HMS *Royalist* and organize a ship's boat and detachment of marines. Walker then returned to Government House, where the warrant for the ship's detention was waiting for his signature. Once the warrant was in his hands, the receiver general acted with speed. He joined Inspector Sutton in HMS *Royalist's* cutter and was rowed out through the eastern channel towards the *Salvador*.

The *Salvador* was keeping a close lookout, and the naval party was spotted seven hundred yards off as it rounded Fort Montague. Carlin immediately had the anchor hauled and ordered the water boat that was still alongside to be pushed off. There were a few men left behind on the beach, but the loading was almost complete and the little ship's decks were crowded.

When the cutter was within one hundred yards of the *Salvador*, the marines hailed the vessel and fired three rifle shots across its bows as a signal to stop. Carlin took no notice and the *Salvador* steamed away, dragging the partly raised anchor as he made off, leaving Receiver General Dumaresq empty-handed, unable to follow them in a headwind and "short rough sea."[6]

Mate Wells said that while he was concentrating on getting the ship underway he saw a boat approaching. He turned to touch the ship's bell and noticed that the boat had turned back. Then he heard a shot but thought that someone in the boat was shooting "Milk Ducks for what I know, I had no idea that they were coming after us for we had Cleared from the Custom House." Commander Loftus Jones later commented that "no other force was resorted to, which perhaps under the circumstances was only prudent as she had a large number of armed Cubans on board."[7]

Carlin calculated that if he left the western harbor on the falling tide, the British warships were too deep-drafted to follow him through the eastern exit channel and would be blocked from taking the twenty-mile route around the outside by the stiff north wind. He had effectively trapped the Royal Navy again and had given the *Salvador* enough time to take on water and get a clear start.

His kindly fates had helped again. Although the water boat was delayed, so too was the response of the Nassau authorities, giving him a morning to refresh his tanks. He could not have set out for an indeterminate period with his existing crew of eighteen, plus forty-two passengers, let alone an additional ninety more men, without sufficient drinking water. He must surely have feared that the island police would at least have stopped the night embarkation from the beach or found a way to enforce the law during the course of the daylight hours.

Chapter 32

# The Cuban Shore, May–June 1869

. . .

Carlin took the *Salvador* straight to the cays on the northern coast of Cuba, arriving early on the morning of Friday, 14 May. These cays were a line of off-shore, low-lying sandy banks sheltering much of the shoreline of Puerto Principe, now Camaguey Province. Mate Wells said that they were at Marritea about twelve miles south of the Port of Nuevitas. They had protection from the wind, but they "did not make any extra concealment of the vessel being behind the Cays, it was landlocked." This suggests that they tucked into the entrance to Babaí de Manati, described as a "typical pocket bay having a deep water, straight and quite lengthy entrance channel leading into a largely shoal water basin fringed . . . by fields of mangroves."[1]

The *Salvador* stayed behind the cays for two days. The "passengers" were issued uniforms on board the vessel and then landed on the cays and crossed immediately to the mainland. The cases of arms were opened on board and sent onshore. Within ten hours the Cubans had established a battery of six field guns, and had put out a screen of skirmishers.

The *New York Herald* reported that "the Cuban boys manoeuvred like regular soldiers . . . and the Cuban flag was unfurled to the breeze amid the cheers of those brave Cubans who will soon show its colors to the enemy . . . repeated cheers and hurrahs echoed too in the heart of the far distant hills." The *Herald* showed an obvious bias against the Spanish colonial authorities. The story continued: "The success of the enterprise reflects credit on James Carlin, the commander of the steamer, and it would not surprise us if before long we hear that he is in command of a Cuban man-of-war and then he will have occasion to chase the Spanish instead of being chased by them, as might happen with such vessel [*sic*] like the *Salvador*." The paper commented that the Spanish consul and a few supporters in Nassau were "quite low-spirited at [the ship's chances of] success and had even made bets that she would be caught."[2] This report differs from official accounts as to dates and numbers, but makes up for it in its enthusiasm for the Cuban cause.

While hidden behind a cay, James Carlin and the crew of the *Salvador* spotted a Spanish cruiser passing by and promptly made for the shore, abandoning their ship with the intention of setting it on fire if necessary. But the Spanish passed without noticing the *Salvador,* and they returned on board. Carlin had tweaked the Spanish navy too. In New York it was said that the gunrunner had sighted six Spanish men-of-war as the ship limped back to Nassau at five or six knots with the bottom out of one of its boilers.

The *Salvador* left the Cuban coast on Sunday, sailing brazenly back into Nassau Harbor on Tuesday afternoon at 5:00 P.M. News of its safe arrival soon spread around the town, and the wharves were thronged with sightseers keen to hear of the expedition. Receiver General Dumaresq was not going to be caught out again. In contravention of the quarantine regulations, he immediately rushed over and seized the *Salvador.* Similarly, the Royal Navy sent two boats from HMS *Favourite,* which was lying off the harbor bar. Captain John D. McCrea, the senior naval officer, was determined not to lose his prize this time and went over to the *Salvador* himself. "The vessel was held by a body of Marines as if they had fallen upon a legal prize."[3] Armed sentries were put in place with two on either side of the gangway. It was later reported that Captain McCrea and his officers treated Carlin and his officers "in a most polite manner and regretted to have seen the steamer come into harbor again." But Receiver General Dumaresq behaved towards the captain and officers "as if they were men about to be hung."[4] The seizure caused great excitement among "all classes of people," and Dumaresq's action had caused a general feeling of indignation. The *New York Herald,* partisan to the end, even claimed that "three or four ill-intentioned people" had put about a rumor and given sworn evidence to the police of eighty persons going on board the vessel just before its departure. As the affair was in the hands of good lawyers, the newspaper expected that the vessel would soon be cleared and that "Mr. Dumaresq's prize would slip from his hands."[5]

The next morning Carlin reported the arrival of the vessel to the port authorities in the normal way and confirmed that he did not have clearance from any Cuban port. He also related all these activities in Cuba to Robert Butler, the collector of customs in Nassau, who passed the news to the authorities. Carlin commented that the men were in "good training" and soon had the battery up to repel any Spanish military that might appear.

On 13 May, Captain McCrea, the senior naval officer, had sent Commander Loftus F. Jones in HMS *Royalist* and Commander J. H. Coxon in HMS *Philomel,* to look for the *Salvador* and patrol the Old Bahamas Channel. They were instructed to detain the *Salvador* and put a strong prize crew on board and were given authority to fire blank charges from their guns as a warning or fire shot into the vessel if necessary.

Meanwhile, Loftus Jones had headed south to Ragged Island on the direct route to the eastern end of Cuba and instructed the local customs officer to inform all British and Spanish vessels about the escape of the *Salvador* and what it was about on the Cuban shore. He then called at the Cuban port of Nuevitas and spoke to the officers of two Spanish naval steamers leaving the harbor. With Mr. Sanchez, the British consul, he called on the military, informing them of the situation with the *Salvador*. He learned from the commandant that fishermen had seen a steamer go into "Port Bayamo," a creek twelve miles to the east. It emerged that the two Spanish naval vessels were on their way to Bayamo, so he joined them, anchoring off the creek.[6]

Loftus Jones went on board the Spanish naval vessel *Juan de Ulloa* to give information about his mission, offering Royal Navy help in finding and detaining the *Salvador*. (This creek may now be called Bahía de Manati as no Bayamo Creek appears on the map.) The Spanish had sent their ships' boats into the creek to look for traces of the *Salvador* or the landing party, but had found only the remains of a letter stating that a large expedition might be expected soon. They believed that only dispatches had been put ashore by the steamer as the fishermen had reported.

The *Royalist* then made for Lobos Cay, searched around Ragged Island again, and communicated with Nurse Cay on the twentieth and the pilot station at the Port of Nuevitas on the twenty-second but received no further news of the *Salvador*.

Loftus Jones seems to have doubted the Spaniards' bland assurance that no landing had taken place, for he reverted to his original view that the *Salvador* had made a successful landing at Bayamo on the sixteenth and had then left Cuba. His opinion was strengthened by the commander of the *Juan de Ulloa*, who told him that he had steamed past the entrance to Bayamo on the night of the sixteenth on the way to Nuevitas.

This neatly confirms Carlin's story of sighting a Spanish cruiser while hidden behind the cays. Loftus Jones also noted that the whole coast was "closely guarded by Spanish Cruisers and I should deem it not easy to elude them." HMS *Royalist* then sailed to Havana for coal.[7] There were limited supplies in Nassau, and the coal was of poor quality, expensive at fifty British shillings per ton, plus another eleven shillings per ton for delivery to the anchorage.

Dispatches were sent to Madrid outlining the action the British government was taking to prevent incidents like that of the *Salvador*. The Spanish officials, on behalf of the Spanish Regent and council of ministers, expressed their satisfaction at "this friendly act," and returned very fulsome praise and thanks.

Captain McCrea was particularly discomfited by the navy's failure to stop the *Salvador* from leaving the anchorage of Fort Montague. On 22 October he wrote to Vice Admiral George G. Wellesley, the commander in chief in Halifax, Nova Scotia, explaining his actions on that day back in May.[8] His explanation was accompanied by two detailed maps showing the relative positions of the *Salvador* and HMS *Royalist* at different times in the incident. His difficulty had been that the *Royalist* drew 14 feet 6 inches and there was a bar of 11 feet at spring high-water between the two vessels. The *Salvador* was out of gunshot, and to get to the ship, he would have had to leave the harbor and go twenty-five miles around to Cochrane's Anchorage. By the time the *Royalist* could have raised steam and made the trip, it would have been after nightfall, and the vessel would have been unable to enter Cochrane's Anchorage behind Rose Island in the dark. And, at any rate, the *Salvador* would have been far over the horizon.

Carlin's later defense suggests that he believed he had stayed within the provisions of the Foreign Enlistment Act or at least those with which he was familiar. Governor Walker and his receiver clearly thought otherwise, as they immediately detained the *Salvador* on its return, arguing that the ship was liable to forfeiture under the seventh section of the act.

Chapter 33

# The Queen v. *Salvador* and British Foreign Enlistment Act 59, Geo. III 1819 c.69., May 1869

. . .

With the *Salvador* safely back under the control of the port authorities, the colony's legal officers set to work. On 31 May they started with a preliminary hearing in the judge's chambers of the Vice-Admiralty Court. The attorney general agued that James Carlin of Liverpool, as owner and commander of the *Salvador,* had contravened various sections of the Foreign Enlistment Act by fitting out or equipping a ship in British dominions for a warlike purpose. He stated that Carlin had knowingly and willingly taken on board numerous persons who had agreed to enlist in the service of persons "exercising or assuming to exercise the powers of government in Cuba with the intention of conveying them there to be employed in the service of those persons and was thus liable to forfeiture."[1]

These points were argued in a series of legal "informations" and "protests" between Carlin's counsel, Bruce Lockhart Burnside, and George Campbell Anderson, the attorney general. In the meantime, the receiver general in his capacity as a customs officer had proceeded under section 6 of the act, which allowed for penalties against James Carlin as master. This empowered the island's provost marshal, James A. Thompson, to serve a writ on Carlin for eighty penalties of £50 each under Statute 59th, Geo. III, section 6, chapter 69, totaling £4,000. Today this is in the region of £300,000, if measured by the retail price index.[2] Carlin was being charged £50 a head, as laid down as the penalty in the act for taking on board the eighty-odd Cubans. Similarly, the *Salvador* was seized under the same section 6 as surety for these penalties on the ship's master. The attorney general later changed this to seizure under section 7 of the act.

Thompson's deputy said that he knew Carlin by sight, and seeing him in the street, he had served the writ. It emerged that it had been handed to the wrong person, and the writ had not actually been served in due form. Carlin was fortunate or was warned beforehand. The crew had been paid and discharged. Carlin had departed the Bahamas well before the end of May and was soon back in New York, staying at 29 William Street around the corner from Wall Street. The size of this penalty would explain why he did not reappear in Nassau and changed his residence from England to Scotland. The Scottish legal system differs from that in England and would have complicated any attempt to extract the £4,000 from him. At this point Carlin may well have sympathized with William Gleason's U.S. expansionist scheme to wrest the Bahamas from the British.

During the trial of the *Salvador* in July 1869, the Vice-Admiralty Court examined the precise meaning of clauses 5 and 7 in the Foreign Enlistment Act. Clause 5 covered the question of provisioning and fitting out a transport for the purpose of conveying men or munitions in support of insurrectionary forces that held or purported to hold jurisdiction over part of the territory of a power with which Britain was not at war. Clause 7 dealt with the recruiting or conveying of persons who could be proved to have been enlisted to aid insurgents against a friendly foreign power.

The case was heard on 13 August 1869 by Charles F. Rothery, the deputy judge in the Vice-Admiralty Court in Nassau, the chief justice having left the colony. Carlin was in New York City, but he had given Tunnell his power of attorney, and Bruce Lockhart Burnside, a local public notary, represented the little ship.

Even with the windows open to catch the sea breezes and with fans moving the hot summer air, it must have been a stifling experience. Doubtless the eighteen witnesses were pleased to be as brief as possible and to escape to the open shade of any available veranda.

The barrister for the *Salvador* based his main defense on the claim that Captain Carlin did nothing to fit out the vessel as a transport or store ship as described in section 5 of the act. It was a merchant ship going about its normal business. No addition or alteration was made to the vessel. It was resupplied in the normal way in Nassau. He also argued that no state of war existed between Great Britain and Spain. Britain had not declared a state of neutrality as contemplated by the act, and the insurgency was not a state of war between the Spanish and the inhabitants of the island.

Deputy Judge Rothery stated that he had read all the authoritative English and American texts concerning the meaning of section 7 and had found them unhelpful, as they all referred to vessels of war and the meanings of the terms were difficult to apply to a transport. Rothery believed that he had to follow his own construction, or interpretation, for judgment in this case.

The judge found that the vessel had been fitted out in the sense that it was reprovisioned and thus enabled to make the voyage. Similarly, the purpose of the expedition was clearly against British interests. But he ruled against the Crown on a very narrow point of law, focusing on a particular phrase in section 7: "That if any person in any part of Her Majesty's dominions beyond the seas shall equip, furnish or fit out any vessel with the intent or in order that such a vessel shall be employed in the service of any persons assuming to exercise the powers of Government in and over any Foreign Colony." It was the narrow point of assuming powers of government that decided the case.

Rothery questioned in whose service the *Salvador* was provisioned or fitted out for, and in whose service the men who were embarked had been employed. He acknowledged that there were numerous insurrections in Cuba and cited the evidence of Wells, the mate, on the state of Cuba. But he decided that he had no evidence of the identity of any insurgents, nor that any of them were in possession of any part of Cuba. He noted that the Spanish governor had indeed assured the British authorities that the insurrections had been put down.

He ruled that the "the *Salvador* as a military expedition was set on foot in Nassau for the purpose of attacking the dominions of a friendly Power" but not as coming under the seventh section of the 59th Geo. III, Cap. 69. He ordered the restitution of the vessel. On the question of costs, he held that as the ship had steamed off to Cuba when "the English man-of-war's boats" were trying to stop it, they were right to detain it for inquiries on its return. No costs or damages were thus awarded.[3]

The attorney general immediately gave notice that he would appeal to the Privy Council and suggested that the law officers of the Crown should be consulted. Meanwhile the Queen's proctor had obtained a writ to prevent the return of the vessel to Carlin pending the appeal. The vessel was also still being held awaiting proceeding in the Nassau court under section 6 of the act concerning James Carlin and the recovery of the £4,000 penalty for conveying the eighty Cubans. By 28 September, London knew that the writ had been served on Carlin in New York.[4]

The Nassau judge's dismissal of the case caused dismay in Whitehall and across Horse Guard's Parade at the Admiralty. The *Salvador* was immediately detained afresh pending the appeal. By April 1870 the ship had been condemned and was in a sinking condition.

In October the Spanish legation in London wrote a stiff note to Lord Clarendon, the foreign secretary, stating that any delay in hearing an appeal against the Nassau judgment may encourage "dealers in the contraband of War" to turn "the Bahamas into a veritable arsenal from whence the enemies of Spain might provide themselves." The Spanish were "surprised beyond measure" that the governor in Nassau would not take the same measures as the governor of Jamaica to prohibit such exports. He threatened that the severity of the Spanish cruisers would have to make up for the leniency of the Bahamas authorities and lawful commerce might suffer consequently.[5]

The Foreign Office hastened to assure the Spanish that an appeal was underway and that the law officers were looking at the comparison with Jamaica. By 9 October the law officers had decided that the Nassau judge's decision would not hold up and that the case should go to appeal in London. They even suggested that such an expedition carried out under a flag of some self-styled government could be considered piratical under the Laws of Nations. They held that the proceeding for penalties under the sixth section of the act in relation to the eighty Cubans should go ahead.

However, in January 1870 Lord Granville postponed the recovery action against James Carlin for loading and transporting the Cuban insurgents until the appeal in the case of forfeiture was decided. Governor Walker and his attorney general called for this delay as they foresaw difficulties with finding sufficient evidence to bring the case. They pointed out that the action would have had to rely on Carlin's own admissions on his return to Nassau after the landing in Cuba. Granville also believed that he would be unlikely to extract any penalties if they succeeded. Carlin was well away from their jurisdiction and took care to give up such adventures. The case was quietly dropped.[6]

Commander John Newland Maffitt, CSN.
Courtesy Hampton Roads Naval Museum.

The *Salvador* was sold at auction in Nassau for five shillings more than the appraised value of £180. Governor Walker regretted that it was bought by Cuban agents but noted that the Spanish government had two Spanish warship commanders, a Spanish colonel of artillery, and the Spanish consul, all in Nassau at the time. None of them attended the sale nor tried to stop it.

The ship was again loaded with arms and munitions in Nassau with help from Tunnell and Loinaz and set out for another trip. Customs cleared it for La Plana on San Domingo Island, but everyone in Nassau knew that it was on its way to Cuba with forty crew and no passengers under the command of Captain William Walker, who had probably been Carlin's colleague when Carlin had run the blockade in the *Ruby* and *Orion*.

The authorities in Nassau were unable to prevent the *Salvador*'s departure, as there was no Royal Navy vessel in the port at the time, although a Spanish warship on station was informed and left harbor to try to find the ship.[7]

Given the damning report on the condition of the vessel and its very modest value, it seems likely that these Cubans set out more in hope than expectation. The *Salvador* was discovered ashore on the south coast of Cuba between Cienfuegos and Trinidad, where it was captured by Spanish land forces. The mate was caught by the Spanish authorities along with some ten crewmen, who were described as "Negroes from the Bahamas." The captain and thirty men had made good their escape.[8]

John Newland Maffitt, too, was tempted by the Cuban junta in New York. Acting on behalf of the junta, J. W. Barron had asked him to inspect their ship the *Hornet* (renamed *Cuba*) then lying in Wilmington, and assess its seaworthiness for a trip to New York.[9] This 1,800-ton, brig-rigged screw-steamer, pierced for eighteen guns, had been purchased in the interests of the junta to operate as a naval vessel off the Cuban coast. It had been seized by the U.S. Treasury for being in violation of American neutrality but after a protracted court case was released. Maffitt agreed to convoy it to New York but wisely declined to command a mission to Cuba.[10]

Defying the Spanish authorities was an exceptionally dangerous business and far removed from the due legal process Carlin went though in the hands of the U.S. Navy. In the Spanish dominions it was accepted that rebels, taken *flagrante delicto*, were liable to immediate execution under government decree. According to Ian Robertson, "Killing prisoners is no murder, it is termed '*asegurar*', to make sure of them: they are provided for without the expense of prisons or provisions."[11] In 1869 the Spanish issued a further harsh decree providing for the immediate execution of all crew members of vessels caught running weapons to the insurgents. This was to be played out with the fate of another ex-runner, the steamer *Virginius*, in 1873, when the Spanish authorities set about the serial execution of some forty-one of its British and American crew and filibusters in Santiago de Cuba over a number of days. The rest only survived because a passing British warship, HMS *Niobe*, threatened to bombard the town unless the firing squad stopped the executions—an excellent result for gunboat diplomacy.

But that was not quite the end of the story of the *Salvador*. The colony's attorney advocate and prosecutor-general, George Campbell Anderson, had notified Judge Rothery that it was his intention to appeal to the Judicial Committee of the Privy Council in London and that he was prepared with sureties for the costs. Carlin's attorney, Burnside, protested the appeal in a hearing in the judge's chambers. However, it was allowed to proceed on the basis of a £100 bond in lieu of the ship, issued in favor of James Carlin, who, pending the appeal, was again the lawful owner of the ship and its tackle. This ruling illustrates the difference between the Admiralty Court case against the ship as a legal entity in its own right and the Civil court demand for damages or penalties from Carlin for his infringement of the act with regard to the eighty Cubans.

The hearing took place in London on 27 and 28 June 1872 in front of four judges headed by Lord Cairns. Carlin did not attend, nor was he represented. In an admirably clear elucidation of the obscure wording of the Foreign Enlistment Act, Lord Cairns held that the argument turned on the question of whether there were insurgents acting together in a province of Cuba and whether the ship was employed by them and acting in their service.[12]

Taking the evidence presented to the court in Nassau by all the witnesses, including that of Receiver Dumaresq, William Butler, Diejo Loinaz [Diego Loynaz y Arteaga], William Wells, and John Mama, the Spanish consul in Nassau, their lordships concluded that the decision of the Vice-Admiralty Court in Nassau should be reversed and judgment pronounced for the Crown. They rested their decision on the evidence that there was an insurgency in Cuba even if they did not purport to exercise government over any portion of the island. Thus, the first part of the clause in section 7 was fulfilled, even if the second part relating to governance was not proved.

By this time the *Salvador* was long gone. Of the sale price, the amount of £168, 4 shillings, and 8 pence was used to reimburse Her Majesty's Commissariat chest in the Bahamas for keeping the vessel while it was under arrest. The fate of the remaining balance of some £17 is lost in the bureaucracy.

In mid-July Mr Thomas W. Tandy, the chief engineer of HMS *Favourite*, had surveyed the *Salvador* and produced a damning report. He considered the hull so decayed that a hammer could go through the plates. It was unseaworthy without extensive repairs. The single-cylinder steeple engines of about 120 horsepower had two boilers pressurized to twenty-five pounds and originally cost about £6,000. They appeared to be in fair working order with the after-boiler in very good condition. This may have been repaired in Key West during the ship's two-month stopover in Florida. The foremost boiler had been "burned" recently and bulged; it had also been "salted" by the use of seawater. Tandy estimated that the machinery was unlikely to bring £200 in a good market, and he considered the hull beyond repair. The Cubans, who bought the vessel and took it on its final run, were taking enormous risks with the ship, as well as with the Spanish.

# Chapter 34

# Caribbean Repercussions
The Governor Tenders His Resignation, 1869–1878

• • •

James Carlin tweaked the nose of the United States Navy for four years during the Civil War. This time he had foiled the British Royal Navy, too, and they were not amused at all. Even though they had sent a warship to chase after the *Salvador* and bring it back to Nassau and had alerted the British Caribbean fleet, he had run rings around them on both his outward voyage to Cuba and his trip back. He had also irritated the Spanish and run around their navy, too.

By 24 May 1869 Governor Walker had his steam up. Writing again to Lord Granville on the ship's return, he confirmed that the *Salvador* was being held on the basis that it was security for the penalties imposed under section 5 of the act—namely, procuring for foreign enlistment. He then complained of Carlin's "effrontery and the defiant nature of his conduct" in opening suits for damages against the receiver general and Captain McCrea, who had supplied a small force under Lieutenant John Phillips to seize the vessel and disconnect its machinery. Six seamen were placed on board as sentries with orders to prevent any contact with the shore. He had also sent for a marine guard, as well as engineers and stokers.

After advice from the attorney general, Captain McCrea himself had boarded the *Salvador* and withdrew most of the ratings, leaving only a sergeant and six men. However, the "strap of the connecting rod" was also removed. Captain McCrea wrote that "the Master made no secret about the success of their raid on the Cuban coast beyond disguising the point where the force disembarked." The greatly disgruntled McCrea then complained "that after defying our laws and outraging the flag, he [Carlin] has boldly sailed in here to hold us accountable for any interference with his outrageous acts."[1]

By the end of May 1869, communications regarding the "Salvadora Affair" were flying around Whitehall and even reached Downing Street. Letters sped between the Colonial Office, the Foreign Office, and the Admiralty. At the direction of their lords and masters Lord Granville, the Earl of Clarendon, and the commissioners of the Admiralty, ministry officials worked to deflect blame and dampen Spanish reaction.

The governor, Sir James Walker, had written to Lord Granville while the *Salvador* was still in the western harbor before escaping on its first trip to Cuba, explaining that he was very uneasy about its commander's intentions. He had consulted the attorney general as to whether there was any colonial or imperial law they could use, but the attorney general was clear that they had no grounds to detain the ship on departure for St. Thomas, the ship's master having completed all the customs formalities correctly. The governor even called in John Moma, the Spanish consul, and in the presence of Captain McCrea, questioned the consul as to whether he had any information that would enable them to hold the ship. To their astonishment, the consul "professed total unacquaintance with what was going on, and the impression that he was not anxious to interfere."[2] Walker confessed that the whole episode bore an ugly aspect and was likely to make the Spanish very angry.

Walker's dispatch was sent with HMS *Cupid* to Havana for the mail boat to London. Although the governor went through the correct process and took action as and when the law allowed, London thought that he should have been more dynamic and taken executive action rather than await due process.

On 18 June, Lord Granville wrote a strong letter of censure to Governor Walker. He was very critical of the governor's action, picking up on his four-hour delay in waiting for a sworn police statement before the cutter from HMS *Royalist* was dispatched with the warrant to arrest the *Salvador*. Lord Granville wanted to know why, "from the moment the *Salvador* came into British Water with the notorious purpose of receiving arms and ammunition . . . and of embarking men," he did not explore what legal powers he had to hold the vessel and why it was not constantly attended by a British warship. Granville made the point that if the *Salvador* had been under the guns of the *Royalist* rather than rifles, the *Salvador* would not have escaped. He also claimed that the reports he had received from the governor were undated and times were given without saying whether they were A.M. or P.M., thus confusing matters. He protested to Lord Clarendon that the local authorities had shown a "want of due vigilances and promptitude."[3] Lord Granville must have been rather tired of James Carlin by then.

On 24 July 1869 Governor Walker had replied, saying that he was mortified by the criticism of his superior. The governor deeply regretted forfeiting Lord Granville's confidence and being criticized by another secretary of state as well. He could but "see the hand of Calumny strong at work against" him. He felt he had no option but to ask Lord Granville to accept his resignation from this government.

His resignation was not accepted, and Lord Granville, having received further details of the affair, told him that he had his "perfect confidence" and that the only thing he had done wrong was to not make it clear that the fault lay with his subordinates in the police. Lord Clarendon also approved this view. Walker was still governor of the Bahamas in 1871. He ended his career as president of the Royal Statistical Society.

Whitehall was especially irritated by the legal action for damages that Carlin's barrister had opened against the receiver general and Captain McCrea. They were determined that the Crown would defend their colonial officials and indemnify them against any penalties. The government law officers believed that "the English Law had been publicly defied in the Bahamas under circumstance of great aggravation."[4] They clearly felt embarrassed in front of the Spanish and believed that the colonial authorities had shown weakness and lack of vigor.

Meanwhile, in Cuba, General Manuel de Quesada and Carlos Manuel de Céspedes continued to receive reinforcements, including large bodies of men from the United States. In July, General Puello, at the head of three hundred Spanish marines, was attacked by a force of patriots near Baga (San Miguel de Baga) on the same bay as Nuevitas and near that city. This is close to where Colonel Rafael Quesada landed from the *Salvador* and may well have involved his troops. When the rainy season arrived in mid-1869, General Quesada had eight thousand men who were properly armed and regularly drilled.[5]

In October the revolutionary volunteers controlled the affairs of this part of the island and the captain general seemed powerless to prevent them. General Thomas Jordan, an American (and ex-Confederate) who was adjutant general of the Cuban (insurrectionary) Army, wrote that he had 26,000 men in the Cuban Army and 40,000 liberated slaves armed with machetes and that all he needed were 75,000 stands of arms to complete the war in ninety days. By the end of 1869, the rebels were recognized by both Chile and Peru and also received a letter of "sympathy" from the U.S. president, Ulysses Grant, implying his support. In March 1870 General Quesada, in a letter to the *New York Tribune,* substantially exaggerated the size of the forces under his control. Doubtless propagandists were at work, but the revolt was a very large-scale operation with large numbers of casualties on both sides.

By September 1870 the Foreign Enlistment Act of George III had been repealed and new measures introduced, although these, too, proved impossible to enforce. Governor Walker made serious efforts to rid his government of Cubans and "their Confederates," through which it seemed that Carlin and his Cuban associates had achieved the unexpected result of the *Salvador*'s trial and the eventual dropping of the case against him for loading insurgents.

The Cubans continued to use Nassau as a staging post for their struggle. The governor was hampered by a shortage of naval vessels and was often unable to do much to halt them. In October 1869 the American steamer *Lillian* also carried a large quantity of munitions to the rebels. Starting from New Orleans, the vessel moved to Cedar Key, north of Tampa, Florida, where it loaded six hundred men, cannons, and arms, and then made the run to Cuba, landing its party successfully. It then made for Nassau, where it was impounded but released a little later. The *Lillian* made a second run to Cuba at the end of the year and was also detained in Nassau for a time. This, too, caused waves back in London, where the Colonial Office was receiving reports of armed men loading in Jamaica.[6]

Was Carlin recruited to the Cuban cause by the lure of an exhilarating trip in the style of his previous escapades, or were the Cubans paying on the same scale as the merchants of Charleston during the heady days of the blockade? Did that colorful bunch in Titusville turn his head with their tales of filibuster daring? Or was he responding to a request from his wife's possible cousin, Mercedes de Montejo, the secretary of the Cuban junta in New York City? The outcome was that he lost the *Salvador*, and from then on he had to avoid the Bahamas, the Spanish, and perhaps some officers of the Royal Navy, too.

The Ten Years' War continued until it was formally concluded by the Pact of Zanjón of February 1878, although some resistance continued in the East. There was a further "little war" in 1879–80. The Third War of Cuban Independence of 1895–98 culminated in American intervention, and the three-month Spanish-American War led to Spain's defeat, the Treaty of Paris of December 1898, and Cuban independence.

Chapter 35

# What Happened Next, 1870–1891

• • •

C aptain James Carlin kept his head down after his excitements in Cuba and the Privy Council action that followed, and there were few further sightings. Family letters and the activities of his wife, Ella Rosa, suggest that he changed his life and moved his operations ashore for a while. Rare mentions are found in scattered records, and we can only speculate on what he was doing on the basis of these snippets of information and family legend.

There were rumors from an old colleague on the *Torch* that Carlin had a little sugar plantation in Louisiana. These are supported in part by Ella Rosa's 1871 claim that he was a cotton planter. Land records from St. May's Parish, in the south of Louisiana, show that he formed a partnership with William Leslie in May 1871 to operate the three-thousand-acre Chatsworth Plantation. They had already taken a five-year lease from Abraham and Jacob Sypher on this sugar plantation at the beginning of 1870. Maximum capital was set at $60,000, with half that amount being paid in installments over the following years. A proportion of the capital came from William Bee and Company of Charleston.

By December 1870 Carlin was staying at Butterworth's Pavilion Hotel on Meeting Street in Charleston in the company of William Leslie, then said to be from Georgia. He was again at the Pavilion Hotel at the end of January 1871, listed as having arrived from New Orleans.[1] But Carlin was still no planter, and the whole project ended after a couple of years and was followed by lawsuits, including a case brought and won by William Bee and Company in 1876. Any hopes he had of tempting Ella Rosa and his family to join him in Louisiana would have vanished in the legal fallout.

In April 1871 Carlin sent a paper to the State Agricultural Society of South Carolina comparing the cost of plantation labor in Louisiana and the western, southern, and middle states of the Union. He showed that labor in Louisiana was 20 percent higher, causing a constant drain of labor to the West, and proposed that Chinese workers be imported to fill the demand.[2]

The previous item before the society's committee had been a letter to Roach and Company, Charleston shipping agents, from Spofford Brothers (Tileston) and

Company of New York City, also shipping agents. Spofford had suggested the provision of "roomy sailing ships" to bring workers directly from the Chinese mainland to South Carolina.

James Carlin was clearly behind this suggestion and using his shipping contacts to promote this project. The question of imported Chinese workers was a constant theme in both Cuba and the wider Caribbean after the banning of the official slave trade. Many Chinese came to the British West Indies as indentured labor to work the sugar plantations in the years after emancipation. There were numerous scandals about indentured labor, and British parliamentary commissions were sent out to report on labor conditions.

Carlin continued his lifelong pattern of extended absences abroad and short periods at home with his ever-growing family. The Carlins lived in a series of houses they leased for a few years before moving on. From Liverpool, the Carlins moved to Garmouth at the mouth of the Spey River in northeastern Scotland, where the 1871 census shows the family living with a governess for the older children, a nursery nurse for the babies, and other domestics. Meanwhile, James, Willie, and Sam were boarders with the headmaster of Milnes Free School in nearby Fochabers. Alexander Milne, a local boy from Fochabers, had used a fortune made in New Orleans to endow a fine neo-Gothic academy in his hometown.

In 1875 the family lived at Balblair House, a large house on the Contary Estate near Nairn. Their youngest daughter, Louise, who was born there, used to tell friends a striking tale about it in her rambunctious, slightly ribald manner. When in middle age, she was firmly established as proprietor of one of the smartest of London's smaller nursing homes in Beaumont Street near Harley Street. She drove north for a touring holiday to find the old family residence she had left as a babe in arms. She was directed to a large, detached house on the outskirts of Nairn.

Louise was an impressive figure: snow-white hair, fur coat, and Armstrong Siddeley motorcar, complete with a leather-gaitered *chauffeuse* named Irene. A forbidding female in a matron's uniform answered her knock, and Louise asked if she might come in and have a brief look round. "You see, I was born here," she said. The stern matron gave her a very odd look and said, "Oh! Is that so?" and moved to one side. Louise then noticed that beside the door was a large brass plate reading, "Glasgow Corporation Home for Unmarried Mothers."[3] The Nairn "Poor's House" was the Scottish equivalent of the work house of Victorian legend.

The joke continued for some sixty years as other members of the family, attempting to locate these traces of the families' life in Scotland were similarly misdirected to the Nairn Union Poor's House at Trades Park before finding the original, substantial, Balblair House farther down the same road on the Estate of Contray. The Nairn Union workhouse became a hospital and local authority nursing home after 1930, when it was known also as Balblair House.

The family was thriving in the 1870s after the excitements of the Cuban adventure. Carlin survived the loss of the *Salvador* and the legal costs of the court case in Nassau. A family story relates that James and Ella Rosa Carlin made a very exotic couple as they tore through the Scottish country in a pony-trap on their way to the kirk in Nairn on a Sunday. Ella was said to be sporting Spanish-style clothes with flamboyant colors more suited to a Caribbean Sunday morning than to the drizzly east coast of Scotland.

Balblair, Nairn, Scotland.
From the author's collection.

The Civil War was long over, and the rich proceeds of blockade-running long spent. Carlin had clearly found an alternative enterprise. The Chicago-based family of James Carlin's son Samuel believes that James, "old red beard" as they call him, was trading on the Greenland coast from a steam whaler, buying sealskin tobacco pouches and slippers, carvings in bone and tooth, and model kayaks in exchange for trade goods. Samuel Carlin used to enjoy telling tales of his time with his older brother and his father in the Arctic. David Carlin, Sam's son, died in 2016 but had clear memories of those evenings with his father. The teenage brothers were introduced to tough seaboard life and also the hospitality of the local hunters and their wives.

Sam's sister-in-law Anne Malcher recalled those times in a letter to her great-nephew:

Now let us go into the Life of your grandfather Samuel Edward Carlin. He was one of seventeen children, 11 boys and 6 girls! Their father was an exploring captain of a whaler vessel who dealt with Esquinmeaux and Northern Races where he traded blubber, whale oil, tusks of animals and oils (formally burned in lamps like kerosene). He came home only once a year, his family saw him rarely, but he must have had a good sense of business, because to keep such a large family must have been an enormous job! Sam told me that after a child was 6 years old it was sent away to school. Their father believed in an education for every one of them, he believed in their going to a university! When Sam Edward was eighteen he was taken along on one of their trips on a whale boat for a year or two, just for the experience, after that he went to the University in London and later spent several years in Gottingen from where he graduated, that was in Germany. (as an aside here) the father before him, an English Officer in the English Navy, ran through that famous blockade down along our Southern Coast Line, took a girl hidden in between bales of cotton with him to England and she became his wife although she never saw her native land again! . . .

[Sam] often came back to his days sailing up in Greenland and Iceland, the awful storms through which his father had to guide the whaler. He told me about the pride his father took in his long red beard all in curls! He must have been a picture. After a few trips like this Samuel had to go back to school, his father the sea Captain had wanted to toughen his son by taking him along up North. Some years later the Captain went on another voyage to the North and was never heard from again. We assume he and his ship are sleeping at the bottom of the sea.[4]

There was indeed a large Greenland fleet of whalers, sealers, and traders that left the northeast coast of Scotland each spring and headed north as the ice retreated under the summer sun. Garmouth and Nairn would have given Carlin easy access to the Greenland fleet centered on Dundee and other east coast ports in Scotland. While the fleet was largely composed of sealers, it would have made good sense for traders to sail with them. Sam would have been eighteen years old in 1880, and this date fits with the little we know of the family at that time.

The Royal Greenland Trade Company (Det kongelige danske Handelskompagni) held a monopoly over all trade with Greenland, so his business was technically illegal and clandestine. But the Danish navy did not station ships in Greenland, and the company had no means to enforce its monopoly. The settlements were so scattered and the coastline so long that the Danish administration was quite unable to impose its rule, and in practice whalers and sealers traded freely with the local inhabitants they encountered. There are no recorded cases of these summer visitors being prosecuted. All the authorities could do was to ban contact between the Greenlanders and whalers and "occasionally fine those who disregarded this prohibition."[5] James Carlin had found a quiet free-for-all and prospered again.

Whalers were permitted to call into Greenland harbors for supplies, but they were not registered by the Danish administration, as whaling normally took place out of Greenland waters. As far as practical, visiting vessels were warned, in English and Danish, that trade was prohibited. This was a formal document laying out the regulation of 18 March 1776 and the relevant punishments. The masters of vessels were obliged to sign that they had received a copy. There is no record of a visit by James Carlin.

As for Ella Rosa, she is in many senses the only hero of this tale. Somehow, through all the ups and downs and comings and goings, she kept the family going and ensured that ten out of her thirteen children survived to adulthood with a good measure of education along the way.

The following letter was written to her just-widowed daughter-in-law Horatia Carlin (known in the family as Ray), who was then in San Francisco. Ella Rosa had received news of the death from tuberculosis of her first-born son, James, in a clinic in faraway Salt Lake City.

47, Almack Road
Clapton Park
London Dec. 16th 1881
My Dearest Ray,
The sad news which your last letter brought us, I need not say is almost unbearable. You can understand I am sure, although we were in a measure prepared for the worst the sting was none the less severe. Poor soul what must you have been suffering to witness the departure of one I feel you loved dearly. It is heartbreaking to me & I can hardly believe my own darling boy is gone, that he is happy there is no question, his life was too pure and full of well doing to admit of doubt on the subject!

No one but a mother (which you have experienced) can know the depth of that affection. Darling Jim how much would I have given to see him once more, and the saddest and I may add bitterest grief to me, is that I could not assist the darling boy in anyway. God provided for him friends I am more than thankful to learn in the hour of need. He saw fit to remove him from this world so soon so young.

We must try and bear this heavy affliction with Christian resignation— Oh dear Ray the only thing we here can do is to strive to live that we may be united with him in that happy abode where he now rests. God help us I earnestly pray. Do write soon as you are able, and let me have full particulars of all that related to him in his illness and death. Where is he buried & how, by whom also.

Did you keep a lock of his hair for me? I hope so—We have nothing belonging to our darling, if you have a likeness or any of his work to spare I should be indeed glad to have something he was recently associated with. There is so much I would like to say—That you nursed him faithfully and did all in your power to save him I am satisfied. So are we all agreed and believe. How is his little darling? What must your affection be for her I well know, God sent her to be comfort in your bereavement! Which you no doubt find her. How I wish dearest Ray (for you will ever be that to us) for your own worth as well as dear Jim's sake)—I could send you the means to bring you home among us which we all desire very much.

It may yet be in our power/God grant it I add if you could join us and that angel of yours, we will all welcome you most heartily. You are to understand our home is yours to share at all times—and whatever we have—Jim's Father keenly feels his loss and is very sad to be in such a helpless position just now.

He unites with me in dear love and sympathy for you and experience the hope that fortune may soon favour us, and enable him to do that which he should by one so highly esteemed as your own dear self.

The children all love you although unknown to them. Write to me and let me know how you manage and what your own wishes are for the future—you might also say if dearest Jim ever expressed his wishes in respect to your future.

Awaiting a reply

I am Dearest Ray Your affectionate but sorrowing Mother, Ella Carlin [6]

Ella Rosa de Montijo Carlin died in London in 1913 surrounded by her daughters and friends.

The Carlins' large family scattered and made their way in London, San Francisco, and Johannesburg, South Africa. Miss Louise de Montijo Carlin thrived in fashionable London society, while her older brother William Yates became a prosperous City of London wine and whiskey merchant. Samuel registered patents for the first mechanical calculator to divide in one operation, which he sold to Underwood Typewriter Company for $82,000. Later he exhibited a form of perpetual motion machine at the Chicago World's Fair of 1933; it was said to have run unaided for the duration of the fair. Other sons started out as City of London stockbrokers and brokers clerks, and the youngest was a mining engineer in Johannesburg. The two other daughters married in London. Ella's son was commissioned into the Indian army after Sandhurst, eventually dying of tuberculosis contracted in Mesopotamia at the end of the First World War. Susan's son was the artist Robin Bartlett, who worked with Ian Fleming and others in British naval intelligence during World War II.

Tradition has it that James Carlin left for America after a dispute with Ella Rosa about the careers of their sons and was never heard from again by the family. Carlin's activities in the years between 1882 and 1890 remain a complete mystery. Between 1881 and 1908 Charles Carlin and his wife, Mary, of Jupiter, Florida, sold some twenty-nine plots of land in Brevard County.[7] Carlin and his old associates in the Florida Provision Company finally revoked the agency agreements with both Francis Sollee and Edward Tattnall Paine in 1882. There have been no other sightings of him in any record, census (he avoided these all his life), or newspapers until the New York census of 1890. This states that he had been living in the United States since 1882; so, whatever else he was doing, he had abandoned England.

Ella Rosa Carlin (center), next to her daughters and friends in
West London in 1912. Courtesy of Mrs. Bea Savory

We are only left with family legends that tell of James Carlin moving between railway survey work in Florida in winter, trading on the Greenland coast in summer, and spending a few weeks in between with his family wherever they happened to be in Britain. He may well have joined his two older sons on the West Coast of the United States in 1880.[8] One son reports him surveying on the Pacific Coast. Horatia Carlin's brother Alfred Richardson was lost overboard on an Arctic voyage in 1879. Thus, there may be a hint of some culpability in James and Ella Rosa naming their last-born son Alfred Richardson Carlin in 1880.

The story then has Carlin and his ship lost in an Arctic storm and never heard from again. Indeed, there was an Arctic tragedy in the harsh winter of 1889, when an ice barrier formed very early across the Davis Strait between Labrador and Greenland to the south of Baffin Bay. Some three hundred whaling and sealing vessels were trapped in the northern waters. The rapidly forming ice crushed many whalers, and their crews had to set out on foot across the ice to the open water to the south, where rescue steamers waited. Greenland was a dangerous place for a man in his later years, if this is in fact where Carlin spent the last years of his seafaring life. An excess of early ice seems to have been his final undoing—where the "kindly fates" that he had chanced so outrageously all his life finally abandoned him. But, as is the way with family stories, this may be an attempt to cover a sad truth.

The reality is that Carlin emerges in the 1890 New York Police Census, apparently washed up in a seaman's hostel on the Bowery waterside in New York City. He was then committed to Ward's Island Asylum on the East River with a "paranoiac condition," where he remained for thirty years until his death in 1921.

If Carlin lost his ship and perhaps his crew in the Arctic incident, it is hardly a surprise that he would be found in a seaman's hostel in the Bowery. Nor is it surprising that he was in a poor way and ended up in Ward Island, which also served as a refuge for the destitute. What is astonishing is that he survived some thirty years in this asylum with his mind reasonably intact and that, aged eighty-seven, his handwriting is still recognizable as that of the young man we met in the Coast Survey.

Given the trouble he had caused to British, American, and Spanish officialdom, it is not too surprising that he was feeling a touch of paranoia by this stage in his career. A 1920 letter he wrote to his sister-in-law Mary Moorer Carlin in Florida shows that he continued to display an entrepreneurial spirit and optimistic outlook.

Whether he was indeed shipwrecked and lost everything is unknown. He had friends in New York, and they may have eased his way into Ward Island, which in those days housed some interesting characters, including the world's first chess champion and also English actresses down on their luck. For someone who had spent almost his entire life in the institutional surroundings of a ship's wardroom, the family can only hope that Ward Island was not too uncomfortable a retirement home. At least it would have been better than Fort Lafayette. It would also have been kept warm enough in the bitter New York winters, and the food was inspected regularly. They even had weekly cinema shows, gymnastic displays by the inmates, and open days for New Yorkers. It was a model institution staffed by doctors who went on to make their names as noted New York psychiatrists. New York State "patient confidentiality" restrictions keep his Ward Island file out of reach.

James Carlin was a driven man who was prepared to take extraordinary risks to achieve his goals. He was on the losing side in the American Civil War but was soon risking his life for the Cuban junta, a largely emancipist movement. He appears to have been a pragmatist and not an idealist, trusting that his skills and kind providence would see him though. All those stresses and strains preyed on his mind, if not his physique, and led to this final demand to his widowed sister-in-law Mary Moorer Carlin, née Joyner, in Jupiter, Florida.

To Mrs. M Carlin                                   20th May 1920
My dear Sister in Law
Would have written since my letter of December 1919, but from time to time fully expected to hear from you, all the same I kept hoping in this instance that no news might prove to be good news meanwhile earnestly praying that your good self with your daughter and son in law would soon be quite restored to their previous good health.

The fact may be mentioned that my present circumstances almost precludes the possibility of writing therefore concluded to wait, but now partly because I am in full enjoyment of a vigorous condition of good health, this fact coupled with certain very favourable considerations exist which serve . . . to constrain me once more to write and let you know that the field of my expected future business activities and possibilities could not be most inviting than they are at present.

So that all I need to make a beginning and thereby take advantage of the present opportunity, and if you can aid me in doing this much you can depend upon, that I can and will—(please God)—make good, as has been stated in my previous letters.

Sincerely hoping that this will find you all well in health, I remain with kindest and best wishes your affectionate Brother in Law.

James Carlin

[*Note on cover*] P.S. Please enclose your reply as follows and oblige, Mrs Henry Holt, C/o Mr Hauley, 306 third Av. N. York City[9]

James Carlin died at Ward Island on 11 March 1921 at the age of eighty-eight. There is no record that Mary Carlin responded to this letter. However, she kept it safe with other family documents that suggests that some help was sent.

> My ship has struck, my mast's gone,
> My soul has fled the deck;
> And here beneath this cold grey stone,
> My body lies a wreck.

But still the Promise standeth sure,
It shall refitted be,
And sail the seas of endless bliss,
Through all eternity.[10]

(Memorial to an old mariner in Brancaster Church Yard,
Norfolk, England)

# Appendix 1:
## Additional Documents

. . .

**James Carlin's Service with the Coast Survey Department**

Hon. W. H. Seward Coast Survey Office
Secretary of State Dec. 15. 1862
Sir,
I have the honor to acknowledge the receipt of yours of Dec, 12'th & to state in re-
ply that James Carlin, was employed as a Pilot, on board the Schr. Gallatin, Lieut.
J. N. Maffitt Commanding, from April 1st. 1856 to the end of 1857. On board the
Schr. Crawford Lieut. J. B. Huger commanding from January 1, 1858 to Oct 15th.
On board the Schr. Varina, Lieut. C. H. Fauntleroy Commanding, from Oct 16th
1858 to April 30th 1860. The vessels were surveying the coasts of North and South
Carolina & Georgia, under the command of Naval Officers of the U.S.
Very respectfully, yours
A. D. Bache, Supd't. US Coast Survey.[1]

**Report of Acting Volunteer Lieutenant Budd,
U.S. Navy, commanding U.S.S. Magnolia.**

USS MAGNOLIA
*Navy Yard, New York, August 4, 1862.*
SIR:      I have the honor to inform the Department that on the morning of July
31, 1862, about 6 o'clock a.m., while in 32° 50′ north latitude, 78° 35′ west longitude, Cape Romain bearing W. by N., 40 miles distant, a steamer was made about
6 miles to the westward. She was then steering about N.E. by E. Upon which I immediately gave chase. As soon as the stranger perceived that I intended to overhaul
him, he made every effort to escape, hauling more to the eastward, so as to make
his fore-and-aft canvas draw (the wind being southwest), firing up and driving his
vessel as fast as possible. After having chased him for about an hour and a half I
fired a shotted gun, throwing the projectile between his masts and about two hundred yards beyond him, upon which he showed English colors, but still persevered
in his efforts to escape. Steadily gaining on him I fired a second time, the shot

dropping close alongside of him; then finding that he would not heave to I threw a shell, which exploded close to his starboard quarter, the fragments flying over his poop. At this he stopped his engines, and I, ranging alongside, hailed and found he was the British steamer *Memphis,* of London, bound ostensibly from Nassau to Liverpool. For some time before coming up with him he was observed to throw wood (Southern pine) overboard, and just before boarded a package loaded for sinking was thrown over the port quarter. I boarded him myself, and finding that he could not produce either a manifest, clearance, or log, immediately took possession, putting a prize crew on board in charge of Acting Master Charles Potter. Learning that an attempt had been made to sink or otherwise destroy the ship just before her capture, and that her crew consisted of nearly fifty persons, independent of officers and passengers, I determined upon removing them all to the Magnolia and convoy the *Memphis* to New York, arriving safely yesterday afternoon.

By a little tact I was enabled to secure a number of papers and letters, fully explaining the true character of the *Memphis* and her port of departure. She had come out of Charleston the night previous with nearly sixteen hundred bales of cotton and five hundred barrels of resin aboard. These documents I have placed in the hands of the prize commissioners, with the necessary affidavits and libel.

The Memphis was captured at 8 a.m., July 31, 1862, in 20 fathoms of water, about 25 miles E.N.E. of where she was first seen.

On board of her, among her passengers, I found J. C. Carlin, a resident of Charleston, and formerly attached for a number of years to the United States Coast Survey. He is intimately acquainted with the whole Southern coast, has been captured once before while running the blockade, and lately commanded the Confederate steamer *Cecile.* He carried the *Gladiator's* cargo from Nassau to Mosquito Inlet, Florida. There were also aboard of her two others, one of whom I know to be a Charleston pilot named Lea, the other I have reason to think belonged to the same class. I have notified the marshal to detain these three persons for the present.

I enclose a list of all the persons on board the Magnolia at the time of the capture, with their rates attached. Hoping that the Department will approve of my course in the matter, I remain, very respectfully, your obedient servant,

WILLIAM BUDD,

*Acting [Volunteer] Lieutenant, Commanding Magnolia.*

Hon. GIDEON WELLES,

*Secretary of the Navy, Washington, D.C.*[2]

## Report of Captain Carlin, commanding the Confederate torpedo ram.

CHARLESTON, [S.C.], *August 22, 1863.*

GENERAL: I have the honor to report that I attacked the *Ironsides* on the night of the 20th, but regret to say, however, it was not accompanied with any beneficial result.

I communicated with Fort Sumter at 10 p.m. and obtained a guard of 11 men, under command of Lieutenant [Eldred S.] Fickling. At 11:30 p.m. I passed the obstructions, and at 12 sighted the *Ironsides* lying at anchor in the channel off Morris Island, with five monitors moored immediately in a S.S.W. direction from her, and about 300 yards distant. One monitor was anchored in the direction bearing upon Battery Gregg and about half a mile distant. When I came within quarter of a mile of the *Ironsides* I lowered the torpedoes and proceeded directly for the ship, feeling at the same time fully confident of striking her in the right place. At this time she was lying across the channel and heading for Morris Island. I steered up, keeping the object on our port bow, and when within 40 yards from the ship I stopped the engine and ordered the helm put hard astarboard.

I attribute my failure to the want of proper execution of this order. I noticed the slow obedience of the ship to her helm, and again gave the order, repeating it three times. It was a moment of great anxiety and expectation, and not doubting but I would strike her, I was obliged to attend to the proper command of the officers and men and restrain any undue excitement. In this I was ably assisted by the cool, courageous bearing of Lieutenant Fickling, who commanded the force stationed for defense. I discovered as we ranged up alongside that in consequence of the *Ironsides* being in the act of swinging to the ebb we must miss with our torpedoes, but feared that her chain cable would either ignite them or detain us alongside. In either case we must have been captured. A kind Providence, however, intervened and saved our little band from such disaster. When about 50 yards distant we were hailed, "Ship ahoy!" After deliberating whether I should not give him some warning, I felt so sure of striking him, I finally answered "Hello," and in an official and stern tone as possible. Another hail, "What ship is that?" I answered almost immediately, "The steamer 'Live Yankee.'"

We were still moving slowly past the bow. I gave the order to go ahead with the engine, and was informed at the same time that the enemy were boarding us. Without looking to see whether such was the case, I gave the order to defend the ship and got my arms ready in time to prevent the firing upon some sailors that were looking at us from the ports. I saw they were not boarding and I immediately ordered the men to hold and not fire. They dropped immediately, showing specimen of the effect of good discipline. Just at this time he hailed again, "Where are you from?" Answered, "Port Royal." I found that we had ranged just clear of his bow and out of danger of being boarded except by launches. I then went to the engine room to see what was the matter, as fully two minutes had elapsed since the order had been given to go ahead. I found that the engine had caught upon the center and notwithstanding a continued effort for at least four or five minutes, they failed to get started ahead. I was again hailed, "What ship is that?" Answered, "The United States steamer 'Yankee.'"

I again went to the engine room, and by encouragement to the engineers found her in the act of starting. Another hail and another called me to the deck and as none of my officers heard the question, I surmised it to be an order to come to anchor or to surrender. I answered, " Aye, aye, sir; I'll come on board." I found we were moving ahead slowly, and in two minutes must have passed out of his sight, as he commenced firing in the opposite direction. He afterwards fired, sweeping the horizon, two shots passing on either side about 20 feet off.

It was my intention to attack one of the monitors, but after the experience with the engine, I concluded it would be almost madness to attempt it. I therefore steered back to the city.

General, in consequence of the tests to which I have put the ship in the two late, adventures, I feel it my duty most unhesitatingly to express my condemnation of the vessel and engine for the purposes it was intended, and as soon as she can be docked and the leak stopped, would advise making a transport of her.

I beg to remain, respectfully, your obedient servant,

J. CARLIN.

To: General G. T. BEAUREGARD

*Commanding at Charleston, S.C.*[3]

General Beauregard replied immediately:

HDQRS. DEPT. SOUTH CAROLINA, GEORGIA AND FLORIDA,
*August 20 [23]. 1863*

CAPTAIN: your report of operations in the attempt to destroy the *Ironsides* during the night of 18th [20th] instant has been received. I regret exceedingly that you should have met with so many difficulties in your disinterested and praise-worthy enterprise, but I am happy to learn that you are still willing to retain command of the torpedo ram, for I know of no one whose skill and experience I would sooner trust the boat on so bold and gallant an undertaking. I feel convinced that another trial under more favorable circumstances will surely meet with success, notwithstanding the known defects of the vessel.

Respectfully, your obedient servant,

G. T. BEAUREGARD,

*Commanding*

To: Captain JAMES CARLIN

*Commanding Torpedo Ram, Charleston, S.C.*[4]

## James Carlin's Report of His Activities in England and Scotland

Wm C. Bee Esquire. President. Port Muck, Isle Magee, Ireland,
Feb 10th 1864

My Dear Sir

I have the honour to report my proceedings so far since, my arrival here on the 10th Feb. and enclose copy of an agreement between the Messrs Denny and myself (on the part of the Co) for the construction of three ships. I trust, after you have seen my full explanation, it will meet with your entire approval and likewise that of the board of Directors.

We landed in London on the 10th [January] and arrived in Liverpool on the 12. Called on Mr Calder and after a delay of two days Mr Sly & Myself started to the N.E. England a place highly recommended by Capt Pick, Lessier and others as combining cheapness with strength of construction etc. We brought up at Stockton on Tees where we called at the different builders who were so pressed with work that they could not entertain the matter at all under 10 months. This was the case at two firms at Middlesboro on the same river, at Hartlepool in three yards, thence wise in all, and in contemplation for building some 27 ships to be completed by the end of the year. One of the Firms promised to send me an estimate for two such ships as I wanted.

I returned to Stockton and Mr Sly started for Hull the next day, with instructions to see what was offering & what could be done. He was to visit London and meet me (after going to Liverpool and being on the trial trip of Fraser's new steel ship under command Capt. Harrison, at Glasgow).

I then after delay of one day to get the estimates promised started for Sunderland and Newcastle. Precisely the same state of things existed at these places that I found at the former. One Firm could build the Hull and not the Engines. They offered to send estimates to my address and although they have never come I am under the impression that His price would have been so exorbitant as to frighten us all.

I visited 4 building firms and found all alike. After a short run to Newcastle upon Tyne I felt satisfied that nothing could be done at any of the places visited. So I started forthwith for the Clyde, against which place I have been prejudiced since hearing Capt. Rollins experience. I called upon Messrs. L & G Thompson the builders of the Giraffe and other fast ships. He showed me two ships to draw 7 ft and go about 14 knots with I suppose a capacity of 500 Bales at outside. He offered to build facsimiles and deliver first in 7 months for say 18 or 19,000 Pounds each. He did not mention these figures but I inferred that he would have placed them in the water for less than 20,000 pounds. The time was however very long and I preferred making efforts elsewhere, so I sent for Mr Sly to Liverpool and called at Mr Denny found him quite full but building on speculation for himself. He could not build the Engines and Boilers but sent to his friends the Messrs Napier and found them ready to undertake the work. I asked for estimates of ships 225 x 28 x 13. I regarded this size as combining certain coasting advantage in point of draft and length that would place them on the same list with the Ruby in particular but carrying 3 times her cargo over 6 to 6½ ft. at about from 6 to 800 bales on 6½ ft. They will have Engines of 54 inch Oscillating Cylinders and Boilers constructed after Mr Sly's and my own plans for light consumption, consuming smoke etc. etc. The first estimate was £22,500. pounds but by some mistake in his calculation it was reduced afterwards in completing it to 22,000. Each. The Engines having to be built out of his own works cost more than if he had been able to build them himself. He had two offers to build the Engines & Boilers, but as Napier had the best name and stood the highest I chose him in preference to the others at precisely £1000 pounds more than I could have had them done by the other people.

The two ships would have stood £21,000 each, they now stand 22,000 each, but the ships and Engines come from the men bearing the highest reputations on the Clyde and when we get them we will be satisfied that they are from the best hands. Mr Calder approved of my above decision as he knows the parties.

Now the next ship is approaching about the size of the maximum I spoke to you about, and upon 8 ft should carry about twice what the A&F would or say 1600 to 1800 bales. The estimates sent to Mr Calder from two of the parties in England & from Caird on the Clyde for one 5 ft shorter than the larger one contacted for. One was from Caird & [unreadable] at £37,500 pounds One is 10 months from parties in England at £38,000 pounds & another same dimensions at £40,000 pounds. Denny's was as the contract reads 35,500. So calculating from Cairds which was the lowest estimate I found that the three could be built for the money that two at that price would taking all things into consideration, that the price of materials has gone up and also labour. I have regarded the enclosed as very far better that can be done anywhere I have heard of. Mr Denny showed me figures [from] 6 months ago for Iron and labour and at that time he could have built the first two at 19 or 19,500 each and delivered a month sooner & and the larger one in proportion. You will read on the agreement that they are to be fitted in every way for the trade & no extras. The larger one I have been anxious to build and when done would with your permission name her after your good lady.

I hope that the above hurried letter may be satisfactory to you. I am obliged to write in a hurry to save the mail. You must not think of deserting us in our infancy & with the State as a partner. I have seen everything there is here, that looks like a suitable vessel for the trade but none comes up to the required stamp.
Yours respectfully
J. Carlin

Finding that I have the time to add a few words more to my hurried letter. I hasten to do so and would now like to finish about the new ships. The most important reason for building with Messrs. Denny is that I can get what we want and with Messrs Thompson we would be obliged to take what he would give which are the dimensions I have mentioned. I think the difference in price is more than counterballanced [*sic*] by the difference in time of delivery & in the quality of ship when finished. The small ones will accommodate say 12 to 15 passengers & be furnished with everything necessary for sea except provisions and coal.

The large one will have steam winches & windlass etc.etc. and be in every way complete with accommodations for say double the former 25 to 30 with all the necessary outfits etc.etc. I deemed it an advantage to build in the manner above stated as the best way of dividing the facilities for transportation with you while the larger would run to the main port. The others could go almost anywhere that the tide ebbed and flowed.

Not anticipating your suggestion of purchasing one vessel and making use of her while the others were building I have nevertheless been to several places to look at the steamers but none that I have seen will do so far. The Dover boats are the nearest to what would be suitable for our business they would cost a great deal & need various alterations for the trade that would be expensive and take a great deal of time. I am to hear all particulars very soon in reference to some others that are for sale and may meet with something that is suitable.

I should not like to buy unless there was a near approach to perfection. The ship built for Fraser's at Liverpool is a failure in speed and draft and instead of drawing 8 ft will draw 10. Otherwise she is a fine ship very far from perfection however. I enclose a Photograph of the S.S. Infanta Isabelle. She is the ship we took passage in from Havana to Cadiz and built by Messrs Denny. One of the finest ships afloat.

Your letters in duplicate commissioning me as Superintendent have come to hand for which please accept my sincere thanks. The general instructions are duly noted and shall be observed as written. In dispatching ships it has been my intention to deliver them in person. After completing my arrangements for building and getting the work started I have run over here to see my Father and Friends. They are all well thank God and enjoying content & happiness with the blessing of health - all of which I trust may fall largely to your lot.

Yours respectfully

J Carlin[5]

# Appendix 2:
# Reflections on Confederate Finance

. . .

In the first stage of the war, foreign currency was sent to Europe in the form of specie, being gold and silver coins, bills of exchange drawn on Europe or the North, and whatever foreign notes could be bought from Southern banks. Initially, the specie came from the Confederate Treasury confiscations from United States mints and U.S. customs houses throughout the South. Later U.S. dollars became available as payment for the large quantities of cotton smuggled over the land borders from Southern plantations to feed the mills of the North.[1]

Blockade-runners carried these special cargoes to the overseas purchasing agents to support letters of credit issued to the suppliers of armaments and other necessities. In addition, the treasury shipped cotton on its own account to Fraser, Trenholm and Company in Liverpool, which sold it and deposited the proceeds to the credit of the government. Armaments and other essential supplies were then paid for by warrants drawn on these deposits.[2]

As the premium on foreign currency increased, this method of financing became more difficult. After eighteen months, the treasury resorted to issuing "cotton certificates," or bonds, redeemable in Europe on the proceeds from the sale of exported cotton. To attract sufficient investment, bonds were offered on the London market at a discount of fifty cents on the dollar. Because much of the cotton was in the western Gulf states, cotton certificates were denominated East or West cotton so that purchasers could gauge the difficulties of realizing their investment. But those difficulties weighed heavily on the minds of potential European investors. Those with long memories remembered the Mississippi state bond issue that the Confederate president, Jefferson Davis, when a state senator "had insisted that the state simply repudiate."[3] Others close to the cotton trade were well aware that cotton planters throughout the South had stock to spare and could find the means to circumvent government controls.

Further foreign financing was facilitated by a $15 million loan. This was a floating, twenty-year, 7 percent loan raised by Baron Emile Erlanger and Company, bankers of Paris, and negotiated by John Slidell and Caleb Huse, the Confederate agents in France. Erlanger in Paris and Frankfurt, Schroeders in London and Amsterdam, and Trenholm in Liverpool all managed the issue. Opened on 19 March 1863, it was quickly oversubscribed to £16 million in two and a half days and even went to a 5 percent premium, although only a total of £3 million was permitted to be sold. The loan was redeemable in government cotton held in the Confederacy, thus encouraging the runners to even greater efforts on behalf of the bondholders.

Within two weeks, the bonds had dropped to 85 percent of the face value. After the disaster of the Confederate defeat at Vicksburg, the price had dropped to 36 percent. While these and other financial devices were used to fund continued purchases, U.S. Consul Dudley in Liverpool remarked to his astonishment at the naivety of European merchants in their ready acceptance of the Confederate paper. While it underpinned the viability of the blockade-runner's business, they did not know that Erlanger was secretly supporting the value of their bonds by active repurchases on the European markets. Government procurement between August 1862 and February 1864 had been almost entirely paid from the $7,675,501 actually raised by the loan.

The Erlanger bonds denominated in £500 Sterling or 12,500 French Francs or 20,000 pounds of cotton. The actual value of the bonds fluctuated with the fortunes of the Confederacy—usually downward. From the private collection of Barto Arnold, Institute of Nautical Archaeology.

The eventual failure of these measures led to an acute funding crisis. The Richmond government's mid-1864 attempt to introduce a system of payment in cotton at the port of dispatch led to a multitude of contracts being hawked around the exchanges of Europe and further reduced Confederate credit. Deliberately set rumors and blatant lobbying by Confederate agents in Europe artificially buoyed Confederate currency and bonds. The legend was that when the war ended, Washington would honor the financial commitments of the breakaway government. This did not take into account the resolution of President Lincoln and his Northern supporters to finish the business, nor did they take account of the weakness of President Davis's position and his empty, poorly managed treasury.

Economist David Surdam argues that the Confederacy held a vital economic advantage: its price-setting power in the world market for raw cotton. According to Surdam, "The antebellum South faced an inelastic and growing demand for its raw cotton. By reducing the crop by one-third, the South could have increased revenue by enough to have financed a strong navy. Concurrently, the South could have freed up 170,000 man-years of labor."[4]

The Confederate states had failed to impose a government monopoly on cotton supply and was unable to control sales. Excess production depressed local prices. Planter interests had prevailed again, and revenues from minimal cotton taxes produced negligible revenues.[5] At the end of the day, the South failed dismally to exploit "King Cotton," and Charleston and Wilmington exported only some 1.5 percent of the 4,056,000 bales shipped from the South before the war, or 11.5 percent of the total bales estimated to have been dispatched from the South during the war years.[6]

# Appendix 3:
# Alexander D. Bache's Correspondence with James Carlin

. . .

J. Carlin to Dr. A. D. Bache.
A.D Bache,                    Fort Lafayette, Sept 30th 1862.
Superintendent, U.S.C. Survey
Dear Sir,
I beg under the circumstances you will excuse the liberty I have taken of using your name in the enclosure (to the Hon. Sec. of War) as a referee. I have been induced to take this liberty feeling confident that you would not refuse one of your old followers in Science such a indulgence. You will easily remember my Service in the Hydrographic Branch of your great work on board the Schooners Crawford and Varina—and in command of the Fire Fly, at a later date. I have [hope] that, that service and our social acquaintance would entitle me to your favour at this time, that is so far I ask, which is your assistance to obtain a Parole of a few days for me, when I could make further explanations. In hoping for your favour in this matter and reply to this at your earliest convenience, I remain respect. and sincerely yours
James Carlin

Dr. Bache to J. Carlin
October 4 1862                    Philadelphia
Dear Sir, Are you prepared to take the oath of allegiance or not? If not I see no use of any representations to be made to the government orally. I am under the impression that you are a secessionist and cannot assist you while that impression remains upon my mind. Please give me a detailed statement of your acts since the breaking out of the rebellion. If you desire assistance with the government from me I must first be satisfied that you are a loyal citizen of the United States,
Yours respectfully A. D. Bache
(Copy)

James Carlin to Dr Bache

Fort Lafayette, Oct 7, 1862

Dear Sir [ Dr. Bache] Your favour of the 4th in reply to my note of the 1st has been received and I cannot but regret, that a simple request, which no one Gentleman ought to refuse another—of whose honor he had—at least some slight proof, should have met so uncourteous a reply.

I think that you are under a mistake with regard to my nationality. I am a Foreigner. Your Government prevents me from establishing that fact, I simply wanted a parole to satisfy the authorities upon that point, and to be taunted in reply, with being a Secessionist, and challenged to take an Oath, (which to say the least of will never reflect much credit upon its framers) is not the courtesy I should have expected.

With regard to my acts, they are my own private property. An oath of allegiance to the United States I have never taken, nor never will. If my favour cannot be granted without it Please Pardon my intrusions and permit me to remain, Respectfully, James Carlin[1]

# Appendix 4:
## Bahamian Exports, 1861–1865

· · ·

The *Report of the Governor of the Bahamas in the Colonial Office Blue Book for 1865* demonstrates the effect of the Union blockade of the Southern states on the economy of the colony.

In 1860 Bahamian imports totaled £234,029 and exports amounted to £157,350. In 1864 imports were £5,346,112. Exports in 1864 were £4,672,398, of which cotton amounted to £3,584,587. Most of the 62,898 bales of cotton originated in Charleston and Wilmington.

### Running the Blockade, 1861–1865

| | Imports £s | Exports £s | Ships Arriving | | Ships Departing | |
|---|---|---|---|---|---|---|
| | | | Sail | Steam | Sail | Steam |
| 1860 | 234,029 | 157,350 | | | | |
| 1861 | 274,584 | 195,584 | 2 | 2 | 1 | 3 |
| 1862 | 1,250,332 | 1,007,755 | 74 | 32 | 109 | 46 |
| 1863 | 4,295,316 | 3,308,567 | 27 | 113 | 48 | 173 |
| 1864 | 5,346,112 | 4,672,398 | 6 | 105 | 2 | 165 |
| 1865 | | | 0 | 35 | 0 | 41 |

Official Bahamian Import-Export Figures during the Civil War.
From *History of the Bahamas* by Michael Craton, 228.

These figures indicate the extent to which the blockade-runners changed tactics after the *Gladiator* affair diverted the direct transatlantic trade from Southern ports to the British Caribbean Islands. They should also be seen in the context of the 4 million bales of cotton that had been shipped directly from Charleston and Wilmington, bypassing Nassau in the prewar years.

# Notes

...

## Preface

1. Letter, Ethel Jones (James Carlin's granddaughter) to author Willard R. Espy of New York, 7 December 1977.

2. "The Case of James Carlin," FO 5/1269, the National Archives of the UK, Public Record Office (hereinafter abbreviated as TNA). This large file contains a collection of Foreign Office (FO) documents relating to the trial of the *Memphis* and the diplomatic tussle for Carlin's release from Fort Lafayette.

3. For more on these points, see Marcus W. Price's series of articles in *American Neptune*, with further analysis by Stanley Lebergott in the *Journal of Economic History* and *Journal of American History*. Their findings are reanalyzed by Bruce W. Hetherington and Peter J. Kower in the *Journal of Economic History*.

## Introduction

1. Thomas, *The Confederate Nation*, 1–12.

2. Thomas, *The Confederate Nation*, 8, 9.

3. *Economist*, 19, no. 948 (26 October 1861), 20.

4. Merli, *The* Alabama, *British Neutrality, and the American Civil War*, 13.

5. Price, "Masters and Pilots Who Tested the Blockade," 81.

6. Wise, *Lifeline of the Confederacy*, 111, and Stanley Lebergott, "Wage Trends, 1800–1900," 452.

7. Introduction, *Charleston Directory*, 1866.

8. Clark, *Railroads in the Civil War*, 5–7.

9. Maffitt, *Life and Services of John Newland Maffitt*.

## Chapter 1: Early Days, 1833–1848

1. Baptismal Records of St. Mary's Church, Old Hunstanton, Norfolk.

2. Coast Guard Staff Records, ADM 175/6, ADM 175/18, and ADM 175/19, Seaman's Tickets, BT113/71, all in TNA. The ADM (Admiralty) and the BT (Board of Trade) series contain extensive Coast Guard records detailing the staff movements.

3. Coast Guard Nominations for Service, ADM 175/77, and Seaman's Ticket no. 141,845, BT 113/71, TNA.

4. Customs and Excise Administration Papers, ref. 2 442–2 448, National Archives of Ireland, Dublin. The Dublin archives hold material from the pre-Independence period, when Ireland was part of the United Kingdom. This includes staff letters and other materials that have been weeded from the parallel records in London.

5. Hipper, *Smugglers All*, 164.

6. Customs and Excise Records, Series CUST 1 and CUST 2, Public Record Office of Northern Ireland, Belfast.

## Chapter 2: Navigation School, the Apprentice, 1850–1856

1. "Death of Mr. William Larmour," *Carrickfergus Advertiser*, 5 October 1883.

2. Register of Greenwich Hospital School, London, ADM 161/2, TNA.

3. *Illustrated London News*, 19 February 1848.

4. Registry of Shipping and Seamen, Index of Apprentices, Outports, BT 150/24, TNA.

5. Registry of Shipping and Seamen, Ticket no. 443.135, BT 113/222, TNA.

6. Reports in *Shipping News*, 1 January 1900, and the *Belfast Commercial Chronicle*, 5 February 1812.

## Chapter 3: United States Coast Survey, 1856–1860

1. Weddle, "Blockade Board of 1861 and Union Naval Strategy," 128.

2. Slotten, *Patronage, Practice, and the Culture of American Science*. See also the National Archives and Records Administration at College Park for microfilm of Record Group 60 for Bache's correspondence between 1862 and 1863. Record Group 23 holds his General Correspondence between 1844 and 1865 and includes some letters relating to James Carlin. Subsequent references to the U.S. National Archive and Records Administration are abbreviated NARA, followed by the city in which the particular branch is located (that is, NARA, College Park; NARA, Philadelphia).

3. Odgers, *Alexander Bache*.

4. Sutherland, *Whistler: A Life for Arts Sake*.

5. Hearn, *Tracks in the Sea*, 180–81.

6. Letter, Carlin to Bache, 30 September 1862, Records of the Adjutant General's Office, 1860–65, (Turner-Baker Records), RG 94.2.5 NARA, College Park. This group contains further correspondence between Carlin and Bache.

7. Miscellaneous Letters, 1789–1906 (Letters Received), General Records of the Department of State, vol. 380, December 1862, Record Group 100, NARA, College Park.

8. *Charleston Courier*, 1 April 1862.

9. *Report of the Superintendent of the Coast Survey During the Year 1856*, 58–59.

10. National Archives at College Park, College Park, MD. 23.2.2 Records of the Office of the Superintendent (1816–1920) Carlin to Bache, Dec. 15, 1858, letter numbered 4573.

11. *Report of the Superintendent of the Coast Survey During the Year 1859*, Appendix no. 29, 321.

12. *Report of the Superintendent of the Coast Survey During the Year 1859*, Appendix no. 29, 321.

13. Silverstone, *Civil War Navies, 1855–1883*, 180.

14. Lt. Cm. C. M. Fauntleroy to Alexander Bache 16 May 1860, No.82, Records of the Coast and Geodetic Survey, Entry 5, Bache correspondence 1860 Vol IX Naval Assistants, Record Group 23; NARA, Washington DC.

## Chapter 4: A Romantic Interlude, 1857

1. Jacob Schirman Diary, May 1857, South Carolina Historical Society (hereinafter cited as SCHS).

2. *Charleston News and Courier*, 13 July 1882.

3. 1860 Comal County census of New Braunfels, Texas.

4. Carlin, *William Kirkpatrick of Málaga*, 146.

5. Villiers, *A Vanished Victorian*, 261–62.

6. McCusker, *How Much Is That in Real Money?*, updated to 2014 using the U.S. Bureau of Labor's CPI Inflation Calculator, available online at http://www.bls.gov/data/inflation_calculator.htm (accessed 30 June 2014). Subsequent citations are shortened to McCusker, *How Much Is That*/CPI.

7. Kurtz, *The Empress Eugénie.*

8. Will of Joseph Gallego, 1818, Will Book 2, Richmond City Hustings Court, Library of Virginia.

9. http://www.lib.noaa.gov/noaainfo/heritage/coastsurveyvol1/CW1.html#COMING or NOAA Central Library, The Coast Survey in the Civil War, Section One, Introduction.

## Chapter 5: Transition, 1860

1. Bill of Sale, vol. 6E, 217, Series: S213050, South Carolina Department of Archives and History (hereinafter cited as SCDAH).

2. McCusker, *How Much Is That*/CPI.

3. *Henry Dietz v. James Carlin*, 23 February 1866, Comal County Court Record for Spring Term 1866; *New Braunfels Zeitung*, 23 February 1866.

4. McCusker, *How Much Is That*/CPI.

5. Eaton, *History of the Southern Confederacy*, 14.

6. Wise, *Lifeline of the Confederacy*, 69.

## Chapter 6: The Blockade Is Declared, 1860–1861

1. Burton, *Siege of Charleston*, 50.

2. Mowat, *Diplomatic Relations of Great Britain and the United States*, 169–70.

3. Weddle, *Lincoln's Tragic Admiral*, 111–12.

4. Davis and Engerman, *Naval Blockades in Peace and War*, 110.

5. Savage, *Policy of the United States*, 1:176–77.

6. White, *Law in American History*, 434–35.

7. Skelton, "Importing and Exporting Company of South Carolina" (thesis), 2.

8. Goldsmith and Posner, *Limits of International Law*, 46–48. Goldsmith and Posner expand on the principle of "free trade and free ships" that underlay Union thinking at this point in the conflict and the Union's subsequent departures from this principle.

9. Savage, *Policy of the United States*, 1:87–88.

10. Robert Bunch, Consul at Charleston, General Correspondence before 1906, United States of America, series 2, FO 5/780, TNA.

11. Merli, *The* Alabama, *British Neutrality, and the American Civil War*, chapter 3.

12. Quoted in Price, "Ships That Tested the Blockade of the Carolina Ports," 201.

13. Weddle, "Blockade Board of 1861," 126.

14. Quoted in Massey, *Ersatz in the Confederacy*, 11.

15. Quoted in Davis and Engerman, *Naval Blockades in Peace and War*, 109.

16. Massey, *Ersatz in the Confederacy*, 11–20.

17. See discussion of Kalmia Mills in chapter 29.

18. Lebergott, "Why the South Lost," 58–74.

## Chapter 7: Wildcatter, Blockade Running Under Sail, 1860–1862

1. Craton, *History of the Bahamas*, 228.

2. General Pay and Receipt Roll, Savannah Station, July–September 1861, Naval Records Collection, Record Group 45, NARA, College Park. See also Muster Rolls, etc., Confederate

Vessels, in U.S. Naval War Records Office, *Official Records of the Union and Confederate Navies,* ser. 2, vol. 1: 322–23. Subsequent references to this source will be abbreviated as *ORN.*

3. Quoted in Buker, *Blockaders, Refugees, and Contrabands,* 40.

4. Price, "Ships That Tested the Blockade of the Carolina Ports," 215–22.

5. Admiralty Case, *United States v. the Schooner* Alert *and her Cargo:* Interrogation of James Carlin and others, Record Group 21, NARA, Philadelphia (hereinafter shortened to *U.S. v.* Alert). The description of the capture of the *Alert* and the events that followed are drawn from the records of this case. This gives a full account of the trial, but the pages are not numbered. The U.S. Navy account is from *ORN,* ser. 1, vol. 6: 295–96, 332.

6. *U.S. v.* Alert.

7. Wise, *Lifeline of the Confederacy,* 9.

8. Moore, ed., *Rebellion Record,* 4:72.

9. Ship number 42766, Port 37 (Nassau), Registry of Seaman and Shipping, BT 108/288, TNA.

10. Blachford, *Reports of Cases in Prize,* 187.

11. *U.S. v.* Alert.

12. United Daughters of the Confederacy, *Patriot Ancestor Album,* 164.

13. Craton, *History of the Bahamas,* 225–37.

14. *Bahamas Chart Kit* and local knowledge from Christopher M. Carlin.

15. Nepveux, *George A. Trenholm,* 235.

16. *U.S. v.* Alert.

## Chapter 8: First Gunfire

1. *U.S. v.* Alert.

2. *Daily National Intelligencer,* 31 October, 1861.

3. *Daily National Intelligencer,* 31 October, 1861.

4. U.S. v. Alert.

5. *Daily National Intelligencer,* 31 October, 1861.

6. *U.S. v.* Alert.

7. *U.S. v.* Alert.

8. ORN, ser. 1, vol.6: 296.

9. U.S. v. Alert.

10. Craton, *History of the Bahamas,* 249.

11. *ORN,* ser. 1,vol. 6. 295-96, 332. and Deposition of H. W. Rylea, U.S. v. Alert.

12. Deposition of Charles Carlin, U.S. v. Alert.

13. Captain Matthew C. Perry Jr. was the son of Commodore Perry who led the famous U.S. expedition to Japan in the 1850s.

14. ORN, ser.1 vol.6: 332.

15. Witness statement by Midshipman John Weidman, 21 October, 1861. *U.S. v.* Alert.

16. Drake, "Cuban Background to the Trent Affair," 29–49.

17. *U.S. v.* Alert.

18. Boys entering the Royal Navy were then classified as first, second, or third class. First and second class boys were identified as potential officers, sailing masters or petty officers, while the others were expected to remain as ratings.

## Chapter 9: The Confederacy Confronts the Blockade

1. Guelzo, *Fateful Lightning,* 291.

2. Lebergott, "Through the Blockade," 881–82.

3. Jones, *Union in Peril,* 43–44.

4. Skelton, "Importing and Exporting Company of South Carolina" (journal article), 24–32.

5. *ORN,* ser. 1, vol. 2: 480–81.

6. Robinton, *Introduction to the Papers of the New York Prize Court, 1861–1865,* 150–51.

7. Lebergott, "Through the Blockade," 867–88.

8. Lebergott, "Through the Blockade," 867.

9. Hetherington and Kower, "A Re-examination of Lebergott's Paradox," 528–32.

10. Nepveux, *George A. Trenholm,* 12.

11. Nepveux, *George A. Trenholm,* 64.

12. Price, "Masters and Pilots Who Tested the Blockade," 81.

13. Letter, Mr. James M. Mason in London to Earl Russell, 7 July 1862. Correspondence with Mr. Mason respecting blockade, and recognition of the Confederate States by Great Britain. Foreign Office (Pamphlet), London, 1863.

14. Weddle, "Blockade Board of 1861," 125.

15. *ORN,* ser. 1, vol. 1: 224–85.

16. Wise, *Lifeline of the Confederacy,* 59.

17. Savage, *Policy of the United States,* 1:450.

18. *Charleston Mercury,* 15 April 1861.

19. Letter, Department of History, University of South Carolina, to Dr. Charles Peery of Charleston, S.C., 7 May 1981.

20. Price, "Masters and Pilots Who Tested the Blockade," 88.

## Chapter 10: Running through the Blockade for Trenholm and Company, 1861–1862

1. Shingleton, *High Seas Confederate,* 39–40.

2. Burton, *Siege of Charleston,* 246.

3. Register of Shipping and Seamen, Nassau, Register 177, BT 108/291, TNA.

4. Shingleton, *High Seas Confederate,* 40–41.

5. Wise, *Lifeline of the Confederacy,* 59–60.

6. *New York Tribune,* 29 April 1862.

7. Horner, *The Blockade-Runners,* 189–90.

8. Price, "Ships That Tested the Blockade of the Carolina Ports," 198.

9. Price, "Blockade Running as a Business," 36.

10. Horner, *The Blockade Runners,* 190.

11. *Nassau Guardian,* 16 and 19 April 1862.

12. For another version of this story and Maffitt's high jinks with the U.S. Consul in Nassau, see James Sprunt, "Derelicts: An Account of Ships Lost at Sea in General Commercial Traffic and a Brief History of Blockade Runners Stranded along the North Carolina Coast, 1861–1865, available online at *Internet Archive,* http://archive.org/stream/derelictsaccountoospru/derelictsaccountoospru_djvu.txt.

13. Price, "Masters and Pilots Who Tested the Blockade," 81.

14. Roberts, *Never Caught,* 37.

15. *New York Times,* 18 September 1892.

16. Roberts, *Never Caught,* 11.

17. *West Australian,* 23 January 1915.

18. Still, Taylor, and Delaney, *Raiders and Blockaders,* 137–38.

19. Taylor, *Running the Blockade.*

20. Wise, *Lifeline of the Confederacy,* 69.

21. Horner, *The Blockade-Runners,* 190.

22. Letter, Bee to Carlin, 3 May 1862, W. C. Bee & Company Records, 1848–1912, SCHS.
23. Horner, *The Blockade-Runners*, 190.
24. *New York Times,* 14 July 1862 (dateline Nassau, 7 July).
25. Nepveux, *George Alfred Trenholm and the Company That Went to War,* 45.

## Chapter 11: The *Memphis* Affair, July 31–August 1, 1862

1. Graham, *Clyde Built,* 71.
2. Graham, *Clyde Built,* 74.
3. *ORN,* ser. 1, vol. 7: 373.
4. *ORN,* ser. 1, vol. 7: 258.
5. Graham, *Clyde Built,* 74.
6. *ORN,* ser. 1, vol. 13: 226.
7. Graham, *Clyde Built,* 75.
8. *Charleston Courier,* 24 June 1862.
9. List contract envelope relating to the *Memphis,* Ship No. 82, 1862, William Denny and Sons Ltd., UGD 3/5/0014, University of Glasgow.
10. Wise, *Lifelines of the Confederacy,* 71.
11. Bunch to Russell 24 June, 1862, FO5/1269, TNA.
12. Wise, *Lifeline of the Confederacy,* 71–72.
13. Bunch to Russell 24 June, 1862, FO5/1269, TNA.
14. Theberge, "The Coast Survey and Army Operations during the Civil War," pt. 3, sec. 2, from an online history of the National Oceanic and Atmospheric Administration (accessed 10 August 2013).
15. Log entries, 31 July and 1 August 1862, log book of the USS *Magnolia,* U.S. Navy Log Books, Microfilm 18W4 6-6-c, Washington National Record Center.
16. *ORN,* ser. 1, vol. 13: 226.
17. *ORN,* ser. 1, vol. 13: 225–26.
18. McCusker, *How Much Is That*/CPI.
19. Underwood, *Waters of Discord,* 38.
20. *ORN,* ser. 1, vol. 13: 225.
21. Acting consul Charles Edwards to Foreign Office, London 7 August 1862.FO 5/1267 7, TNA.

## Chapter 12: Trial of the *Memphis,* August–September, 1862

1. Microfilm Prize Case 116-1 to 116-58, Papers of the New York Prize Court during the Civil War, United States District Court, New York (Southern District) , Columbia University. Law School Library, New York.
2. Price, "Ships That Tested the Blockade of the Carolina Ports," 212n47 (letter from Welles to Admirals commanding North Atlantic Blockading Squadron).
3. FO 5/1269, TNA. The British Consul attended the court and made a record of the proceedings.
4. Microfilm Prize Case 116-1 to 116-58, Papers of the New York Prize Court during the Civil War, United States District Court, New York (Southern District) , Columbia University Law School Library, New York.
5. Microfilm Prize Case 116-35, Papers of the New York Prize Court during the Civil War, United States District Court, New York (Southern District) , Columbia University Law School Library, New York.
6. Quoted in Robinton, *Introduction to the Papers of the New York Prize Court,* 183–84.

7. Microfilm Prize Case 116-1 to 116-58, Papers of the New York Prize Court during the Civil War, United States District Court, New York (Southern District) , Columbia University Law School Library, New York.

8. Edwards to Foreign Office, London FO 5/1269 7, 7 August 1862.

9. "A peep into the Star Chamber at the custom house," *New York Express* June 6, 1863.

10. Robinton, *Introduction to the Papers of the New York Prize Court, 1861–1865.*

11. Robinton, *Introduction to the Papers of the New York Prize Court, 1861–1856,* 101.

12. Microfilm Prize Case 116-60, Papers of the New York Prize Court during the Civil War, United States District Court, New York (Southern District) , Columbia University Law School Library, New York.

## Chapter 13: Recriminations and Fall Out, 1862

1. FO 5/1269, 17, TNA.

2. FO 5/1269, 28, TNA.

3. Robinton, *Introduction to the Papers of the New York Prize Court, 1861–1865,* 82.

4. FO 5/1269, 49, TNA.

## Chapter 14: Fort Lafayette

1. Berwanger, *British Foreign Service and the American Civil War,* 54.

2. FO 5/1269, TNA.

3. While the letter gives the name as Samuel Carlin, this appears to be a misreading. The original letter may have been signed "Jas." and incorrectly transcribed.

4. FO 5/1269, 12, TNA.

5. Letter in the file "Case of James Carlin," FO 5/1269, 11, TNA.

6. Negus, "A Notorious Nest of Offence," 350–85.

7. Murray to British Consul Archibald, 5 September 1862. FO 5/1269 72, TNA.

8. Berwanger, *The British Foreign Service and the American Civil War,* 53.

9. See Lord Newton, *Lord Lyons: A Record of British Diplomacy,* vol. 1, for more on this pivotal figure.

10. Barnes and Barnes, *American Civil War Through British Eyes,* 2:iv.

11. Report in the Dutch newspaper *Middelburgsche courant* of the 15 April, 1862.

12. Maynard, "Thomas H. Dudley and Union Efforts to Thwart Confederate Activities in Great Britain."

13. FO 5/1269, 67, TNA.

14. FO 5/1269, 96, TNA.

## Chapter 15: Still a Captive, Late 1862

1. Letter, Lyons to Archibald, 19 November 1862, FO 5/1269, 100, TNA.

2. Letter, Welles to Seward, 6 December 1862. FO 5/1269, 106, TNA.

3. Letter, Seward to Bache 9 December 1862, Baker Turner, Record Group 94.2.5 NARA, College Park.

4. Letter, Bache to Seward, 11 December 1862, Adjutant General's Records War Department Division, Letters in the files of Brigadier General Lafayette C. Baker Provost Marshall and Levi C. Turner, Judge Advocate of the U.S. War Department (known as the Baker-Turner papers, 1852–65), Record Group 94.2.5, NARA, College Park.

5. Baker Turner papers, Record Group 94.2.5, NARA, College Park.

6. Baker Turner papers, Record Group 94.2.5, NARA, College Park. These two revealing letters between Carlin and Bache are given in full in appendix 3.

7. Bache writing to Seward on 11 December 1862, Baker Turner papers, Record Group 94.2.5, NARA, College Park.

8. Letter, Bache to Welles, 4 December 1862, Baker Turner papers, Record Group 94.2.5, NARA, College Park.

## Chapter 16: Diplomatic Power Play, Christmas 1862–January 1863

1. Correspondence between Lyons and Seward, FO 5/1269, 111–15, TNA.
2. Mowat, *Diplomatic Relations of Britain and the United States,* 170.
3. Foreman, *World on Fire,* 348–51. Amanda Foreman gives a lively account of the hostility Seward faced from Senators and other members of the cabinet.
4. *Charleston Courier,* 17 February 1863.
5. Letter, Seward to Lyons, 16 December 1862, FO 5/1269, 119, TNA.
6. Letter, Seward to Lyons, 16 December 1862, FO 5/1269/ 119, TNA.
7. Letter, Lyons to Archibald 26 December 1862, FO 5/1269 123–27, TNA.
8. Letter, Lyons to Archibald 26 December 1862, FO 5/1269 126–27, TNA.
9. Letter, Lyons to Russell, 10 January 1863, FO 5/1269, 76–82, TNA.
10. Letter, Lyons to Russell, 10 January 1863, FO 5/1269, 76–82, TNA.
11. Letter, Lyons to Archibald, 10 January 1863, FO 5/1269 131,TNA.
12. Letter, Lyons to Archibald, 10 January 1863, FO 5/1269 132, TNA.
13. Letter, Seward to Lyons, 12 January 1863, FO5/1269, 150, TNA.
14. Letter, Lyons to Russell, February 1863, FO5/1269, 151, TNA.
15. Letter, Delafield Smith to Seward, 7 January, 1863. Baker Turner papers, Record group 94. 2.5, NARA, College Park.
16. *Charleston Courier,* 17 February 1863.
17. Fetzer and Mowday, *Unlikely Allies.*
18. *Charleston Courier,* 17 February 1863.

## Chapter 17: Carlin Stakes His Claim, January–July 1863

1. Letter, Carlin to Archibald, 7 January 1863, FO 5/1269, 152–54, TNA.
2. Letter, Lyons to Russell, 1 March 1863, FO 5/1269, 146, TNA.
3. McCusker, *How Much Is That/*CPI.
4. Letter, Carlin to Archibald, 16 January 1863, FO 5/1269, 150–51, TNA.
5. Letter, Foreign Office Law Officer to Lord Lyons, 22 April 1863, FO 5/1269, 161, TNA.
6. Letter, Foreign Office Law Officer to Lord Lyons, 22 April 1863, FO 5/1269, 162, TNA.
7. Letter, Lyons to Archibald, 9 May 1863, FO 5/1269, 169, TNA.
8. Letter, Lyons to Russell, 25 May 1863, FO 5/1269, 173, TNA.
9. Letter, Archibald to Lyons, 25 May 1863, FO 5/1269, 173–74, TNA.
10. Letter, Law Officer to Lord Lyons, 9 July 1863, FO 5/1269, 175, TNA.
11. Claims 157 and 178, *Return of Claims of British Subjects Against the United States Government,* 745.

## Chapter 18: Resumption of Trade

1. Albury, *Story of the Bahamas,* 153.
2. Craton, *History of the Bahamas,* 236.
3. Roberts, *Never Caught,* 164.
4. Dundas, "Blockade Running During the War Between the States."
5. Johnson, *Rose O'Neale Greenhow and the Blockade Runners,* 71.
6. Graham, *Clyde Built,* 198.

7. *ORN*, ser. 1, vol. 3: 3.

8. *Nassau Guardian*, 18 April 1863.

9. *ORN*, ser. 1, vol. 14: 157.

10. Wise, *Lifelines of the Confederacy*, 256

11. Bill of Sale, vol. 6F, 24, Series: S213050, SCDAH.

12. Wilkinson, *Narrative of a Blockade-runner*, 62.

13. *Wilmington Journal*, 16 June 1863.

### Chapter 19: The "Commodore" of the South Carolina I&E Company

1. Price, "Blockade Running as a Business," 36–38.

2. Skelton, "Importing and Exporting Company of South Carolina" (thesis). I have drawn heavily on this detailed account for this chapter.

3. Price, "Blockade Running as a Business," 37–38.

4. *Charleston Mercury*, 1 May 1863.

5. Price, "Blockade Running as a Business," 39.

6. Skelton, "Importing and Exporting Company of South Carolina" (thesis), 29.

7. McCusker, *How Much Is That*/CPI.

8. Skelton, "Importing and Exporting Company of South Carolina" (thesis), 31.

9. Skelton, "Importing and Exporting Company of South Carolina" (thesis), 78.

10. Lebergott, "Through the Blockade," 871.

11. Skelton, "Importing and Exporting Company of South Carolina" (thesis), 34. Skelton used reports in the local newspapers for her detailed examination of these events, and I have drawn on her account.

12. Jervey, *Charleston During the Civil War*, 176.

13. Price, "Blockade Running as a Business," 39.

14. Skelton, "Importing and Exporting Company of South Carolina" (thesis), 37.

15. The I&E Company referenced as W.C. Bee & Co. (Charleston, S.C.). W.C. Bee & Company records, 1848-1912. (23/298-301) South Carolina Historical Society.

16. Civil War Reminiscences, Henry W. Feilden papers, 1025.00, SCHS.

17. Jervey, *Charleston During the Civil War*, 175.

18. Skelton, "Importing and Exporting Company of South Carolina" (thesis), 97.

19. Skelton, "Importing and Exporting Company of South Carolina," (thesis) 49, quoting *Nassau Guardian* of 9 May 1863.

20. Wise, *Lifeline of the Confederacy*, 114.

21. *Charleston Daily Courier*, 25 May 1863.

22. *Charleston Courier*, 15 June 1863.

23. Inward manifest for *Alice*, June 1863, from Skelton, "Importing and Exporting Company of South Carolina, 1861–1865" (thesis), 51.

24. Price, "Blockade Running as a Business," 39.

### Chapter 20: Charleston Under Siege

1. Gibbons, *Warships and Naval Battles of the Civil War*, 33–34.

2. Beauregard, "Torpedo Service in the Harbor and Water Defences of Charleston," 151.

3. Perry, *Infernal Machines*, 73.

4. Willis, *Fighting Ships 1850–1950*, 65.

5. *ORN*, ser. 1, vol. 13: 824.

6. *ORN*, ser. 1, vol. 13: 824.

7. *ORN*, ser. 1, vol. 13: 824.

8. *ORN*, ser. 1, vol. 13: 826.

9. Burton, *Siege of Charleston*, 136.

10. Burton, *Siege of Charleston*, 138.

11. Burton, *Siege of Charleston*, 143.

12. United States War Department, *The War of the Rebellion: A Compilation of the Official Records of the Union and Confederate Armies*, ser. 1, vol. 28, pt. 2: 195. Hereinafter this source is cited as *ORA*.

13. *ORA*, ser. 1, vol. 28, pt. 2: 208–9.

14. *ORA*, ser. 1, vol. 28, pt. 2: 229.

15. *ORA*, ser. 1, vol. 28, pt. 2: 229.

16. *ORA*, ser. 1, vol. 28, pt. 2: 230.

17. "Winans' model" refers to the "cigar ships"—so called because of their pointed, streamlined hulls—that were developed in the mid-1800s by Ross Winans and his sons, a family of marine engineers based in Baltimore.

18. *ORA*, ser. 1, vol. 28, pt. 2: 230.

19. Beauregard, "Torpedo Service in the Harbor and Water Defences of Charleston," 150.

20. Burton, *Siege of Charleston*, 218–20.

21. *ORA*, ser. 1, vol. 28, , pt. 2: 229–30.

22. Burton, *Siege of Charleston*, 216.

23. *ORA*, ser. 1, vol. 28, pt. 2: 229.

24. *ORA*, ser. 1, vol. 28, pt. 2: 251.

25. *ORA*, ser. 1, vol. 28, pt. 2: 251–52.

26. *ORA*, ser. 1, vol. 28, pt. 2: 254.

27. *ORA*, ser. 1, vol. 28, pt. 2: 254.

## Chapter 21: The CSS *Torch* Incident

1. *ORN*, ser. 1, vol. 14: 498.

2. Luraghi, *History of the Confederate Navy*, 259.

3. Price, "Blockade Running as a Business," 51.

4. A detailed version of this event is found in Campbell, *Hunters of the Night*, 42–52.

5. Beauregard, "Torpedo Service in the Harbor and Water Defences of Charleston," 150.

6. *ORN*, ser. 1, vol. 14: 420.

7. *ORN*, ser. 1, vol. 13: 240–41.

8. Scharf, *History of the Confederate States Navy*, 698.

9. *ORN*, ser. 1, vol. 14: 498.

10. *ORN*, ser. 1, vol. 14: 498–99.

11. Tomb, *Engineer in Gray*, 189.

12. Poulnot in the *Charleston News and Courier*, January 27, 1895

13. *ORN*, ser. 1, vol. 14: 499.

14. *ORN*, ser. 1, vol. 14: 498.

15. Perry, *Infernal Machines*, 80.

16. Poulnot in the *Charleston News and Courier*, January 27, 1895.

17. Poulnot in the *Charleston News and Courier*, January 27, 1895.

18. ORN, ser. 1, vol. 14: 500.

19. Wise, *Lifeline of the Confederacy*, 257.

20. Perry, *Infernal Machines*, 98–108.

21. Burton, *Siege of Charleston*, 217.

22. Scarborough, *Diary of Edmund Ruffin*, 156.

## Chapter 22: Trouble in Bermuda

1. *Charleston Mercury,* 26 May 1863.
2. Quoted in McNeil, *Masters of the Shoals,* 39.
3. Skelton, "Importing and Exporting Company of South Carolina" (journal article), 28.
4. Skelton, "Importing and Exporting Company of South Carolina" (thesis), 90. Much of this chapter uses material from Skelton's detailed study of the company.
5. Skelton, "Importing and Exporting Company of South Carolina" (thesis), 41–49. Skelton draws on the I&E Company papers in the SCHS, supplemented by contemporary Charleston newspaper reports. The company papers include the letters of Bonneau and William Bee.
6. Letter, Bonneau to Bee, 13 October 1863, W. C. Bee & Company Records, 1848–1912, SCHS.
7. *ORN,* ser. 1, vol. 2: 450.
8. Letter, Stansbury to J. T. Bourne, 17 August 1863, *The Authentic Campaigner A Web Site for the Authentic Living Civil War Historian* (website), http://www.authentic-campaigner.com/forum/archive/index.php/t-14324.html (accessed 2 December 2014).
9. Wise, *Lifeline of the Confederacy,* 136.
10. Letter, Walker to Bee, 16 October 1863, W. C. Bee & Company Records, 1848–1912, SCHS.
11. Skelton, "Importing and Exporting Company of South Carolina" (thesis), 45. Skelton references these quotes to Vandiver, *Confederate Blockade Running Through Bermuda.*
12. *New York Times,* 18 September 1892, 17.
13. *ORN,* ser. 1, vol. 9: 291–92. This account draws on the reports of the commanders of the USS *Niphon* and USS *Shenandoah.*
14. Letter, Bee to Bonneau, 12 December 1864, W. C. Bee & Company Records, 1848–1912, SCHS.
15. Letter, Bonneau to Bee, 15 December 1864, W. C. Bee & Company Records, 1848–1912, SCHS.

## Chapter 23: Preparing for Change, December 1863

1. As quoted one page 1 of the *Daily Constitutionalist* (Augusta, Georgia) of April 29, 1864.
2. Letter, Bee to Memminger, 4 February 1864 (C.S. Treasury letters), Record Group 365.2.1, NARA, College Park, quoted in Skelton, "Importing and Exporting Company of South Carolina" (thesis), 91.
3. Letter, Bee to Memminger, 4 February 1864, Treasury letters, Record Group 365.2.1, NARA, College Park, quoted in Skelton, "Importing and Exporting Company of South Carolina" (thesis), 91.
4. Skelton, "Importing and Exporting Company of South Carolina," (thesis), 88.

## Chapter 24: Appointment in Scotland, December 1863–1864

1. W. C. Bee and Company records, 1848–1912, 23/298–301, SCHS. For the full text of Carlin's report, see appendix 1.
2. "William Denny and Brothers," *Grace's Guide to British Industrial History* (website), http://www.gracesguide.co.uk/William_Denny_and_Brothers (accessed 22 May 2014).
3. Lyon, *The Denny List,* 1:107–10.
4. Correspondence with Graham Hopner, Dumbarton District Library, 13 December 1983.
5. Wise, *Lifeline of the Confederacy,* 164.
6. *Nassau Guardian,* 8 June 1864, and *The Index,* 7 July 1864, cited in Skelton, "Importing and Exporting Company of South Carolina" (thesis), 62.
7. Le Scelleur, *Channel Islands' Railway Steamers,* 191.

**Chapter 25: Liverpool and the Last Days of the Confederacy, March 1864–June 1865**

1. Maynard, "Thomas Dudley and Union Efforts to Thwart Confederate Activities in Great Britain," 44n5.
2. Nepveux, *George Alfred Trenholm and the Company That Went to War*, 35.
3. Mays, *Mr. Hawthorne Goes to England*, 57.
4. *Gore's Directory of Liverpool and Its Environs*, 1867.
5. Letter, Carlin to Bee, 30 July 1864, W. C. Bee & Company Records, 1848–1912, SCHS.
6. Letter, Carlin to Bee 25 August 1864, W. C. Bee & Company records, 1848–1912, SCHS.
7. Letter, Carlin to Bee 30 July 1864, W. C. Bee & Company Records, 1848–1912, SCHS.
8. Taylor, *Running the Blockade*, 97.
9. Skelton, "Importing and Exporting Company of South Carolina" (journal article), 29.
10. *Dumbarton Herald*, 24 November. 1864.
11. Spence, *Treasures of the Confederate Coast*, 64-12-US-NC-1,340. Spence references various sources for this including ORN, Ser. 1, vol. 11, 125-134,151, 416, which give a full account of the capture.
12. Spence, *Treasures of the Confederate Coast*, 64-12-US-NC-1, 340.
13. Skelton,"Importing and Exporting Company of South Carolina," (thesis) 70.
14. References to ship sailings in this chapter are drawn from Skelton and Wise unless otherwise credited.
15. Skelton, "Importing and Exporting Company of South Carolina," (thesis) 72.

**Chapter 26: The Last of the Cotton, April–May 1865**

1. Letter from "Baltimore June 4, 13," CA32, Mariners' Museum Library, Newport News, Va. A note in different handwriting states: "from A. J. Forrest." Transcribed with valuable help from Walter E. Wilson, Captain, USN (ret.).
2. *ORN*, ser. 1, vol. 22: 34.
3. Annual Report of Bahamas Governor Rawson, *Liverpool Daily Post*, 29 Sept 1866.
4. Wise, *Lifeline of the Confederacy*, 273.
5. *Cincinnati Daily Enquirer*, June 1865.
6. Savage, *Policy of the United States*, 1:94.
7. This chapter is based on the British Admiralty Case *Prioleau v. Carlin*, Court of Chancery Pleadings, Cause number: 1865 P85, C 16/293, TNA.

**Chapter 27: Financial Matters, 1864–1866**

1. The named directors were Charles Kuhn Prioleau of Liverpool, Theodor Dehon Wagner, James Thomas Welman, William Lee Trenholm of Charleston, South Carolina, and John Richardson Armstrong of Liverpool, all merchants trading under the firm of Fraser, Trenholm, and Company. See Inspectorship 12,518, *Perry's Bankrupt Weekly Gazette*, 16 November 1867, 1075.
2. *Blackburn Standard*, 18 March 1868.
3. Skelton, "Importing and Exporting Company of South Carolina" (thesis), 104–5.
4. Skelton "Importing and Exporting Company of South Carolina" (thesis), 100, 103. Marcus Price estimates that the number of bales carried by the company was at least fifteen thousand. See his "Blockade Running as a Business," 40.
5. Dividend Account no.3 with James M. Calder, W.C. Bee and Company records, 1848–1912, SCHS.
6. Skelton, "Importing and Exporting Company of South Carolina," (thesis), 107–8.
7. Skelton, "Importing and Exporting Company of South Carolina," (thesis), 128–30.

8. Price, "Blockade Running as a Business," quoting from Notice of Declaration of Dividends, published in the *Charleston Mercury,* 28 December 1865.

9. Price, "Blockade Running as a Business," 48.

## Chapter 28: Life in England, June 1865–1871

1. Graham, *Clyde Built,* 99–100.

2. Jervey, *Charleston During the Civil War,* 171.

## Chapter 29: Charleston and Florida Ventures, 1865–1869

1. The absence of other Carlins of an appropriate age and origin in the census returns for the eastern United States suggests that the James Carlin who appears in the records cited in this chapter is Captain James Carlin, born in Hunstanton, Norfolk, England, in 1831.

2. *Charleston Courier,* 11 November 1865. Advertisement.

3. Charleston Dredging and Wharf Building Company. General Assemble Petitons ND 5623, SCDAH..

4. *Charleston Daily News,* 12 March 1868.

5. Appointment of Additional Magistrate, Pickens County, General Assembly Petitions No. 5207, SCDAH.

6. *Charleston Mercury,* 14 December 1866.

7. *Charleston Daily,* 12 April 1867.

8. "Historical Development of Titusville," *North Brevard History* (website), accessed February 12, 2016, http://www.nbbd.com/godo/history/NBrevHist/.

9. Burnett, *Florida's Past,* vol. 3, 23.

10. de la Cova, "Cuban Filibustering in Jacksonville in 1851," 17.

11. de la Cova, "Cuban Filibustering in Jacksonville in 1851," 24.

12. Iona Spencer, "Colonel Henry T. Titus," *Bald Eagle* 7, no. 4 (1981): n.p., available online at *Historic Lecompton* (website), http://www.lecomptonkansas.com/wp-content/uploads/2015/04/Bald.Eagle_.Vol7_.No4_.Winter.1981.pdf. Accessed February 12, 2016.

13. "Col. Henry T. Titus," *North Brevard History* (website), http://nbbd.com/godo/history/ColTitus.html (accessed 7 August 2013).

14. Register of Contracts, 31 May 1867, 91–94, Brevard County Courthouse, Titusville, Fl.

15. Cowart, *Crackers and Carpetbaggers,* 121.

16. Hebel, "Colonel H. T. Titus, Founder of Titusville, Florida," typescript, 1969.

17. *Official Register of the United States,* 2:700.

18. Transcript of Record (16,276), Supreme Court of the United States, October 1895, no. 986, in Carlyle, Calderon, *Report to the Spanish Legation, 1896.*

## Chapter 30: The Steamer *Salvador* and the Cuban Revolution, 1869

1. Peter Dalleo, "A Bold Captain, a Swift Steamer, and a Noiseless Crew," *Journal of the Bahamas Historical Society,* 1 (1979): 20.

2. *New York Herald,* 21 May 1869 (report from Nassau dated 10 May 1869).

3. See appendix 4 for statistics on Bahamian imports and exports for this period

4. A good overview of the Cuban Ten Years' War is found in Hugh Thomas's authoritative history of the island, *Cuba, or The Pursuit of Freedom,* 157–55.

## Chapter 31: The Cuban Run, May 1869

1. Wise, *Lifeline of the Confederacy,* 301.

2. Details are drawn from the trial in the Vice-Admiralty Court in Nassau and British Co-lonial, Foreign Office, and Royal Navy records in TNA and contemporary newspaper reports. Royal Navy records are in ADM 72/ 1270 where the best summary of this extensive file is Sir James Walker's Memorandum on the Case of the Salvador. The other extensive file is PCAP1/417.

3. *The Queen v. Salvador*, Vice Admiralty Court of the Bahamas, 13 August 1869, CO 884/2, TNA.

4. *New York Herald*, 21 May 1869.

5. Letter, Walker to Granville, 24 July 1869, FO 12/1270, TNA.

6. Letter, Receiver General to Colonial Secretary, 11 May 1869, FO 12/1270, TNA.

7. Letter, Commander Loftus F. Jones to Captain McCrea, 12 May 1869, FO 12/1270, TNA.

## Chapter 32: The Cuban Shore, May–June, 1869

1. Sailing Directions 2015, Caribbean Sea, volume 1. Publication 147, National Geospatial-Intelligence Agency, Springfield, Virginia. Cuba North Coast, 59. Accessed February 14, 2016, http://msi.nga.mil/MSISiteContent/StaticFiles/NAV_PUBS/SD/Pub147/Pub147bk

2. *New York Herald*, 3 June 1869 (report from Nassau, N.P., dated 22 May 1869).

3. *New York Herald*, 3 June 1869 ( report from Nassau, n.p. dated 22 May 1869)

4. *New York Herald*, 3 June 1869 ( report from Nassau, n.p. dated 22 May 1869).

5. *New York Herald*, 3 June 1869 and 21 July 1889.

6. Town names in Cuba have changed over the years. Bayamo is now an inland city well to the south of Nuevitas, so the exact location of the *Salvador*'s landing place remains obscure.

7. Report of Commander Loftus F. Jones to Captain McCrea, 24 May 1869, FO 72/1270, TNA.

8. ADM 128/69 folio 817–19, and CO 27/196, with maps in MFQ 1/641, TNA.

## Chapter 33: The Queen v. *Salvador* and British Foreign Enlistment Act 59, Geo. III 1819 c.69. May 1869

1. The Steamship *Salvador* v Our Lady the Queen. Act on Protest, 32 May 1869, PCAP1/417,TNA.

2. Value obtained from *Measuring Worth* (website), http://www.measuringworth.com/ukcompare/, using its Purchasing Power Calculator based on Retail Price Index (accessed 30 June 2014).

3. Decree of Deputy Justice Rothery of the Vice Admiralty Court, Bahamas 10 August 1869, PCAP1/417, TNA.

4. Letter, E. Hammond to Lord Granville 28 September 1869, FO 12/1270, TNA.

5. Letter, Spanish Legation to Lord Clarendon, 5 October 1869, FO 12/1270, TNA.

6. Letter, Earl Granville to Sir James Walker, 22 January 1870, FO 12/1270 TNA.

7. Letter, Acting Governor George C. Strahan to the Earl of Kimberley, 9 September, 1870, ADM, 72/1270, TNA.

8. *New York Times,* 19 September. 1870.

9. Letter, J. W. Barron to Maffitt, 4 June 1870, Wilson Library, University of North Carolina, Chapel Hill.

10. Shingleton, *High Seas Confederate,* 101–2.

11. Robertson, *Richard Ford,* 88.

12. Blake, *Weekly Reporter,* 1054–56.

## Chapter 34: Caribbean Repercussions

1. Letter, McCrea to Secretary of the Admiralty, 23 May 1869, FO 72/1270, TNA.

2. Letter, Walker to Granville, 10 May 1869, FO 72/1270, TNA.

3. Draft for Lord Granville and covering letter dated 18 June 1869, FO 72/1270, TNA,.

4. Foreign Office to Colonial Office, 21 June 1869, FO 72/1270, TNA. There are a large number of letters in a similar vein that I have drawn on for this chapter.

5. *American Annual Cyclopaedia and Register,* 219.

6. Colonial Office Letter Book, West Indies, 1869–70, CO333/6, TNA.

## Chapter 35: What Happened Next, 1870–1891

1. *Charleston Daily News,* 27 January 1871.

2. *Charleston Daily News,* 14 April 1871.

3. John Carlin, "Grandmothers 1913."

4. Letter, Ann Malcher to her nephew Scott Carlin, grandson of Samuel Edward Carlin, 20 Nov. 1967.

5. Correspondence with Niels H. Frandsen, archivist, Greenland National Archives, Nuuk.

6. Letter in possession of Mrs. Sally Purinton. Jim is James Cornelius [Montijo] Carlin, Ella's eldest son. Ray is Horatia Carlin, née Richardson, of San Francisco. The "little darling" is her daughter Imogene. Jim's father is Captain James Carlin—the sudden change in the tone of the letter suggests that James dictated this passage. The lock of hair is now with the author.

7. Real Estate Conveyances, Brevard County, Florida Grantor's Index, 1881–1908.

8. Stevens, *Dear Medora,* 138.

9. Letter in the Carlin White Collection of the Loxahatchee River Historical Society, Jupiter Inlet Lighthouse and Museum, Jupiter, Florida.

10. Brancaster Churchyard, memorial for Thomas Blocking, master mariner, died 24 September 1865, aged 89 years. Composed by an old man-of-war sailor just before he died. Originally from *The Shipwrecked Mariner* 8 (January 1861).

## Appendix 1: Additional Documents

1. Miscellaneous Letters, 1789–1906 (Letters Received), vol. 380, December 1862, General Records of the Department of State, Record Group 60, NARA, College Park.

2. *ORN,* ser. 1, vol. 13: 225–26.

3. *ORN,* ser. 1, vol. 14: 498–99.

4. *ORN,* ser. 1, vol. 14: 500.

5. 23/298–301, W. C. Bee & Company Records, 1848–1912, SCHS.

## Appendix 2: Reflections on Confederate Finance

1. Lebergott, "Through the Blockade," 881.

2. Todd, *Confederate Finance,* 177.

3. Lebergott, "Why the South Lost," 58–74.

4. Surdam, *Northern Naval Superiority* (book), 6–7, and Surdam, "Northern Naval Superiority" (journal article), 473–75.

5. Lebergott, "Why the South Lost," 69–73.

6. Lebergott, "Through the Blockade," 880–81.

## Appendix 3: James Carlin's Correspondence with Dr. Bache

1. Carlin–Bache letters, 30 September, 4 October, and 7 October 1862, Records of the Adjutant General's Office, Baker-Turner Records, 1862–1865, 370–81, Record Group 94.2.5, NARA, College Park.

# Selected Bibliography

. . .

## Primary Sources

### Republic of Ireland

The National Archives, Dublin

Customs and Excise Administration Papers, series 2 442–2 448.

### United Kingdom

The National Archives of the U.K., Public Record Office, Kew, London

ADM 128/69, folio 817–19. Correspondence, Reports and Memoranda, North America and West Indies.

ADM 161/2. Register of Greenwich Hospital School, London.

ADM 175/6. Records of Service, Coast Guard, Establishment Books by station.

ADM 175/18–19. Records of Service, Coast Guard, Establishment Books by station.

ADM 175/77. Records and Nominations of Service, Coast Guard.

BT 108/288. Registry of Shipping and Seaman, Plantation Copies, Nassau, N.P.

BT 113/71. Registry of Shipping and Seamen Registry of Seaman's Tickets.

BT 113/222. Registry of Shipping and Seamen, Register of Seamen's Tickets.

BT 150/24. Registry of Shipping and Seamen, Index of Apprentices, Outports.

C 16/293/. Court of Chancery Pleadings, Cause number: 1865 P85. *Prioleau v. Carlin*. Plaintiffs: Charles Kuhn Prioleau and others.

CO 23/196 . Bahamas Dispatches 1868, June–August. For maps form this file see MFQ 1/641. These show the relative positions of the *Salvador* and the British Naval vessels in Nassau Harbor at the time of the *Salvador's* escape.

CO 333/6. Bahamas: Register of Correspondence, West Indies, 1869–70.

CO 884/2. *The Queen v.* Salvador, Vice-Admiralty Court.

FO 5/780. General Correspondence before 1906, United States of America, Series II. Consul at Charleston. Bunch.

FO 5/1269. Claims arising out of the Civil War, vol. 34, *Memphis,* etc.

FO 72/1270. Aid to Cuban insurgents: Case of the *Salvador,* 1869.

MFQ 1/641. Maps relating to CO 27/196 showing the position of the *Salvador* in Nassau Harbor.

### The Public Record Office of Northern Ireland, Belfast

Series CUST 1 and CUST 2, Customs and Excise Records.

**St. Mary's Church, Old Hunstanton, Norfolk**

Baptismal Records, 1830–1840.

**University of Glasgow, Archive Service**

William Denny and Brothers, shipbuilders, Dumbarton, 1844–1952, for shipbuilding contract envelopes.

## United States

**Brevard County Courthouse, Titusville, Florida**

Register of Contracts, 31 May 1867.
Real Estate Conveyances, Brevard County, Florida Grantor's Index, 1881–1908.

**Columbia University in the City of New York, Law School Library**

United States District Court, New York (Southern District). Papers of the New York Prize Court during the Civil War. Case of the *Memphis*. Microfilm Prize Case 116–1 to 116–58.

**Comal County Court, New Braunfels, Texas**

*Henry Dietz v. James Carlin.* Comal County District Court Record for Spring Term 1866.

**Library of Virginia, Richmond**

Will of Joseph Gallego, 1818, Richmond City Hustings Court, Will Book 2.

**Jupiter Inlet Lighthouse and Museum, Jupiter, Florida**

Letter, James Carlin, Ward Island, N.Y., to Mary Moorer Joyner, 20 May 1920, Jupiter, Fla.

**Mariners Museum Library, Newport News, Virginia**

Letter ref. CA32 written from A. J. Forrest, 4–13 June 1865.

**National Records and Archives Administration at College Park, Maryland**

Record Group 23. Records of the Coast and Geodetic Survey. General Correspondence of Alexander Bache, Microfilm M642, roll 253.
Record Group 45. Naval Records Collection. General Pay and Receipt Roll, Savannah Station, July–Sept 1861.
Record Group 60. General Records of the Department of State. Miscellaneous Letters, 1789–1906 (Letters Received), vol. 380, December 1862.
Record Group 94.2.5. War Department Division. Adjutant General's Records, 1780–1917. Turner-Baker Papers.
Record Group 365.2.1. Treasury Letters. Bee to C. G. Memminger, 4 February 1864.
Record Group 23. Records of the Coast and Geodetic Survey, Entry 5, Bache correspondence 1860 Vol IX Naval Assistants, Lt. Cm. C. M. Fauntleroy to Alexander Bache 16 May 1860, No.82.

**National Records and Archives Administration, Mid-Atlantic Region, Philadelphia**

Record Group 21. U.S. Court for the District of Maryland. Admiralty Case *U.S. v. the Schooner Alert and her cargo.*

**South Carolina Department of Archives and History, Columbia**

General Assembly Petitions ND 5207. Appointment of Additional Magistrate, Pickens County.
General Assembly Petitions ND 5623. Charleston Dredging and Wharf Building Company.
Series: S213050. Bill of Sale (Slaves), vol. 6E, 1860, and vol. 6F, 1863.

# Bibliography

## South Carolina Historical Society, Charleston

W. C. Bee and Company Records, 1848–1912. SCHS 23/298–301.

Henry Wemyss Feilden Papers, 1851–1949. SCHS 1025.00. Civil War Reminiscences.

Jacob Schirman Diary, May 1857.

## University of North Carolina, Chapel Hill, Wilson Library

Letter, J. W. Barron of the Junta Central Republicana de Cuba y Porto Rico 71, Broadway, New York, to Captain Maffitt, 4 June 1870.

## U.S. Government Records and Reports

1860 Comal County census of New Braunfels, Texas.

Records of the Coast and Geodetic Survey, Entry 5, Bache correspondence, 1860, vol. 9, Naval Assistants.

*Report of the Superintendent of the Coast Survey During the Year 1856.* Washington, D.C.: A. O. P. Nicholson, Printer, 1856. This and other Coast Survey annual reports (below) are available online at the National Oceanic and Atmospheric Administration (NOAA) Central Library website, http://www.lib.noaa.gov/collections/imgdocmaps/cgs_annual_reports.html.

*Report of the Superintendent of the Coast Survey During the Year 1859.* Washington, D.C.: Thomas H. Ford, Printer, 1860.

*Report of the Superintendent of the Coast Survey Showing the Progress of the Survey During the Year 1860.* Washington, D.C.: Government Printing Office, 1861.

United States Naval War Records Office. *Official Records of the Union and Confederate Navies in the War of the Rebellion.* 30 vols. Washington, D.C.: Government Printing Office, 1894–1922. These volumes and those of the army records (below) are available online at Cornell University's *Making of America* website, http://ebooks.library.cornell.edu/m/moawar/index.html.

United States War Department. *The War of the Rebellion: A Compilation of the Official Records of the Union and Confederate Armies.* 128 vols. Washington, D.C.: Government Printing Office, 1880–1901.

## Washington National Record Center, Textual Reference Branch, Suitland, Maryland

Ship's Logs 1839–1920. Log book of the U.S.S. *Magnolia,* 31 July–1 August 1862. From microfilm 18W4 6-6-c.

## Unpublished Letters, Correspondence, etc., in Private Collections

Author's correspondence with Graham Hopner of Dumbarton District Library, Helenslee Road, Dumbarton, Scotland.

Author's correspondence with Niels H. Frandsen, archivist, Greenland National Archives, Nuuk, 2013.

Carlin, John. "Grandmothers 1913." Typescript, 1960. Copy in possession of the author.

Letter, Ann Malcher of Chicago to her nephew Scott Carlin, grandson of Samuel Edward Carlin, 20 November 1967. Copy in possession of the author.

Letter, Ethel Jones to author Willard R. Espy, 7 December 1977. Collection of Mrs. Sydney Stevens of Oysterville, Washington.

Letter, Mrs. Ella Rosa Carlin, London, to Mrs. Horatia Carlin, San Francisco, 16 December 1881. Collection of Mrs. Sally Purinton.

Letter, University of South Carolina, Department of History, to Dr. Charles Peery of Charleston, S.C., 7 May 1980. Copy in possession of the author.

Notes of family conversations in Johannesburg. Recorded by John Cushnie for Murray Carlin, 1960s. Collection of Vuyelwa Carlin, Craven Arms, U.K.

## Secondary Sources

**Books**

Albury, Paul. *The Story of the Bahamas*. London: Macmillan Caribbean, 1973.

*The American Annual Cyclopaedia and Register of Important Events*. Vol. 9. New York: Appleton and Company, 1869.

*Bahamas Chart Kit*. 3rd edition. Boston: Better Boating, 1984.

Barnes, James J., and Patience P. Barnes, eds. *The American Civil War through British Eyes: Dispatches from British Diplomats*. Vol. 2. *April 1862–February 1863*. Kent, Ohio: Kent State University Press, 2003.

Berwanger, Eugene H. *The British Foreign Service and the American Civil War*. Lexington: University Press of Kentucky, 1994.

Blachford, Samuel. *Reports of Cases in Prize Argued and Determined in the Circuit and District Courts of the United States for the Southern District of New York, 1861–65*. Washington, D.C.: Government Printing Office, 1866.

Blake, Martin Joseph (Privy Council Reporter). *The Weekly Reporter Containing Cases Decided in the Superior Courts of Equity and Law in England and Ireland*. Vol. 18. London, 6 August 1870.

Buker, George E. *Blockaders, Refugees, and Contrabands: Civil War on Florida's Gulf Coast, 1861–1865*. Tuscaloosa: University of Alabama Press, 1993.

Burnett, Gene M. *Florida's Past: People and Events That Shaped the State*. Vol. 3. Sarasota, Fla.: Pineapple Press, 1991.

Burton, E. Milby. *The Siege of Charleston, 1861–1865*. Columbia: University of South Carolina Press, 1976.

Campbell, R. Thomas. *Hunters of the Night: Confederate Torpedo Boats in the War Between the States*. Shippensburg, Pa.: Burd Street Press, 2000.

Carlin, Colin. *William Kirkpatrick of Málaga: Consul, Négociant and Entrepreneur, and Grandfather of the Empress Eugénie*. Glasgow: Grimsay Press, 2011.

Carlisle, Calderon. *Report to the Spanish Legation, 1896*. Transcript of Record 16,276. Supreme Court of the United States. October Term, 1895. No. 986. Washington, D.C., 1896.

Caskie, Jaquelin Ambler. *Life and Letters of Matthew Fontaine Maury*. Richmond, Va.: Richmond Press, 1928.

*Charleston Directory*. Charleston, S.C.: M. B. Brown and Company, 1866.

Clark, John E. *Railroads in the Civil War: The Impact of Management on Victory and Defeat*. Baton Rouge: Louisiana State University Press, 2001.

Cowart, John W. *Crackers and Carpetbaggers: Moments in the History of Jacksonville, Florida*. Jacksonville, Fla.: Bluefish Books, 2005.

Craton, Michael. *A History of the Bahamas*. London: Collins, 1968.

Davis, Lance E., and Stanley L. Engerman. *Naval Blockades in Peace and War: An Economic History since 1750*. New York: Cambridge University Press, 2006.

Eaton, Clement. *A History of the Southern Confederacy*. New York: Macmillan, 1954.

Fetzer, Dale, and Bruce Edward Mowday. *Unlikely Allies: Fort Delaware's Prison Community in the Civil War*. Mechanicsburg, Pa.: Stackpole Books, 2000.

Foreman, Amanda. *A World on Fire: Britain's Crucial Role in the American Civil War*. London: Penguin Books, 2011.

Gibbons, Tony. *Warships and Naval Battles of the Civil War*. New York: Galley Books, 1990.

Bibliography

Goldsmith, Jack L., and Eric A. Posner. *The Limits of International Law.* Oxford, U.K.: Oxford University Press, 2005.

*Gore's Directory of Liverpool.* Liverpool, 1867.

Graham, Eric J. *Clyde Built.* Edinburgh: Birlinn Ltd., 2006.

Guelzo, Allen C. *Fateful Lightning: A New History of the Civil War and Reconstruction.* New York: Oxford University Press, 2012.

Hearn, Chester G. *Tracks in the Sea.* Camden, Maine: International Marine, 2002.

Hebel, Ianthe (Bond). "Colonel H. T. Titus, Founder of Titusville, Florida," typescript, 1969.

Hipper, Keith. *Smugglers All: Centuries of Norfolk Smuggling.* Dereham, Norfolk, U.K.: Larks Press, 2003.

Horner, David. *The Blockade-Runners.* New York: Dodd, Mead and Company, 1968.

Jervey, Theodore D. *Charleston During the Civil War.* Washington, D.C.: American Historical Association, 1915.

Johnson, George Jr. *Rose O'Neale Greenhow and the Blockade Runners.* Privately printed in Canada, 1993.

Jones, Howard. *The Union in Peril: The Crisis over British Intervention in the Civil War.* Chapel Hill: University of North Carolina Press, 1991.

Kurtz, Harold. *The Empress Eugénie.* London: Hamish Hamilton, 1964.

Le Scelleur, Kevin. *Channel Islands' Railway Steamers.* Wellingborough, U.K.: P. Stephens. 1985

Luraghi, Raimondo. *A History of the Confederate Navy.* Annapolis, Md.: Naval Institute Press, 1996.

Lyon, David John. *The Denny List: Introduction, Ship Numbers 1–1505 and Appendices I–VIII.* Vol. 1. Greenwich, London: National Maritime Museum, 1975.

Maffitt, Emma Martin. *The Life and Services of John Newland Maffitt.* New York: Neale Publishing Company, 1906.

Massey, Mary Elizabeth. *Ersatz in the Confederacy: Shortages and Substitutes on the Southern Homefront.* Rev. ed. Columbia: University of South Carolina, 1993.

Maxwell, Sir Herbert, ed. *Life and Letters of the Fourth Earl of Clarendon.* Vol. 1. London: Edward Arnold, 1913.

Mays, James O'Donald. *Mr. Hawthorne Goes to England.* Burley, Hampshire, U.K.: New Forest Leaves, 1983.

McCusker, John J. *How Much Is That in Real Money? A Historical Price Index for Use as a Deflator of Money Values in the Economy of the United States.* Worcester, Mass.: American Antiquarian Society, 1992.

McNeil, Jim. *Masters of the Shoals: Tales of the Cape Fear Pilots Who Ran the Union Blockade.* Cambridge, Mass.: Da Capo Press, 2003.

Merli, Frank J. *The Alabama, British Nationality, and the American Civil War.* Edited by David M. Fahey. Bloomington: Indiana University Press, 2004.

Moore, Frank, ed. *The Rebellion Record: A Diary of American Events.* Vol. 4. New York: Putnam, 1862.

Mowat, R. B. *The Diplomatic Relations of Britain and the United States.* London: Edward Arnold, 1925.

Nepveux, Ethel Trenholm Seabrook. *George Alfred Trenholm and the Company That Went to War.* Charleston, S.C.: Self-published, 1973.

———. *George A. Trenholm: Financial Genius of the Confederacy.* Anderson S.C.: Self-published, 1999.

Newton, Lord. *Lord Lyons: A Record of British Diplomacy.* Vol. 1. London: Edward Arnold, 1913.

*Official Register of the United States.* Vol. 2. Washington, D.C.: Government Printing Office, 1885.

## Bibliography

Odgers, Merle M. *Alexander Bache.* Philadelphia: University of Pennsylvania Press, 1947.

Perry, Milton F. *Infernal Machines: The Story of Confederate Submarine and Mine Warfare.* Baton Rouge: Louisiana State University Press, 1965.

*Report of the Governor of the Bahamas in the Colonial Office Blue Book for 1865.* London: HMSO for Colonial Office, 1865.

*Return of Claims of British Subjects Against the United States' Government from the Commencement of the Civil War to the 31st of March, 1864.* Presented to the House of Commons by Command of Her Majesty. London: HMSO, 1864.

Roberts, Captain A. *Never Caught.* Bedford: Applewood Books, 1908.

Robertson, Ian. *Richard Ford 1796–1858: Hispanophile, Connoisseur and Critic.* Norwich, U.K.: Michael Russell Publishing, 2004.

Robinton, Madeline Russell. *An Introduction to the Papers of the New York Prize Court, 1861–1865.* Studies in History, Economics, and Public Law, no. 515. New York: Columbia University Press, 1945.

Rogers, Augustus C., ed. *Sketches of Representative Men, North and South.* New York: Atlantic Publishing Company, 1872. Typescript from William Carlin White of Jupiter.

Savage, Carlton, ed. *Policy of the United States Towards Maritime Commerce in War.* Vol. 1. *1776–1914.* Washington, D.C.: Government Printing Office, 1934.

Scarborough, William Kauffman, ed. *The Diary of Edmund Ruffin.* Vol. 3. *A Dream Shattered, June 1863–June 1865.* Baton Rouge: Louisiana State University Press, 1989.

Scharf, J. Thomas. *History of the Confederate States Navy.* New York: Rogers and Sherwood, 1887.

Shingleton, Royce. *High Seas Confederate: The Life and Times of John Newland Maffitt.* Columbia: University of South Carolina Press, 1994.

Silverstone, Paul H. *Civil War Navies, 1855–1883.* New York: Routledge, 2006.

Slotten, Hugh Richard. *Patronage, Practice, and the Culture of American Science: Alexander Dallas Bache and the U.S. Coast Survey.* Cambridge, U.K.: Cambridge University Press, 1994.

Spence, E. Lee. *Treasures of the Confederate Coast.* Charleston, S.C.: Narwhal Press, 1995.

Sprunt, James. "Derelicts: An Account of Ships Lost at Sea in General Commercial Traffic and a Brief History of Blockade Runners Stranded along the North Carolina Coast, 1861–1865." http://archive.org/stream/derelictsaccountoospru/derelictsaccountoospru_djvu.txt.

Stevens, Sydney. *Dear Medora: Child of Oysterville's Forgotten Years.* Pullman: Washington State University Press, 2007.

Still, William J., John M. Taylor, and Norman C. Delaney. *Raiders and Blockaders: The American Civil War Afloat.* Washington, D.C.: Brassey's, 1998.

Surdam, David G. *Northern Naval Superiority and the Economics of the American Civil War.* Columbia: University of South Carolina Press, 2001.

Sutherland, Daniel E. *Whistler: A Life for Art's Sake.* New Haven, Conn.: Yale University Press, 2013.

Taylor, Thomas E. *Running the Blockade.* London: John Murray, 1896.

Thomas, Emory M. *The Confederate Nation: 1861–1865.* New York: History Book Club Press, 1979.

Thomas, Hugh. *Cuba, or The Pursuit of Freedom.* London: Pan Books, 2002.

Todd, Richard Cecil. *Confederate Finance.* Athens: University of Georgia Press, 1954.

Tomb, James Hamilton. *Engineer in Gray: Memoirs of Chief Engineer James H. Tomb, CSN.* Jefferson, NC: McFarland, 2005.

Underwood, Rodman L. *Waters of Discord: The Union Blockade of Texas During the Civil War.* Jefferson, N.C.: McFarland, 2008.

United Daughters of the Confederacy. *Patriot Ancestor Album.* Paducah, Ky.: Turner Publishing, 1990.

Vandiver, Frank Everson. *Confederate Blockade Running Through Bermuda, 1861–1865: Letters and Cargo Manifests.* 1947. Reprint, New York: Kraus, 1970.

Villiers, George. *A Vanished Victorian: Being the Life of George Villiers, Fourth Earl of Clarendon.* London: Eyre and Spottiswoode, 1938.

Weddle, Kevin J. *Lincoln's Tragic Admiral: The Life of Samuel Francis Du Pont.* Charlottesville: University of Virginia Press, 2005.

White, G. Edward. *Law in American History: From the Colonial Years Through the Civil War.* Oxford, U.K.: Oxford University Press, 2012.

Wilkinson, J. *The Narrative of a Blockade-runner.* New York: Sheldon and Co., 1877.

Willis, Sam. *Fighting Ships 1850–1950.* London: Quercus, 2008.

Wise, Stephen R. *Lifeline of the Confederacy: Blockade Running During the Civil War.* Columbia: University of South Carolina Press, 1991.

## Journal Articles and Book Chapters

Beauregard, General G. T. "Torpedo Service in the Harbor and Water Defences of Charleston." *Southern Historical Society Papers* 5 (April 1878): 145–61.

de la Cova, Antonio Rafael. "Cuban Filibustering in Jacksonville in 1851." *Northeast Florida History: The Journal of the Jacksonville Historical Society* (1996): 17–34.

Dalleo, Peter. "A Bold Captain, a Swift Steamer, and a Noiseless Crew." *Journal of the Bahamas Historical Society* 20 (1998).

Drake, F. C. "The Cuban Background to the Trent Affair." *Civil War History,* no. 1 (1973): 29–49.

Dundas, F. de Sales. "Blockade Running During the War Between the States." *United Daughters of the Confederacy Magazine* 15, no. 11 (1952): 18–25.

*Economist* (London) 19, no. 948 (26 October 1861).

Hetherington, Bruce W., and Peter J. Kower. "A Re-examination of Lebergott's Paradox about Blockade Running During the American Civil War." *Journal of Economic History* 69, no. 2 (2009): 528–32.

Lebergott, Stanley. "Through the Blockade: The Profitability and Extent of Cotton Smuggling, 1861–1865." *Journal of Economic History* 41, no. 4 (1981): 867–88.

———. "Wage Trends, 1800–1900." In *Trends in the American Economy in the Nineteenth Century: Studies in Income and Wealth,* vol. 24, by the Conference on Research Income and Wealth, 449–500. Princeton, N.J.: Princeton University Press, 1960.

———. "Why the South Lost: Commercial Purpose in the Confederacy, 1861–1865." *Journal of American History* 70, no. 1 (1983): 58–74.

Negus, Samuel. "A Notorious Nest of Offence: Neutrals, Belligerents, and Union Jails in Civil War Blockade Running." *Civil War History* 56, no. 4 (2010): 350–85.

Price, Marcus W. "Blockade Running as a Business in South Carolina During the War Between the States, 1861–1865." *American Neptune* 9 (January 1949): 31–62.

———. "Masters and Pilots Who Tested the Blockade of the Confederate Ports, 1861–1865." *American Neptune* 21 (April 1961): 81–106.

———. "Ships that Tested the Blockade of the Carolina Ports, 1861–1864." *American Neptune* 8 (April 1948): 196–241.

———. "Ships that Tested the Blockade of the Georgian and East Florida Ports, 1861–1865." *American Neptune* 15 (April 1955): 229–38.

*The Shipwrecked Mariner* 8, no. 29 (January 1861).

Skelton, Lynda Worley. "The Importing and Exporting Company of South Carolina, 1862–1876." *South Carolina Historical Magazine* 75, no. 1 (1974): 24–32.

Sprunt, James. *Derelicts: An Account of Ships Lost at Sea in General Commercial Traffic and a Brief History of Blockade Runners Stranded along the North Carolina Coast, 1861–1865*. Accessed June, 2014.  http://archive.org/stream/derelictsaccountoospru/derelictsaccountoospru_djvu.txt.

Surdam, David G. "Northern Naval Superiority and the Economics of the American Civil War." *Journal of Economic History* 56, no. 2 (1996): 473–75.

Theberge, Captain Albert E. "The Coast Survey and Army Operations during the Civil War." Part 3, section 2, of *The Coast Survey, 1807–1867*. Vol. 1 of *History of the Commissioned Corps of the National Oceanic and Atmospheric Administration*. Silver Springs, Md.: National Oceanic and Atmospheric Administration (NOAA) Central Library, 2007. Available online at http://www.lib.noaa.gov/noaainfo/heritage/coastsurveyvol1/CW2.html#ARMY.

Weddle, Kevin J. "The Blockade Board of 1861 and Union Naval Strategy." *Civil War History* 48, no. 2 (2002): 123–42.

## Unpublished Theses

Maynard, Douglas H. "Thomas Dudley and Union Efforts to Thwart Confederate Activities in Great Britain." Ph.D. dissertation. University of California, Los Angeles, 1951.

Skelton, Lynda Worley. "The Importing and Exporting Company of South Carolina, 1862–1876." Master's thesis. Clemson University, South Carolina, May 1967.

# Index

. . .

# About the Author

· · ·

Colin Carlin, a retired business executive with a strong connection to Africa and latterly an art dealer, is author of *William Kirkpatrick of Malaga, Consul, Négociant and Grandfather of the Empress Eugénie*. He lives in Bath, England.